THE BRADT STORY

In 1974, my (former) husband George and I spent three days sitting on a river barge in Bolivia writing our first guide for like-minded travellers: *Backpacking along Ancient Ways in Peru and Bolivia*. The 'little yellow book', as it became known, is now in its sixth edition and continues to sell to travellers throughout the world. Since 1980, with the establishment of Bradt Publications, I have continued to publish guides for the discerning traveller, covering more than 100 countries and all six continents, and winning the 1997 *Sunday Times* Small Publisher of the Year Award; *Guide to Zanzibar* (3rd edition) is the 137th Bradt guide to be published.

The company continues to develop new titles and new series, but in the forefront of my mind there remains our original ethos – responsible travel with an emphasis on the culture and natural history of the region. I hope that you will get the most out of your trip, and perhaps have the opportunity to give something in return.

Travel guides are by their nature continuously evolving. If you experience anything which you would like to share with us, or if you have any amendments to make to this guide, please write; all your letters are read and passed on to the author. Most importantly, do remember to travel with an open mind and to respect the customs of your hosts – it will add immeasurably to your enjoyment.

Happy travelling!

Hilary Bradt

41 Nortoft Road, Chalfont St Peter, Bucks, SL9 0LA, England
Tel/fax: 01494 873478 Email: bradtpublications@compuserve.com

Guide to
Zanzibar

3rd Edition

David Else

with contributions by Sarah Chanter

Bradt Publications, UK
The Globe Pequot Press Inc, USA

First published in 1993 by Bradt Publications.
This third edition published in 1998 by Bradt Publications,
41 Nortoft Road, Chalfont St Peter, Bucks SL9 0LA, England
Published in the USA by The Globe Pequot Press Inc, 6 Business Park Road,
PO Box 833, Old Saybrook, Connecticut 06475-0833

British Library Cataloguing in Publication Data
A catalogue record for this book is available from the British Library
ISBN 1 898323 65 8

Library of Congress Cataloging in Publication Data
Else, David.
    Guide to Zanzibar / David Else : [text photographs, Christine Osborne
... et al. : illustrations, Rebecca de Mendonça : maps, Steve Munns].
– 3rd ed.
    p. cm.
Includes bibliographical references.
ISBN 1-898323-65-8
1. Zanzibar–Guidebooks. I. Title.
DT449.Z22E57 1997
916.78'1–dc21
                                                                97-35260
                                                                CIP

Cover photographs   Christine Osborne, MEP
Text photographs   Peter Bennett (PB), Chris Bradley (CB), David Else (DE),
Rod Grant (RG), Fungu Mubarak (FM), Christine Osborne/MEP (CO),
Matt Richmond (MR)
Illustrations Rebecca de Mendonça
Maps Steve Munns

Typeset from the author's disc by Patti Taylor, London NW10 1JR
Printed and bound in Great Britain by The Guernsey Press Co Ltd

THE AUTHOR

David Else has travelled in Africa since 1983, using all types of transport, including trains, planes, cars, camels, dug-out canoes and mountain bikes. He has crossed the continent several times, from Cairo to Cape Town, and from Dakar's Atlantic coast to the Indian Ocean shorelines of Kenya and Tanzania. He first reached Zanzibar in 1985, sailing by dhow from Dar es Salaam. He returned in 1992 to write the first edition of this guide, his fifth for Bradt Publications.

David has written or co-written about a dozen books for travellers in Africa, and visits the continent frequently. Between 1994 and 1997, he returned to Zanzibar several times (using more comfortable modes of transport) to collect the information for this third edition.

ACKNOWLEDGEMENTS

I would like to thank the many people who helped me write this guidebook.

Firstly, many thanks to Sarah Chanter, who researched and wrote the *History of Zanzibar* chapter and many of the historical 'boxes' scattered throughout the book. Her endless enthusiasm was contagious and invaluable.

For the first edition, the following people (in Zanzibar and Britain) also provided Sarah and myself with advice, assistance and information: Abdul-Wahed Hassan, Salim Abdullah, Msanif Msanif, Suleiman Hassan, Naila Majid Jiddawi, Abdi Salim Ali, Allis Montensson, Derek Chartres, Paddy Hogan, John Baile, David Gray, Ramadhan Mwinyi (Ministry of Information, Culture, Tourism and Youth, Zanzibar), Mohamed Feruzi (Zanzibar Tourist Corporation, Pemba), Pippa Heylings (Commission for Lands and Environments, Zanzibar).

For the second edition, our thanks go to many of the above people again. We would also like especially to thank Abdul Sheriff (University of Dar es Salaam), John Da Silva and Balkrishna Gorolay, whose insight and deep knowledge helped us enlarge and improve our history sections. Thanks also to Matt Richmond (Institute of Marine Sciences, Zanzibar), Fiona Clark and Jim Boggs, who helped us similarly improve our sections on wildlife and culture, and to Fatma Rashid, Osmo Seppala (Zanzibar Urban Water Supply Project), Timo Vihola (Zanzibar Forestry Development Project), Emerson Skeens, Peter Bennett, Helen Paul, Celia Kissoon (Tanzania Desk, Department of Trade and Industry).

For the third edition, once again my thanks go to most of the people above, plus Tahir Ishaq, Flo and Mike Liebst, Mary Silver, Mahboub Machano, Tim Hendriks, Mubeen Jamal, Andrew Cooke (Zanzibar Protected Areas Project) and Dr Jane Wilson-Howarth.

I am also indebted to the readers of the previous editions, and all the other people, who wrote in with news, ideas, corrections and suggestions. These include Adam Sachs, Rodney Lebow, Paul Lie, Sibylle Riedmuller, A Cotcher, Klaus Richter, Susan Robinson, Jacky Sutton, Anna Asheshov and Sandy Orton.

Thanks also to the many Zanzibaris, and to the travellers from around the world, who willingly (or unknowingly) supplied me with their comments and impressions.

David Else, 1997

CONTENTS

Perspectives on Zanzibar   IX

Chapter One   Zanzibar – A Profile   1

Chapter Two   A History of Zanzibar   5

Chapter Three   Planning and Preparations   39
                   When to go 39, Getting to Zanzibar 39, Arriving
                   and leaving 49, Before you go 50, What to take 54

Chapter Four   Facts about Zanzibar   57
                   Accommodation, food and transport 57, Health and
                   safety 60, Things to buy 62, Business hours, public
                   holidays and festivals 63, Music and dance 64,
                   Geology and soils 65, Vegetation 65, Wildlife 69,
                   The seas and shores of Zanzibar 72

Chapter Five   Zanzibar Town   85
                   Travel around Zanzibar Town 86, Hotels and
                   guesthouses 88, Eating and drinking 100, Travel
                   companies 106, Tour companies 110, Diving, sailing
                   and fishing companies 114, Shopping 117, Local
                   services 120, Places to visit in Zanzibar Town 128,
                   Places to visit near Zanzibar Town 147

Chapter Six   Zanzibar Island   161
                   Travel around Zanzibar Island 161, Hotels and
                   guesthouses 164, Places to visit 177

Chapter Seven   Pemba Island   189
                   Getting to Pemba 190, Leaving Pemba 191, Travel
                   around Pemba Island 192, Chake Chake 194,
                   Mkoani 196, Wete 198, Pango ya Watoro 200,
                   Local services 201, Places to visit 202

Appendix One   Sultans   207

Appendix Two   Language   209

Appendix Three   Further Reading   213

Index   224

VIII

MAPS

Chake Chake	195
Exploration in East Africa	18
Mkoani	197
Pemba Island	188
Wete	199
Zanzibar	XIV
Zanzibar and East Africa: European Territories	28
Zanzibar and the Slave Trade	12
Zanzibar in the Ancient World	6
Zanzibar Island	160
Zanzibar Stone Town	132
Zanzibar Town and surrounding area	84

Perspectives on Zanzibar

Zanzibar is one of those magical African names, like Timbuktu, Casablanca and Kilimanjaro. For many travellers, the name itself is often reason enough to come. And when *you* arrive, you'll discover for yourself many other reasons and the many different faces of Zanzibar.

Some of Zanzibar's early visitors seem to have been favourably impressed:

'This place, for the goodness of the harbour and watering and plentiful refreshing with fish, and for sending sorts of fruits of the country, as cows...and oxen and hens, is carefully to be sought for by such of all ships as shall hereafter pass that way.'

James Lancaster, captain of the *Edward Bonaventure*, first English ship to visit Zanzibar (1592)

'Truly prepossessing was our first view...of Zanzibar. Earth, sea and sky all seemed wrapped in a soft and sensuous repose... The sea of purest sapphire...lay basking...under a blaze of sunshine.'

Richard Burton, British explorer (1856)

'An artist could find genial occupation for years; but your matter-of-fact...tourist would vote the place slow, of course, see nothing in it, and sigh for a future of broad streets and civilisation, broad-cloth, bottled beer and blacking; and from such revilers of the picturesque I trust a kindly Providence may long deliver the quaint, queer, rambling old Arab town of Zanzibar.'

J F Elton, *Travels and Researches among the Lakes and Mountains of Eastern and Central Africa* (1879)

Not all travellers were so impressed, however:

'The stench from the...exposed sea-beach, which is the general depository of the filth of the town, is quite horrible. At night, it is so gross and crass, one might cut a slice and manure the garden with it. It might be called 'Stinkibar' rather than Zanzibar.'

David Livingstone, British explorer (1866)

'February 19th. We anchored off Zanzibar at dawn. A day of fierce heat. The island is said to enjoy a cool season. I have never struck it. An hour's stroll ashore sufficed to revive old memories, then I retired to the ship for a cold bath and an afternoon under the electric fans.'

Evelyn Waugh, *Tourist in Africa* (1959)

The name of Zanzibar crops up in all sorts of places. In popular fiction:

'And then they had reached the town and were threading their way...through streets so narrow that neighbours living on opposite sides...could surely shake hands with each other from their upper windows. Tall whitewashed houses, so high that the streets were deep canyons and crevasses. Hot white walls, hot black shadows...The smell of strange eastern spices and hot dust; the scent of sandalwood...and cloves. A sound of laughter and music and drums...'

M M Kaye, *Death in Zanzibar* (Longmans/Penguin)

In music:

'Why do the wrong people travel, travel, travel,
When the right people stay back home?
What compulsion compels them
And who the hell tells them
To drag their cans to Zanzibar
Instead of staying quietly in Omaha?'

Noel Coward, *Sail Away*

'Then I'll go sailing far,
Off to Zanzibar.
Though my dream places seem,
Better than they really are.'

Popular song (1950s)

In magazines and newspaper travel sections:

'Zanzibar engulfs you. Arabic dhows wait in the harbour. The old Stone Town is heavy with the scent of spice, heat and decay... Muezzins call the faithful to prayer and behind intricately carved doors there is a vacuum of silence, of families and half-empty offices guarding secrets.'

Richard Lutz, *The Independent* (Britain, June 1989)

'Gradually, through the mist, I saw Zanzibar Island, newly-born in the early dawn...glistening in the distance... These are not the crisp whitewashed buildings one sees on travel posters of the Greek islands... The buildings exude an atmosphere of palpable decay; of a still-inhabited, picturesque ruin. If buildings could speak, these would be crying out for restoration.'

Dana Seidenburg, *Signature Magazine* (1990)

'Travellers from far away lands sit alongside the grand Zanzibar wazee (old people) and gaze over the sea to Chunguu Island...where ancient tortoises scuttle about the ruins of a never-used prison. The sea breeze wafts the pungent scent of clove oil...'

Phoebe Vreeland, *Kenya Airways Magazine* (1991)

'Zanzibar gleamed in the late afternoon sun like a fairytale set in a harbour of aquamarine. Zanzibar – even more exotic than its name. It really is a fairytale place. You know you've seen it before, imagined it as a child, when you step from the wharf and find yourself right in the heart of the old Stone Town. Palm trees lean beside Arabic whitewashed houses and against a bright blue sky; men walk by wearing long white robes; women wrap the black bui-bui around bright dresses; and on the harbour Arabic sailing boats – dhows – glide by. Any minute you expect to spot Ali Baba or maybe the odd genie.'

Leanne Logan, *TNT Magazine* (1990)

'Zanzibar is full of ghosts, a time capsule heavily laden with the past.'

Mark Ottaway, *The Sunday Times* (Britain, September 1994)

'In most parts of the world today, the traveler tends to get a sneaking feeling that he has arrived too late; in Zanzibar the traveler is rewarded with that rare feeling that for once he got there in time. The island has been sensitively cleaned up since the Marxist excesses of the seventies, but has not yet been wrecked by Western development.'

William Dalrymple, *Condé Nast Traveler* (USA, April 1995)

'Pemba is like the straight man in a successful double act, the one nobody can remember. It is part of Zanzibar, an entity that consists of two islands. The main island has taken the name, the adulation, the money and all the best architecture, leaving Pemba as its forgotten partner. Most of the tourists who are now busy rearranging Zanzibar's economy have never heard of Pemba. To me, this seemed a pretty good recommendation...'

Stanley Stewart, *The Sunday Times* (Britain, October 1995)

'All your desert island fantasies come true as you approach Zanzibar. Indeed, all the fantasies you ever had about travel suddenly crowd around. The sea is preposterously aquamarine, the sand implausibly golden and the airport impossibly empty. Check the map in the in-flight magazine to make sure you are not dreaming...'

Simon Calder, *The Independent* (Britain, August 1996)

'The insanitary old Stone Town that Burton and others first clapped eyes on was left to crumble...and it might well have done so entirely had not the Aga Khan given a "something must be done" speech...then primed the pump for the restoration process with funds from his Foundation. His involvement has not been without controversy, but anyone who starts such a project not with something flash and showy, but by fixing the drains, gets my vote.'

Mark Ottaway, *The Sunday Times* (Britain, June 1997)

Today's travellers also have a wide range of varying impressions:

'Sailing into the port was like entering a giant Christmas Cake. The smell of cloves and spices is amazing.'

'The history of Zanzibar fascinates me. Sultans, princesses, palaces, explorers, pirates, ivory traders... Wow!'

'Zanzibar Town must rate as the Venice of Africa. Narrow streets of beautiful buildings, all in danger of crumbling away. And after rain these streets turn into canals!'

'I didn't enjoy Zanzibar Town. The decrepit buildings, the dirt and the filth all depressed me. But the beaches. Man! What a great place to hang out.'

'Compared to other African cities and towns, Zanzibar was so clean and airy. I loved it. I could have stayed for weeks.'

'I enjoyed the atmosphere of the town. The history and the romance of the place. I've never been anywhere else like it. And the 'lost palaces' around the island – it was like walking through the pages of Arabian Nights. The beaches on the east coast were great too, but I don't need to go halfway round the world for a good beach!'

'I was completely lost for words when I first saw the beaches on the East Coast. They are beautiful and as yet unspoilt, although there was building galore.'

'Zanzibar has left a great impression on me, mostly favourable, although it did take me a day or so to become accustomed to the squalor, dirt and smells of the Stone Town.'

'Many travellers rave about the beaches on Zanzibar. They are in fact idyllic: clean white sand, palm trees, not many tourists, and photogenic fishing boats. But it seems very narrow-minded to come here just for the beach. There's much more to it than that. If Zanzibar becomes just another beach resort it will certainly cheapen the experience. I hope Zanzibar doesn't go the way of Kenya's Lamu and Malindi.'

'I enjoyed walking around the Stone Town, always getting lost, and taking a different way home every night. I'll always remember the amazing colour of the sea and the beautiful, beautiful sunsets. And no tourists! But it won't stay like this for long. I'm glad I went when I did.'

During my travels, and in the course of writing this guidebook, I have visited the islands of Zanzibar several times over the last ten years. Until recently, the greatest impression the islands made on me was the 'unspoiltness' of it all. This was mainly due to the local political situation and the efforts required by travellers just to reach Zanzibar. In the 1980s, for example, before the days of the high-speed catamarans, the intending visitor had to contend with long and uncomfortable dhow-rides or the vagaries of the Air Tanzania timetable, plus some quite formidable entry requirements and a lack of any decent place to stay (for whatever budget).

However, since the early 1990s, new hotels have been built and the transport services from the mainland have improved. More visitors have started to come to Zanzibar, but it's still only a trickle compared to some other tourist destinations in Africa. Although Zanzibar may have lost some of its isolation, many parts of the islands retain their unique atmosphere of peace, charm and remoteness.

The Zanzibar government department with special responsibility for tourism intends to restrict the development of hotels and other facilities, and hopes to ensure that tourism remains relatively low-key, not too obtrusive, and provides some benefits for the local people without destroying their culture or environment. These are laudable aims, but to keep Zanzibar 'un-spoilt' much of the responsibility lies with us, the visitors (tourists and travellers all).

If we behave in a sensible and appropriate manner, treat the local people with consideration and respect, support local businesses and conservation schemes, travel with an open mind and see the islands of Zanzibar as a community, not a theme-park, our experiences here will be so much the richer for it.

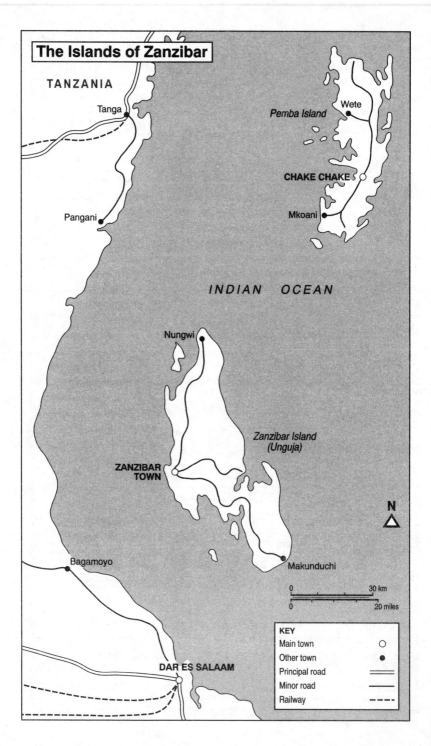

Chapter One

Zanzibar – A Profile

This is an introductory chapter describing in brief many different aspects of Zanzibar. More detailed information on subjects such as history, wildlife and vegetation are given elsewhere in later chapters of this book.

Location
Zanzibar consists of two large islands, plus several smaller ones, about 40km (25 miles) off the coast of East Africa, in the Indian Ocean, about 6° south of the Equator. The two large islands are Unguja (usually called Zanzibar Island) and Pemba.

Size
Zanzibar Island is about 85km long and between 20km and 30km wide, with an area of just under 1,500km² (640 square miles). Pemba Island is about 75km long and between 15km and 20km wide, with an area around 850km² (380 square miles).

Topography
The islands of Zanzibar are generally flat and low lying. The western and central parts of Zanzibar Island have some low hills, where the highest point is about 120m (390ft) above sea level. Pemba Island has a central ridge, cut by several small valleys, and appears more hilly than Zanzibar Island, although the highest point on Pemba is only 95m (310 ft) above sea level. The islands of Zanzibar are surrounded by coasts of rocky inlets or sandy beaches, with lagoons and mangrove swamps, and coral reefs beyond the shoreline particularly on the eastern side of the main islands.

Climate
The climate of Zanzibar is dominated by the movements of the Indian Ocean monsoons, and characterised by wet and dry seasons. The northeast monsoons blow from November/December to February/March, and the southwest monsoons blow from June to September/October. The main rains fall from mid-March to the end of May, and there is a short rainy season in November. Humidity is generally quite high, although this can be relieved by winds and sea breezes. Temperatures do not vary greatly throughout the

year, with daytime averages around 26°C (80°F) on Zanzibar Island from June to October, and around 28°C from December to February. Pemba tends to be cooler and get slightly more rain than Zanzibar Island.

Vegetation and agriculture

The islands were originally forested, but human habitation has resulted in widespread clearing, although a few isolated pockets of indigenous forest remain. The main crops grown in Zanzibar are coconuts and cloves. Bananas, citrus fruits and other spices are also grown commercially. Seaweed is a major export crop. Maize, cassava and other vegetables and cereals are grown for local consumption.

Wildlife

There are no large wild animals on Zanzibar, as found on the African mainland. Forest areas are inhabited by monkeys and small antelopes. Civets and various species of mongoose are found all over the islands. Birdlife is varied and interesting, with over 100 species being recorded, although bird populations are not as high as in other parts of the East African region. The marine wildlife, in the coral reefs that surround the islands, is particularly rich.

History

The monsoon winds that blow across the Indian Ocean have allowed contact between Persia, Arabia, India and the coast of East Africa (including the islands of Zanzibar) for over 2,000 years. The first European arrivals were Portuguese 'navigators' looking for a trade route to India. They reached Zanzibar at the end of the 15th century and established a trading station here and at other points on the East African coast. At the end of the 17th century the Portuguese were ousted by the Omani Arabs. During this period, Zanzibar became a major slaving centre. In 1840, the Omani Sultan Said moved his court from Muscat to Zanzibar, and the island became an Arab state and an important centre of trade and politics in the region. Many European explorers, including Livingstone and Stanley, began their expeditions into the interior of Africa from Zanzibar during the second half of the 19th century.

Zanzibar was a British protectorate from 1890 until 1963, when the state gained independence. In 1964, the sultan and the government were overthrown in a revolution. In the same year, Zanzibar and the newly independent country of Tanganyika combined to form the United Republic of Tanzania.

People

It is thought that the original inhabitants of Zanzibar came from the African mainland around 3,000 to 4,000 years ago, although no descendants of these people remain, having been completely absorbed by later arrivals. During the first millennium AD, African peoples of Bantu origin migrated from central Africa and settled across east and southern Africa. On the coastal area and islands, including Zanzibar, many of these peoples adopted some of the customs and language of the Arabs who were trading on the coast and became known as the Swahili. From the 10th century, groups of immigrants from Shiraz (Persia) settled in Zanzibar and mingled with the local people. In the following centuries, various groups of Arab and Persian peoples settled on the islands and continued to intermarry with the Swahili and Shirazi. In the 18th and 19th centuries, Omani Arabs settled on Zanzibar as rulers and landowners, forming an elite group, while Indian settlers formed a merchant class.

Today, most of the people in Zanzibar are Shirazi or Swahili, although precise definitions and clear distinctions are not always possible. They fall into three groups: the Wahadimu (mainly in the southern and central parts of Zanzibar Island), the Watumbatu (on Tumbatu Island and in the northern part of Zanzibar Island), and the Wapemba (on Pemba Island). There are also groups of people of African origin who are descendants of freed slaves. In recent times, a large number of Africans have immigrated from mainland Tanzania, and some Arabs, who were expelled after the 1964 revolution, have returned to Zanzibar. There are also people from Goa, India and Pakistan, mainly involved in trade or tourism, and a growing number of European expatriates and volunteers, many working in the tour industry, with others employed as teachers, doctors and engineers.

Population and settlement
The population of Zanzibar was around 600,000 in 1988, the last date when reliable figures were available. In 1992, the population was estimated at around 700,000 with a 3% annual growth rate. Based on these figures, the population estimate for 1996 was around 800,000. Zanzibar's largest settlement is Zanzibar Town (sometimes called Zanzibar City), on Zanzibar Island (the correct local name is Unguja), with about 100,000 inhabitants. Other towns on Zanzibar Island include Chaani, Bambi and Makunduchi, but these are small. Outside these towns, most people live in small villages and are engaged in farming or fishing. The overall settlement pattern is similar on Pemba. The largest town is Chake Chake, with a population of about 10,000; other smaller towns are Wete and Mkoani.

Language (see also *Appendix Two*)
The language of Zanzibar is Swahili (called *Kiswahili* locally). Visitors with a basic grasp of this language will be understood anywhere, although there are many forms and dialects found in different areas. Arabic is also spoken. English is widely used in the towns and tourist areas.

Religion
Islam is the dominant religion, and practised by most Zanzibaris. All towns and villages have mosques. In Zanzibar Town there are also churches and

temples for the small populations of Christians and Hindus.

Government

Zanzibar is a separate state within the United Republic of Tanzania, governed by a Revolutionary Council and House of Representatives, whose members are elected or appointed. The president of Zanzibar is also the vice-president of Tanzania.

Economy

For the people of Zanzibar, fishing and farming are the main economic activities. From the beginning of the 19th century to the mid-1970s Zanzibar exported a large proportion of the world's supply of cloves, and the islands' economy was based largely on this commodity. Some diversification has occurred in the last ten to 15 years, but cloves are still a major export, along with coconut products and other spices. In recent years, seaweed has also become an important export commodity. The potential for tourism to be a major earner of foreign currency has been recognised and this is being developed. The number of tourists visiting Zanzibar is increasing every year.

Currency and exchange rates

As part of Tanzania, Zanzibar's unit of currency is the Tanzanian Shilling (TSh). Visitors (non-Tanzanians) to Zanzibar must pay for some items, such as air flights, ship tickets and smarter hotels, in foreign ('hard') currency, usually US dollars ($). The prices for many other items, such as tours or rental cars, are quoted in US dollars, although these are payable in hard currency or in TSh at the going rate. This situation means the US dollar is an unofficial second currency in Zanzibar. Prices in TSh are likely to vary considerably in the future, but prices in US dollars will remain more constant. Both currencies are used in this book. In November 1997, the exchange rates were:

1 US dollar = 600 TSh approx
1 UK pound = 1,000 TSh approx

Visitors should note, however, that exchange rates are not fixed and are likely to fluctuate.

Chapter Two

A History of Zanzibar

Sarah Chanter

First inhabitants and early visitors

The first human beings (*Homo erectus*) evolved in the East African Rift Valley, within a thousand miles of Zanzibar, about 1½ million years ago. They migrated throughout Africa and later Asia and beyond, becoming hunter-gatherers and fishermen. Zanzibar's first inhabitants were probably fishermen who crossed from the African mainland in dug-out canoes sometime before the 1st century AD.

At around the same time, or even earlier, the East African coast (including the islands of Zanzibar) may have received visitors from many parts of the ancient world, including Mesopotamia (present-day Iraq) and Egypt. The Egyptian pharaohs sent expeditions to the land of Punt (present-day Somalia) in around 3000BC and again in 1492BC, which possibly continued southwards down the East African coast. This is supported by carvings on temple walls at Luxor showing sailing boats with slaves unloading gold, ivory tusks, leopard skins and trees of frankincense.

Other visitors may have included Phoenicians, a seafaring people from the eastern shores of the Mediterranean. Around 600BC, a Phoenician fleet sailed south along the coast, past Zanzibar, and is believed to have circumnavigated Africa before returning to the Mediterranean three years later.

During the 2nd century BC the Silk Route, from China to India across the Himalayas, was in constant use: it is likely that Chinese silk and porcelain started to reach Zanzibar via Indian merchants.

By the 1st century AD Greek and Roman ships were sailing from the Red Sea down the East African coast, searching for ivory. Around 60AD, a Greek merchant from Alexandria wrote a guide for ships in the Indian Ocean called *The Periplus of the Erythaean Sea*. This is the first recorded eyewitness account of the East African Coast, and describes 'the Island of Menouthesias' (most likely the present-day island of Unguja, also called Zanzibar Island) as '...flat and wooded' with 'many rivers' and 'small sewn boats used for fishing'. Another Alexandrine Greek, Claudius Ptolemaeus (usually called Ptolemy), also mentioned Menouthesias in his book *Geographike*, written about 150AD.

Trade between Africa and the kingdoms of the ancient world continued to grow. The coastal islands, including Zanzibar, were now part of a vast commercial network, which extended from Egypt, Greece and Rome to the East African coast, and across the Indian Ocean to India and beyond.

Africans, Arabs and Persians

At the beginning of the 1st century AD, Zanzibar and the East African coast were under the sovereignty of the Kingdom of Saba (also called Sheba). The Sabeans were a maritime people, with a large kingdom in southwestern Arabia (now Yemen); they used the seasonal monsoon to travel regularly between Arabia and the East African coast. Their dhows sailed south between November and February, on the northeast monsoon, carrying beads, Chinese porcelain and cloth. Then, between March and September, they returned north on the southwest monsoon, carrying food grains, mangrove poles for timber, tortoiseshell, ebony and ivory.

At about the same time, it is thought that Arab and Persian ships from the Persian Gulf were also sailing down the coast of East Africa. These people traded with the local inhabitants but they remained visitors and, at this stage, they did not settle.

During the 3rd and 4th centuries AD, other groups of migrating peoples started to arrive on the east coast of Africa, having originally come from the area around present-day Cameroon. These people were Bantu (the name comes from the term used to define their group of languages); they traded

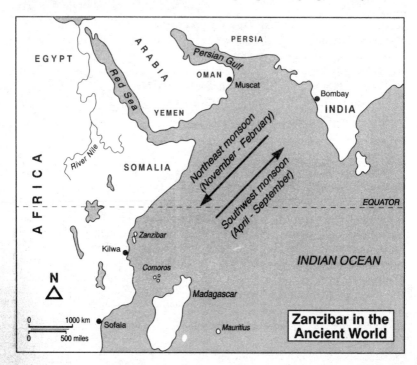

Zanzibar in the Ancient World

with the Arabs, exporting ivory, rhino-horn, tortoiseshell and palm oil, and importing metal tools and weapons, wine and wheat.

The 7th century AD saw the rise of Islam in Arabia. At the same time wars in this area, and subsequent unrest in Persia, caused many people from these regions to escape to the East African coast, this time to settle permanently. The fertile, peaceful area was seen as a haven from their own dry and war-torn countries. Many of the immigrants brought the new Islamic religion with them.

These Arab traders called the East African coast 'Zinj el Barr', meaning land of the black people, from where the modern name Zanzibar is derived. 'Zinj' comes from *zang*, the Persian word for 'black', and *barr* is the Arabic word for 'land'. The Arabs may also have derived the word from *Zayn za'l barr*, meaning 'Fair is this land'. Zanzibar remained the name of the whole coast, including the islands of Unguja and Pemba (which together make up the present-day state of Zanzibar), until the late 15th century.

There are several accounts of the emigrations from Arabia to East Africa. (The history of this period is largely based on stories handed down by word of mouth through generations, which are difficult to separate from myth and legend.) One story tells of two Arab chiefs from Oman who arrived in East Africa with their families around the end of the 7th century, and settled on the island of Pate, near Lamu. Another story tells of a large-scale emigration from Shiraz, in Persia, some time between the 8th and 10th centuries. The Sultan of Shiraz and his six sons migrated with their followers in seven boats. One of the sons stopped at Pemba, while others settled in Mombasa and Kilwa. The Shirazis brought Islamic pottery, Chinese porcelain, dates, spices and cloth.

The 9th century Arab tale of *Sinbad the Sailor*, one of the stories in *The Arabian Nights*, was most probably inspired by accounts of journeys by Arab sailors to East Africa and Southeast Asia. Sinbad was an intrepid sailor from Mesopotamia; he encountered apes and elephants, and brought home gold, cloves and ivory.

Throughout the 8th and 9th centuries, the Arabs and Persians continued to trade with their original homelands. Dhows regularly sailed from Africa to Arabia and Persia carrying gold, ivory, rhino-horn, leopard skins, tortoiseshell and ambergris from whales. African slaves were also carried to the Persian Gulf, probably to work in the marshlands of Mesopotamia.

Trading links between East Africa and Asia also continued to grow. Ivory was exported to India, and later China, while Indian cloth and Chinese porcelain were imported to Arabia and Zanzibar. Between the 8th and 10th centuries, Indonesian sailors from Java and Sumatra are thought to have reached East Africa and Madagascar, possibly introducing coconuts and bananas.

Around this time the Bantu peoples who had settled on the East African coast and islands (over several centuries) started to call themselves the Swahili, taking their name from the Arabic word *sahil* meaning 'coast'.

Their language, Kiswahili, although Bantu in origin, contained many Arabic words. It also included some Persian words, mainly nautical terms. The Swahili people seem to have co-existed peacefully with the Arab and Persian settlers; they gradually intermarried with them and adopted many of their customs and traditions, including the Islamic religion. On Unguja (Zanzibar Island), the Shirazi settlers are believed to have married into the family of the island's king. Several centuries later, the *Mwinyi Mkuu* ('The Great Lord'), the traditional ruler of Unguja, continued to claim descent from a Shirazi prince.

It seems that relations between the Arabs and Shirazis were not always so peaceful: an account from the 11th century tells how the Shirazis of Zanzibar had to defend themselves against a group of Omani Arabs who had also settled on the island. Despite these setbacks, the Shirazi settlement on Zanzibar continued. Early in the 12th century, a mosque (which can still be seen today) was built at Kizimkazi, on the southern part of the island. An inscription is dated 500AH (*Anno Hegirae*), which corresponds to the Christian year 1107AD, making this the oldest known Islamic building on the East African coast. From the end of the 12th century, Omani immigrants also settled in Pemba.

Trade continued to expand and Zanzibar became an increasingly powerful and important commercial centre. Major imports included cotton cloth, porcelain and copper from Dabhol, a port on the west coast of India, and exports included iron from Sofala (in present-day Mozambique). By the 13th century, Zanzibar was minting its own coins, and stone buildings were starting to replace more basic mud dwellings. In 1295, the Venetian traveller Marco Polo wrote 'The people have a king...elephants in plenty...and whales in large numbers', although he never visited the island. Other writers of the time noted that the kings and queens of Zanzibar and Pemba dressed in fine silks and cottons, wore gold jewellery, and lived in stone houses decorated with Persian carpets and Chinese porcelain.

Many Chinese imports had come to Zanzibar via India and the Silk Route, but in the early 15th century the ports on the coast of East Africa were trading directly with China. Gold, ivory and rhino-horn were transported to the East, as well as a small number of slaves, mainly for domestic labour and military service. In 1414, a dhow from the city of Malindi (in present-day Kenya) carried a giraffe to China, as a present for the emperor. A few years later, the Chinese admiral, Cheng Ho, visited Mogadishu, Malindi and possibly Zanzibar. The trade came to an abrupt end in 1443 when the new Ming Emperor banned Chinese merchants from going abroad. However, the demand for ivory remained, which the Arab dhows supplied via markets in India.

By the mid-15th century the islands of Zanzibar, with Mombasa, Malindi, Lamu and Kilwa, formed a chain of thriving Islamic city states, each with its own sultan, spread along the East African coast. Positioned on the coast of Africa, these cities had close trading links with Arabia, Persia, India and

Southeast Asia, but no significant attempts were ever made to penetrate the East African interior. Goods such as gold, iron, ivory and amber were brought to the coastal city states, such as Zanzibar, by African traders, and hence exported further afield.

This flourishing Indian Ocean trade may have continued successfully for many more years but it was severely disrupted at the end of the 15th century by the arrival of the Portuguese on the coast of East Africa.

The Portuguese

By the mid-15th century, Prince Henry 'The Navigator' of Portugal was encouraging voyages of exploration around the African coast. He hoped to find a sea route to the East, as well as the Christian Kingdom of the legendary Prester John (or 'Priest-king') of Abyssinia. With the rise of the Ottoman Empire in 1453, all spices from the East now reached Portugal through potentially hostile Muslim countries. Prices were high as the Sultans of Egypt and the Ottoman Empire charged considerable levies for the passage of goods across their lands.

In 1487, Prince Henry's successor, King John II, dispatched two expeditions to the East: one by sea around the southern tip of Africa, the other overland through Egypt. By 1488, Bartholomew Dias had rounded the Cape of Good Hope (so called because of the hope that it led to a sea route to India) before turning back. Meanwhile, Pedro da Covilhan had sailed across the Mediterranean to Alexandria, crossed Egypt in disguise as a Muslim honey merchant and then sailed from the Red Sea to India. On his way back (around 1489) he made a diversion along the coast of East Africa, sailing past Zanzibar to Sofala (in present-day Mozambique) before returning to the Red Sea.

In 1497, another Portuguese navigator, Vasco da Gama, encouraged by the reports of Dias and da Covilhan, rounded the Cape of Good Hope and sailed northwards up the coast of East Africa, on the way to India. He passed Zanzibar and landed at Mombasa, where he received a hostile reception from the sultan. But he got a warm welcome in Malindi, an old enemy of Mombasa. Da Gama built a pillar of friendship on the shore at Malindi and employed an Omani navigator called Ahmed bin Majid to guide him across the Indian Ocean. On his return from India in 1499 he moored for a day off the island of Unguja (today's Zanzibar Island).

More Portuguese ships followed in the wake of da Covilhan and da Gama. They needed safe provisioning and repair bases for their voyages to and from the Far East, and so garrisons were established in the harbours of Unguja (Zanzibar Island), Pemba and Mombasa.

Any early friendship that may have existed was soon forgotten when the Portuguese took control of Unguja (Zanzibar Island) in 1503. A ship commanded by Rui Lorenco Ravasco moored off the southern end of the island while Portuguese sailors captured over 20 Swahili dhows and shot about 35 islanders. The Mwinyi Mkuu (king of Zanzibar) was forced to become a subject of Portugal, and agreed to allow Portuguese ships free access to Zanzibar to be supplied with fresh food and water. Additionally, the Mwinyi Mkuu was required to pay an annual tribute to the Portuguese crown.

Portuguese domination of the region continued. In 1505 they took control of Mombasa, and in 1506 Pemba came under Portuguese control. Between 1507 and 1511 the Portuguese also occupied territories in the Arabian Gulf, including Muscat and the island of Hormuz.

By 1510 Unguja's tribute had fallen short and the people of Pemba had also become hostile to the Portuguese. Under Duarte de Lemos, the Portuguese looted and set fire to settlements on Unguja, then plundered the town of Pujini in Pemba. They soon regained both islands and by 1525 the whole East African coast, from Lamu to Sofala, was also under Portuguese control and a vital part of their trading empire. Gold, ivory, ebony and slaves from the interior were carried to India or back to Portugal. Iron-ore and garnets from Sofala, and coconut fibre and gum-copal (a tree resin) from the islands were also exported. Cloth, beads, porcelain and metal tools were imported from Oman and Portugal.

Around 1560 the Portuguese built a church and small trading settlement on a western peninsula of Unguja (Zanzibar Island). This was to become Zanzibar Town. But although the Portuguese occupied Unguja, and forced the local people to trade under their supervision, the islanders continued to pay allegiance to the Mwinyi Mkuu, their own king.

Portugal was not the only European power with interests in the Indian Ocean. In November 1591 the *Edward Bonaventura*, captained by Sir James Lancaster, became the first British ship to call at Zanzibar. It was supplied with fresh food and water by the Mwinyi Mkuu. Soon, more British ships were calling at Zanzibar on their way between Britain and the new colony of India.

In 1625 a Zanzibari princess is believed to have escaped with a Scottish sailor called John Henderson who had been captured on the island. Today, their portraits are in the collection of the Scottish National Portrait Gallery in Edinburgh.

With the advent of British ships in the Indian Ocean, the Portuguese needed to strengthen their position on the coast. In 1594 they built a fort at Chake Chake in Pemba, and from 1593 to 1595 Fort Jesus in Mombasa was constructed. Settlers arrived from Portugal, and a Portuguese garrison was established in Fort Jesus, brutally suppressing the local population. Mombasa became known as *Mvita*, 'the place of war', and the Portuguese governor, *Afriti*, 'the devil'.

Despite these fortifications however, the Portuguese position in East Africa began to weaken. In Arabia, Hormuz was regained by the Persians in 1622, and in January 1650 Muscat was regained by the Omani Arabs. Following this victory, the Sultan of Oman's navy then sailed to Zanzibar to help the Mwinyi Mkuu, Queen Mwana Mwema. The Omanis raided the

Portuguese settlement on Zanzibar, killing many people and imprisoning about 400 in the church. They also attacked and burnt the Portuguese settlement on Pemba. By 1668, virtually the entire coastal area was in Omani hands. The only garrisons still held by the Portuguese were Fort Jesus in Mombasa, and Zanzibar.

In 1679 the queen of Pemba, who had given her island to the Portuguese, had become a Christian and was living in Goa. In 1682 the Portuguese persuaded her to return, but this attempt to install a friendly ruler in Pemba was frustrated when her own subjects drove her out. The last Portuguese inhabitants were expelled in 1695.

By this time, Queen Mwana Mwema of Zanzibar Island had been succeeded by her son, Yusuf. After he died, towards the end of the 17th century, the island was divided between his two children, Bakari and Fatuma. King Bakari ruled the southern part of the island, with Kizimkazi as his capital, while his sister, Queen Fatuma, ruled the northern part. Fatuma supported the Portuguese, so her capital was built near the garrison on the western peninsula which later became the site of Zanzibar Town.

When the Omani fleet arrived at Mombasa and laid siege to Fort Jesus in March 1696, Queen Fatuma sent three dhows full of food to help the Portuguese defenders. The dhows were captured and burnt by the Omanis, who then attacked Zanzibar itself, forcing Queen Fatuma and her followers to flee into the interior.

The siege of Mombasa lasted until December 1698, when the Omani forces took Fort Jesus and installed an Omani governor. Once again, the Omanis attacked Zanzibar. They drove out the last of the Portuguese settlers and captured Queen Fatuma and took her to Oman, where she spent the next 12 years in exile before returning to resume her rule. While she was away, her son Hassan took the title Mwinyi Mkuu, but paid allegiance to Oman.

Thus the Portuguese were finally ousted from the whole East African coast, and the Omanis were firmly in control of the entire region as far south as present-day Mozambique (which remained in Portuguese hands until 1972).

Omani rule and the rise of the slave trade

From 1698 the Sultan of Oman ruled the islands of Zanzibar from Muscat, his capital, through appointed governors and occasional armed raids to put down minor rebellions. To consolidate his grip on the islands, a fort was built in Zanzibar Town, on the site of the Portuguese church, and by 1710 about 50 Omani soldiers were garrisoned there.

By this time, Oman had become a major trading nation. One of its major exports was dates, and the expansion of date plantations created a demand for cheap slave labour. The rules of Islam forbade the enslavement of Muslims, so Africans were imported in large numbers, many of them transported through Zanzibar. It is estimated that there were about 5,000

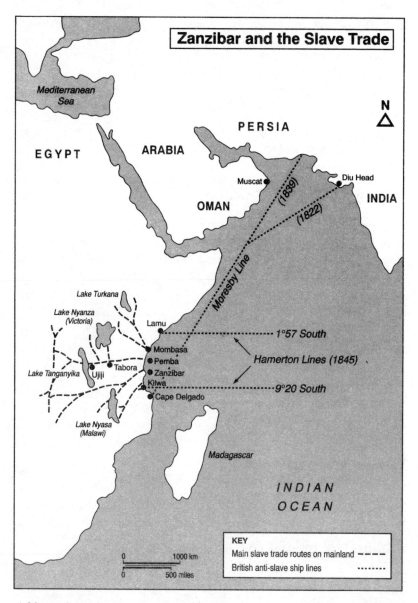

African slaves in Oman at the beginning of the 18th century, with about 500 new slaves arriving each year. Although most slaves were used on the plantations, others were employed as domestic workers or concubines, and some were re-exported to Persia or India.

In 1744, in Oman, the ruling Yaa'rubi dynasty (which had been in power since 1624) came to an end after a long civil war. It was succeeded by the new Busaidi dynasty led by Ahmed bin Said al Busaidi, an Omani merchant and ship-owner. Ahmed was appointed Sultan of Oman and the East African coast; one of his first moves was to install a new governor in Zanzibar.

At this time, the governors of the East African city states paid allegiance to Oman, but in practice they enjoyed a great deal of autonomy. Zanzibar, Pemba, Lamu and Kilwa were all ruled by members of the Busaidi family, but a rival Omani family, the Mazrui, was in control of Mombasa. In 1746 the Mazruis declared Mombasa independent of Oman, and overthrew the Busaidi force on Pemba. In 1753 they tried to capture Zanzibar, but the governor here remained loyal to Oman and repelled the attack.

During this time, the Mwinyi Mkuu, King Hassan, had died and been succeeded by his son, named Sultan, who in turn was succeeded by his son Ahmed, and then by his grandson Hassan II.

Zanzibar was now a major commercial centre and had also become very important strategically. From the middle of the 18th century there was a flourishing trade in slaves from Zanzibar and Kilwa to the Mascarenes (present-day Mauritius and Reunion) where slaves were used on sugar and clove plantations. By the 1770s these numbered about 3,000 slaves a year. In the same period Dutch ships came to Zanzibar in search of slaves to work on plantations in the East Indies.

Until this time African slave traders had brought captured slaves to the coast, but by the end of the 18th century the demand for slaves had increased to such an extent that Arab and Swahili traders from the coast and islands were penetrating the African interior. By the 1770s caravan traders had already travelled inland as far as Lake Nyasa (present-day Lake Malawi). (For more details, see the *East African Slave Trade* box, page 126.)

In Oman a new sultan, whose name was Sultan bin (son of) Ahmed, came to power in 1792. He needed a strong ally to help him combat the Mazrui and also to keep the Persians out of Oman. He found this ally in Britain, who was at war with France and knew that the French Emperor, Napoleon Bonaparte, was planning to march through Persia and capture Muscat, on his way to invade India. So in 1798 Britain and Oman agreed a Treaty of Commerce and Navigation. Sultan bin Ahmed pledged himself to British interests in India, and his territories became out of bounds to the French. He allowed the British East India Company to establish a trading station in the Persian Gulf, and a British Consul was posted to Muscat.

As well as defeating Bonaparte, the British had another motive for the treaty with Oman: they wanted to put pressure on the sultan to end slavery, which had been declared illegal in England in 1772. At this time, the trade from Africa to Oman was still buoyant with about 3,000 African slaves passing through Zanzibar every year.

At the same time, Zanzibar's position as an important trade centre was bolstered further when the supply of ivory from Mozambique to India collapsed due to excessive Portuguese export duties. The traders simply shipped their ivory through Zanzibar instead.

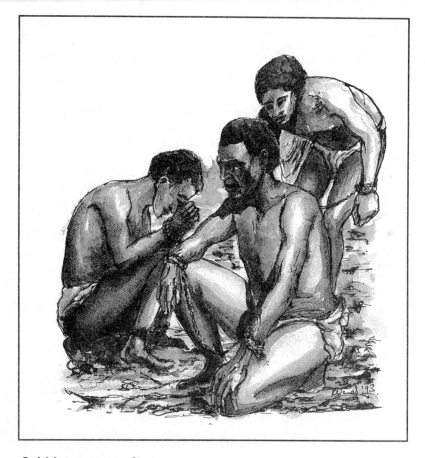

Said becomes sultan

In 1804 Sultan bin Ahmed of Oman was killed in battle, and his sons Salim and Said (aged 15 and 13) jointly inherited his kingdom with their cousin, Bedr, acting as regent. Two years later the young Said killed Bedr, who he believed was plotting to kill him; in 1806 he was proclaimed Sultan of Oman and the East African coast.

Said ruled his kingdom from Muscat and did not visit his African territories for several years. He maintained good relations with Britain; like his father, he hoped for British help against the Persians and the Mazruis. During this period, wars and drought had drained Oman's economy, and many Omani merchants migrated to Zanzibar to participate in coastal trading and the caravans to the interior.

Meanwhile, in Europe, a campaign led by William Wilberforce resulted in the abolition of the slave trade within the British Empire in 1807. The USA passed a law against slave trading in 1808; the French and Germans did the same a few years later.

In East Africa, however, about 8,000 slaves were brought from the mainland to Zanzibar every year, many of them carrying ivory. This led to a surplus of slaves – a serious problem for the traders and for the sultan of Oman. The answer to this problem came in 1812, when a Muscat-born Arab called Saleh bin Haramil al Abray introduced clove trees into Zanzibar from the island of Bourbon (now Reunion). Zanzibar's surplus of slaves was diverted to work on clove plantations and demand increased once again.

As the demand for slaves and ivory continued to expand, Arab traders from the coast pushed further inland. In 1820, they established a trading centre at Kazeh (near present-day Tabora, in Tanzania), over 800km (500 miles) from the coast. From Kazeh, trade routes branched north to the shores of present-day Lake Victoria, northwest to Buganda (now Uganda), and southwest to the southern end of Lake Tanganyika. (See *Zanzibar and the Slave Trade* map, page 12.)

Early British anti-slaving attempts

To combat this expansion in slavery the British Consul in Muscat continued to put pressure on Sultan Said to end the slave trade. In September 1822 Said signed an anti-slavery treaty with the British Captain Fairfax Morseby which prohibited slave transport south and east of the 'Moresby Line' drawn from Cape Delgado, the southern limit of the sultan's domain in Africa, to Diu Head on the coast of India. (See *Zanzibar and the Slave Trade* map, page 000.)

This treaty meant that the transport of slaves from Zanzibar to the Mascarenes and to India was banned, but still permitted between Zanzibar and Oman. The sultan was also banned from selling slaves to Christians, which included the French for their Indian Ocean islands. British warships gained the right to confiscate any dhows found carrying slaves in forbidden waters.

Ironically, British prohibition of the slave trade to the Mascarenes only led to an increased development of the slave trade in Zanzibar itself. Sultan Said lost the revenue he would have received as duty on all slaves sold, so to make up the shortfall he encouraged the development of more clove plantations.

In 1822 Said also attempted to oust the Mazrui sultan of Mombasa. The following year a British ship, *HMS Barracouta*, docked at Mombasa and the sultan asked for British protection against Oman. The ship's captain passed on the request to his senior officer, Captain William Owen of *HMS Leven*, who saw that he could use this local dispute to Britain's advantage: he sailed to Muscat and informed Sultan Said that he intended to grant the Mazrui request for British protection unless Said agreed to end the slave trade. Said refused to do this, so Owen declared Mombasa a British Protectorate, along with the coastline from Malindi to Pangani, on condition that the Mazrui sultan agreed to abolish the slave trade. The sultan agreed, but soon reverted to slave trading so the British Protectorate was lifted in July 1826.

Said consolidates his power in Zanzibar

In 1827, Sultan Said sailed to Zanzibar and was greeted there by Edmund Roberts, an American merchant from Portsmouth, New Hampshire. Roberts suggested a commercial treaty between Said and America. Soon Zanzibar was supplying large amounts of ivory to America and Western Europe. African ivory was soft and easy to carve into combs, piano keys and billiard balls. Asian ivory, in contrast, was hard and brittle. Ivory was exported to America, and cotton cloth (called 'Amerikani'), guns and gunpowder were imported into Zanzibar for distribution along the coast and to Arabia. The Americans also purchased animal hides and gum copal, a tree resin used in the manufacture of varnish. (It is interesting to note that so great was the American demand for ivory in the 1830s that a town called Ivoryton was established in Connecticut, with a factory making piano keys and billiard balls out of ivory imported from Zanzibar.)

Sultan Said realised that trade with Europe and America would increase Zanzibar's wealth and strength, and thereby consolidate his own position, so at the end of the 1820s he decided to further develop Zanzibar's clove industry. His first move was to confiscate the plantations of Saleh bin Haramil al Abray, who had introduced cloves to the island in 1812. Said's reason for this was that Saleh was the leader of a political faction competing for power, and had also continued to send slaves to the Mascarenes after the Moresby Treaty had made this illegal.

Vast plantations were established on Zanzibar and Pemba, and the islands' prosperity soon grew dramatically. Said decreed that three clove trees must be planted for every coconut palm, and that any landowner failing to do so would have his property confiscated. Said became the owner of 45 plantations scattered over the island, with about 50 slaves working as labourers on the smaller plots and up to 500 on the larger ones. Cloves fetched a high price abroad and by the end of Said's reign Zanzibar was one of the world's leading clove producers.

Said valued Zanzibar's large harbour, abundant fresh water supply and fertile soil. He also recognised the strategic importance of a Busaidi power base on the East African coast, and decided to spend several months on the island each year. A large house was built for him at Mtoni, on the west coast of the island about five kilometres north of Zanzibar Town.

Said sailed for Muscat in 1828, leaving his 13-year-old son, Khaled, as governor of his East African territories, but in Said's absence the Mazrui recaptured Fort Jesus again in 1829. Said also came under increased pressure from the British: in 1833 the Emancipation Act abolished slavery throughout the British Empire and all slaves in British territories were freed. Recognising the need for strong allies Said signed a Treaty of Amity and Commerce with Edmund Roberts of the United States of America in 1833. This gave the Americans freedom to set up trading posts at Zanzibar and on the mainland. In return, Said hoped for armed assistance against the Mazrui and for British anti-slavery pressure to ease.

In December 1833 Said sent an envoy to Queen Ranavalona of Madagascar asking for her hand in marriage and for soldiers to help him fight the Mazrui. Ranavalona declined his proposal of marriage, but offered him as many soldiers as he pleased. She also asked Said to send her a coral necklace, which she would pay for, but disappointed by the Queen's rejection Said did not take up her offer of reinforcements.

In 1837, Said finally managed to oust the Mazrui from Mombasa and install his own garrison of soldiers in Fort Jesus. Links between Zanzibar and America became increasingly cordial, and a consul, Richard Waters, was appointed in March the same year. Said presented him with a horse and a boat, and Waters was often the sultan's guest at Mtoni Palace. In November 1839 Said sent his trading ship *El-Sultani* to America. The ship arrived in New York in May 1840, the first Arab boat ever to visit an American port, and returned to Zanzibar with a cargo of arms and ammunition, china, beads and 'Amerikani' cloth.

Zanzibar becomes the capital of Oman

In December 1840 Sultan Said established his capital in Zanzibar, transferring it 3,000 miles from Muscat. He made this move at a time when Zanzibar's prosperity was increasing rapidly, and Oman's was in decline. Many of Oman's most influential merchants were already based in Zanzibar. Said also believed that the dual powerbase of Zanzibar and Oman would help safeguard his territories on the African mainland and maintain his dominance over Indian Ocean trade.

Said's title was now Sultan of Zanzibar and Oman. He ruled Zanzibar directly while his eldest surviving son, Thuwaini, remained in Muscat as governor of Oman. Zanzibar's own king, the Mwinyi Mkuu, presided over local matters but Said's government took control of trade and international affairs.

Zanzibar Town began to expand: when Said had first arrived in the 1820s the buildings were mostly huts of mud thatched with coconut fronds, but by the 1850s many impressive stone buildings had been constructed by the new immigrants from Oman.

Said was also followed to Zanzibar by Captain Atkins Hamerton, who had originally been installed in Muscat to act as British Consul. In December 1841 he became the first British Consul in Zanzibar. France also established diplomatic relations with Zanzibar: a French Consulate was opened in 1844.

Meanwhile, despite the restrictions imposed by the Moresby Treaty, the slave trade continued to expand. In 1841 Arab traders had established a trading colony at Ujiji on Lake Tanganyika, almost 1,600km (1,000 miles) from the coast, and in 1843 the first Arab caravans had reached Buganda (now Uganda) on the shores of present-day Lake Victoria. By the end of the 1840s, Arab traders had gone even further, reaching the Upper Congo (now Eastern Zaire), the Central Highland area around Mount Kenya, the Rift Valley lakes of Baringo and Turkana, and southern Ethiopia. About

13,000 slaves a year were arriving in Zanzibar from the mainland. (See *Zanzibar and the Slave Trade* map, page 12.)

Britain continues to oppose the slave trade

Sultan Said became increasingly concerned that British attempts to abolish the slave trade would weaken his power in the region. In 1842 he sent his envoy Ali bin Nasur to England in the ship *El-Sultani* to plead his case. Said's gifts for Queen Victoria included emeralds, cashmere shawls, pearl necklaces and ten Arab horses.

In reply, Britain told Zanzibar that they wished to abolish the slave trade to Arabia, Oman, Persia and the Red Sea. To soften the blow Queen Victoria gave Said a state coach and a silver-gilt tea service. The state coach arrived in pieces and had to be assembled. It was still unused a year later, as Zanzibar had no roads. The tea service was considered too ornate to use and was taken to the British Consulate for safe keeping.

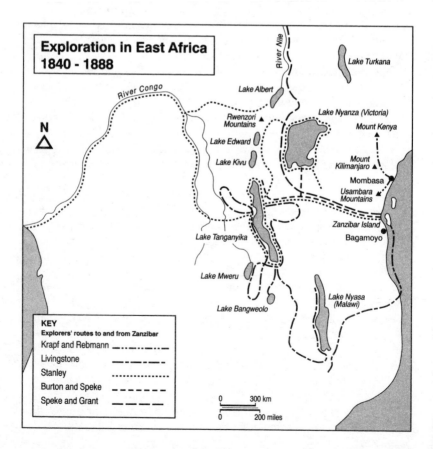

Exploration in East Africa 1840 - 1888

KEY
Explorers' routes to and from Zanzibar
Krapf and Rebmann
Livingstone
Stanley
Burton and Speke
Speke and Grant

Britain continued putting restrictions on the slave trade. In October 1845 Said was virtually forced by Captain Hamerton to sign another anti-slavery treaty, which allowed slave transport only between lines of latitude 1°57" south and 9°2" south (between Lamu and Kilwa, the limits of Said's dominions on the coast). This meant slaves could still be imported into Zanzibar but could no longer be exported to Oman. (See *Zanzibar and the Slave Trade* map, page 12.)

Ships from the British Navy were employed to help enforce the treaty by capturing any dhows carrying slaves. When a dhow was captured, it was set on fire and the slaves were taken to Aden, India, or a free-slave community on the coast, such as English Point in Mombasa. The British navy commanders decreed that no dhow could be destroyed until the ship's papers had been removed. But very few dhows' captains carried any documents and on the rare occasions when papers were produced, they were usually in Arabic or Swahili which few British could read anyway.

With only four ships to patrol a huge area of sea, the British Navy found it hard to enforce the treaty, so the slave dhows continued to sail. Ships from France, Germany, Spain, Portugal and America continued to carry slaves, as there were still huge profits to be made. And on the mainland slave traders continued to push further into the interior.

Early explorers

In the 1840s, European missionaries and explorers began to venture into the East African interior. In Britain, an Association for Promoting the Discovery of the Interior Parts of Africa had been formed as early as 1788, and had since merged with the Royal Geographical Society; it would soon play a leading role in the search for the source of the River Nile. Meanwhile, the English Church Missionary Society, unable to find any British recruits, sent two Germans, Krapf and Rebmann, to East Africa, to convert the locals to Christianity.

At this time, Zanzibar provided the usual starting point for journeys into the interior. Here, the European missionaries and explorers paid their respects to Sultan Said, who 'owned' most of the land they would pass through. They equipped their expeditions with supplies and porters, before sailing to Bagamayo on the mainland. Many explorers followed the established slaving routes into the interior, often employing slave traders to act as guides.

In 1844, the German missionary Johann Krapf arrived in Zanzibar, followed by his colleague, Johann Rebmann, two years later. Rebmann was introduced to Sultan Said by the British Consul, Hamerton, before joining Krapf in Mombasa. They travelled widely across the areas now known as southern Kenya and northern Tanzania. In May 1848 Rebmann became the first European to see Kilimanjaro and in December 1849 Krapf became the first European to see Mount Kenya. (See *Exploration in East Africa* map, opposite.)

Meanwhile on Zanzibar the slave trade continued: by the 1850s about 14,000 to 15,000 slaves a year were being imported into Zanzibar from the mainland, providing Sultan Said with a large income from duties. Zanzibar traders had pushed into the area now called Northern Zambia, and in 1852 a caravan reached Benguela (in present-day Angola) having completely traversed the continent from east to west, while the following year another group reached Linyanti, in the present-day Caprivi Strip of Namibia.

Through the slave caravans Said had become the nominal ruler of a vast commercial empire stretching along the coast from Mozambique to the Somali ports, and inland to the Great Lakes of Nyasa (Malawi), Tanganyika, Nyanza (Victoria) and Turkana. By the end of his reign Zanzibar's empire covered about 2½ million km² (one million square miles), or 10% of the African continent, including the whole of present-day Tanzania, plus sizeable parts of Malawi, Zambia, Zaire, Uganda and Kenya. The Arabs had a saying: 'When the flute plays in Zanzibar, they dance on the lakes.' But it was an empire in name only and Said never attempted to conquer or develop the area.

The end of Said's reign

Sultan Said made periodic visits to Muscat, leaving his son Khaled as governor of Zanzibar in his absence. Khaled had a predilection for French goods and called his principal country estate Marseilles, after the French Mediterranean port. The house had floors inlaid with black and white marble and the inside walls were covered with large mirrors. When Khaled died of tuberculosis in November 1854, an order came from Said in Muscat appointing another son, the 20-year-old Majid, as governor.

In September 1856 Said sailed for Zanzibar again in his boat *Kitorie*. He travelled with his family, including his son Barghash, now 19 years old. Said ordered some loose planks of wood to be loaded on to the ship, saying that if anyone should die on board, the body must not be buried at sea according to Muslim custom, but embalmed and taken to Zanzibar in a coffin. Said seemed to know it was he who was about to die: he began to suffer severe pains from an old wound in his thigh followed by an attack of dysentery. On October 19 1856 he died on board the ship. He was 65 years old.

Barghash put his father's body in the coffin and took command of the fleet. He did not anchor in Zanzibar harbour, but went instead to Chumbe Island, about eight kilometres to the south. That night, Barghash came ashore secretly and tried to take control of the palace at Mtoni and the fort in Zanzibar Town, but he was unable to muster enough supporters.

Barghash's attempt to seize control was thwarted and on October 28 1856, Majid bin Said was proclaimed Sultan of Zanzibar. A ship was sent to Oman with the news, but Said's eldest son Thuwaini refused to acknowledge Majid as sultan, believing that he was the legitimate successor. Majid agreed to pay Thuwaini 40,000 Maria Theresa dollars (the trade currency of the time) annually as compensation, but after a year the payment ceased.

Burton, Speke and Grant

By this time, the reports of early explorers like Rebmann and Krapf encouraged the British Royal Geographical Society to send an expedition to East Africa to search for the source of the White Nile. The leaders were Lieutenant (later Sir) Richard Francis Burton and Lieutenant John Hanning Speke.

In December 1856, on the last day of mourning for Sultan Said, Burton and Speke arrived in Zanzibar. A month later they sailed for Bagamoyo and followed the slave route towards Lake Tanganyika which they reached in January 1858. Burton became ill, so Speke travelled on alone and became the first European to see the great *Nyanza* (meaning 'lake') which he named Lake Victoria (after the British Queen), certain it was the source of the White Nile. Speke and Burton returned to Zanzibar in March 1859, and thence to London.

To verify his theory, Speke returned to Zanzibar in 1860 with the Scottish explorer James Grant. Together they travelled inland to Lake Victoria. Speke reached the waterfalls where the Nile leaves the lake and named them the Ripon Falls after the president of the Royal Geographical Society.

Division of Oman and Zanzibar

Meanwhile, back on Zanzibar, Captain Hamerton, the British Consul, had died and a power struggle was developing between the Omani rulers. Sultan Thuwaini of Oman planned to overthrow Sultan Majid of Zanzibar, as his promised tribute had not been paid. In February 1859 he sailed southwards but was intercepted by a British cruiser on the eastern tip of Arabia. The British government wanted to keep control of the sea route to India, so Thuwaini was persuaded to submit his claims to the arbitration of Lord Canning, the Governor General of India. Thuwaini agreed and returned to Muscat.

But Majid was in danger from another member of the family: his brother Barghash was still plotting to overthrow him and proclaim himself Sultan of Zanzibar. Majid learnt of the plot but Barghash escaped to the Marseilles plantation. He was finally captured and exiled to India for two years. (For more details see *The Escape to Marseilles*, page 154.)

In April 1861 Lord Canning declared that Oman and Zanzibar should be completely separate states. The annual tribute from Zanzibar to Oman was reinstated and in March 1862 Britain and France signed an Anglo-French declaration which recognised Majid as Sultan of Zanzibar and his territories as an independent sovereignty.

Although the Mwinyi Mkuu still lived in the palace at Dunga, his power was now negligible. Hassan II was succeeded by Mohammed, who died in 1865, aged 80. He was succeeded by his son, Ahmed, who died of smallpox in March 1873, leaving no male heir. The line of the Mwinyi Mkuu of Zanzibar had come to an end, and its passing was hardly noticed.

In 1866 one of Majid's sisters, Princess Salme, met a German trader called Heinrich Reute. They became lovers and eloped to Germany, where Salme changed her name to Emily and later wrote a book about her life at the court of Zanzibar. (For more details see *Salme's Story,* page 142.)

In the same year, in Oman, Thuwaini was murdered in his sleep by his son, Salim, who succeeded him. Majid discontinued the payment of the tribute on the grounds that Salim was a usurper, and Oman withdrew into isolation. (This isolation lasted for over a hundred years, until the accession of Sultan Qaboos bin Said, in 1970.)

'Stinkibar'

In 1866 the Scottish missionary and explorer David Livingstone arrived in Zanzibar. He had already travelled across much of central and southern Africa, and written at great length about the horrors of the slave trade. He had now been asked by the Royal Geographical Society to clarify the pattern of the watersheds in the area of Lake Nyasa and Lake Tanganyika and their relation to the source of the White Nile.

By this period, Zanzibar's increasing trade and growing population had created its own problems and Livingstone did not enjoy his stay: 'no-one can truly enjoy good health here,' he wrote, later adding: 'the stench from...two square miles of exposed sea-beach, which is the general depository of the filth of the town, is quite horrible. At night, it is so gross or crass, one might cut a slice and manure the garden with it. It might be called "Stinkibar" rather than "Zanzibar"'. Other European visitors arriving by ship claimed they could smell Zanzibar before they could see it.

In the town itself, the freshwater springs were not particularly fresh. Dr James Christie, an English physician who arrived in Zanzibar in 1869, reported that the springs consisted of the 'diluted drainage of dunghills and graveyards'. Not surprisingly, this led to frequent bouts of dysentery and epidemics of smallpox and cholera. Malaria and bilharzia were also problems. Cholera epidemics had occurred in 1821 and 1836, and smallpox in 1858. Later cholera epidemics in 1858 and 1869 to 1870 killed one sixth of the population of Zanzibar Town, and 35,000 people throughout the island.

At this time, slavery still had not been abolished on Zanzibar. In the early 1860s an average 15,000 slaves a year were being imported into Zanzibar from mainland Africa, and by 1866 this had grown to 20,000 a year. The slave population had reached its peak and clove production entered a phase of overproduction and stagnation, so prices dropped.

The Arabs had invested all their capital in their plantations, many of which were mortgaged to Indian moneylenders, who soon became very wealthy. (The Indians were British subjects, encouraged to settle in Zanzibar by the presence of a British Consul, and so could not own slaves themselves.)

As a result of the declining profitability of clove production, there was a greater interest in the production of coconut and sesame-seed oils, mainly for export to France. There was also a revival of sugar production, and rubber plantations were established on the East African coast.

Livingstone, Stanley, and the relief expeditions

David Livingstone had left Zanzibar in March 1866. Lack of news in the outside world led to speculation on his whereabouts, and in January 1871 the American journalist Henry Morton Stanley arrived in Zanzibar, having been commissioned by *The New York Times* to search for the 'lost explorer'. In November the same year Stanley arrived at Ujiji, where he found Livingstone and greeted him with the now immortal phrase, 'Doctor Livingstone, I presume?'. (For more details on the explorations of Livingstone and Stanley, see the boxes on pages 122 and 121.)

Livingstone and Stanley travelled to Kazeh together, then Stanley continued alone back towards Zanzibar. Livingstone stayed at Kazeh until August, then set off southwards on another expedition which he thought would take no more than a few months. (He had already been in the interior for six years at this stage.)

Meanwhile the RGS in London was unaware of Stanley's 'find' so in February 1872 the Livingstone Search and Relief Expedition, led by Lieutenant Llewellyn Dawson, was dispatched to Zanzibar in the steamship *Abydos*.

Two months later, the expedition arrived in Zanzibar, where their ship was caught in the freak hurricane of April 14. Contemporary accounts record that it began to blow at 11.00pm and continued until 1.30pm the next day, when it abated for about half an hour. The storm then suddenly burst upon the island in greater fury, and raged for another three hours. Every ship and dhow in the harbour was driven ashore except the *Abydos*, although the expedition's accounts were blown away. The town was wrecked, many people were killed, and over two thirds of the coconut and clove trees on the island were uprooted.

A few weeks after the hurricane, in May 1872, Stanley arrived at Bagamoyo, where he met Dawson and told him that Livingstone was safe and would be arriving after a few more months. Dawson cancelled the Search and Relief Expedition and returned to London. But by the end of 1872 Livingstone had still not arrived back at Zanzibar as expected, so in February 1873 a second Relief Expedition, led by Lieutenant Verney Lovett Cameron, set out from Zanzibar to find him.

Unknown to Cameron, and the rest of the world, Livingstone's short expedition had become much longer than he had intended. He had grown ill again, and the attacks of dysentery had returned. On May 2 1873 he died in the village of Chitambo, near Lake Bangweulu (in present-day Zambia), 800km (500 miles) south of Ujiji. Two of his companions carried his body back towards Zanzibar. In August 1873 they reached Kazeh, where they

met Cameron and told him of Livingstone's death.

Cameron decided to march on to Ujiji which he reached in February 1874 and found Livingstone's papers. From Ujiji, Cameron continued westwards, eventually reaching the Atlantic coast in November 1875, thereby becoming the first European to travel across this part of Africa from east to west.

Sultan Barghash and John Kirk

By this time, on Zanzibar, Sultan Majid had died, aged 36. His only child was a daughter so his brother Barghash (who had twice already tried to seize the throne and returned to Zanzibar from exile in India in 1861) was proclaimed sultan on October 7 1870. In the same year, Dr John Kirk (who had originally come to Zanzibar as a medical officer on Livingstone's expedition) was made acting British Consul.

After the hurricane, Sultan Barghash had announced plans to grow new plantations, and the slave trade picked up once again. In 1872 around 16,000 slaves were imported into Zanzibar. (The hurricane only hit the southern tip of Pemba, leaving most of the clove trees on that island untouched. By the 1880s Pemba was producing about 80% of the total clove harvest from Zanzibar and Pemba.)

At the same time, the anti-slavery movement continued to grow, fuelled in America by the publication of *Uncle Tom's Cabin*. In January 1873 Sir Bartle Frere, a special envoy from Queen Victoria, arrived in Zanzibar to negotiate a treaty which he hoped would finally put an end to the Arab slave trade. Sultan Barghash was naturally reluctant to end slavery as he was still earning a great deal of revenue from import duties, and needed the slaves to work in the clove plantations. Frere sailed for England at the beginning of March 1873 without a treaty and almost immediately the British Navy began a blockade of every slave port on the mainland. The number of slaves passing through the Customs House in Zanzibar Town between January and March dropped to 21, compared to 4,000 in the same period the previous year.

In June 1873 Sir John Kirk, the British Consul, informed Sultan Barghash that a blockade of Zanzibar Island was imminent. Reluctantly Barghash signed the Anglo-Zanzibari treaty which provided for the complete abolition of the slave trade in Barghash's territories, the closing of all slave markets and the protection of all liberated slaves. Transport of slaves was forbidden, and slaves could no longer be exported from mainland Africa to Zanzibar and Pemba, except for domestic purposes.

The large slave market in Zanzibar Town was closed immediately. The site was bought by missionaries of the Universities Mission in Central Africa (UMCA), and work started on the cathedral which can still be seen in Zanzibar Town today.

One of the main effects of the treaty, now that slavery was illegal, was to push up the price of slaves and the trade continued in a clandestine manner.

Through the 1870s smugglers were estimated to be exporting between 10,000 and 12,000 slaves a year.

In 1875 John Kirk brought Sultan Barghash an official invitation to visit Britain to ratify the Anglo-Zanzibari treaty. In June the same year Barghash and Kirk arrived in London where Barghash received the Freedom of the City at the Guildhall and attended a state banquet at the Mansion House.

During his visit Barghash went to the Ascot and Doncaster races, Hyde Park and the British Museum. He had guided tours of the General Post Office, Woolwich Arsenal, Aldershot Camp and Brighton. He also went to the manufacturing towns of Birmingham, Liverpool and Manchester, where he witnessed the might of the Industrial Revolution. A firework display was given for him at Crystal Palace.

Barghash also visited Queen Victoria at Windsor, and the Prince and Princess of Wales at Marlborough House. He was surprised to see the young princes Albert and George wearing sailor suits, which he regarded as the uniform of working men.

While Barghash was in London, his sister Salme had come from Germany (where she had gone in 1866 with Heinrich Reute) hoping to be reconciled with her brother. But Barghash refused to meet Salme. The British government supported this action as they thought Salme might persuade her brother to reject the treaty.

On July 15 1875, after four weeks of intensive sightseeing and entertainment, Barghash and his party went from Folkestone to Calais and thence to Paris. A few days later, they travelled by train to Marseilles and sailed for Zanzibar, arriving home in September.

For the British, Zanzibar was no longer a distant obscure island, and links between the two countries became even more firmly established. In 1869 the Suez Canal had opened, making the sea voyage between Britain and the coast of East Africa much shorter and simpler. In 1872 the British India Steamship Navigation Company started a monthly mail service between Zanzibar and Aden. It brought the first scheduled passenger and cargo service to Zanzibar, which allowed merchandise to be exported quickly. Communication was again improved in 1879, when the Eastern Telegraph Company completed their cable from Zanzibar to Europe via Aden, and a telegraphic link with Europe was established.

Inspired by his visit to Europe, Barghash decided to make many changes on Zanzibar. Advised by John Kirk (now firmly installed as the power behind the throne), he appointed Lieutenant William Lloyd Mathews to reorganise his army and enforce his sovereignty over the interior. (For more details see the *Mathews* box, page 146.)

During his exile in India, Barghash had seen the opulent wealth of the Indian palaces and he tried to emulate them on Zanzibar. Many luxurious palaces were built, including Chukwani, to the south of Zanzibar Town, and Maruhubi Palace, to the north, for his harem. Another palace, in the town, became known as the *Beit el Ajaib*, or House of Wonders, as it was the first building on Zanzibar to have electric light. In all his palaces, Barghash upgraded the dinner services from silver to gold. Divan coverings of goat and camel hair were replaced by silks and taffetas, and French carpets covered the floors.

Barghash introduced Zanzibar's first clean water system to replace supplies from local wells and rainwater: aqueducts and conduits brought pure water from a spring at Bububu into Zanzibar Town, a distance of some six kilometres. Other developments introduced by Barghash included a police force, an ice-making factory, electric street lighting, and telephones to connect his city and country palaces. Barghash also built and improved the roads on the island, and every year he provided one of his private steamships for Muslims wishing to make the pilgrimage to Mecca.

The scramble for Africa

In 1884 Dr Karl Peters, founder of the Society for German Colonisation, arrived in Zanzibar then sailed for the mainland where he made 'treaties of eternal friendship' with the local African chiefs in return for large areas of land. By the time he reached Kilimanjaro he had annexed more than 6,000km^2 (2,500 square miles) of land, which were still nominally under the control of Sultan Barghash.

Meanwhile, in January 1885, Khartoum, the capital of Anglo-Egyptian Sudan, fell to the forces of the Mahdi. The British General Gordon was killed and the governor of Equatoria Province, south of Khartoum, was cut off. The governor was a German called Eduard Schnitzer, although he had adopted the name Emin Pasha and was working for the British.

Otto von Bismark, the German Chancellor, saw the Mahdi's victory as a sign of Britain's weakness and believed that Germany could move into East Africa without British opposition. In February the same year the General Act of Berlin, signed by Kaiser Wilhelm of Germany, officially proclaimed a German protectorate over the territories annexed by Karl Peters. Sultan Barghash was only formally told about his loss of land in April of the same year. He hoped for support from the British, but Britain did not want to make an enemy of Germany, and so declined.

In June 1885 the Germans claimed another protectorate over Witu and the mouth of the Tana River, near Lamu, and in August the same year five ships of the German Navy, commanded by Carl Paschen, arrived in Zanzibar harbour. Paschen demanded that Sultan Barghash recognise the German protectorates. Kirk had to obey the recommendations of the British government, which was to persuade Barghash to submit.

A few days after the arrival of the German fleet, another German ship entered the harbour, carrying Barghash's sister Salme (who had eloped to Germany in 1866). She was with her son Said-Rudolph, now 16 years old, and two other children. Kirk believed that the Germans would propose Said-Rudolph as sultan. Then, if Barghash arrested him or Salme, now German citizens, this would justify the Germans in declaring war on

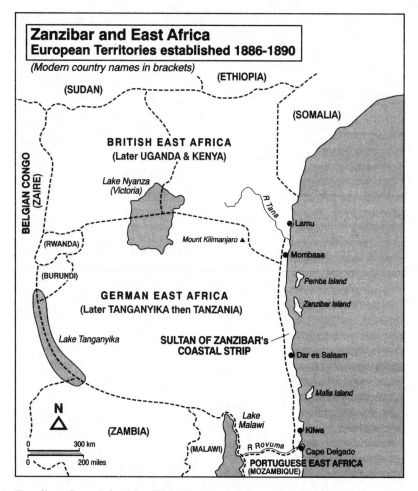

Zanzibar and East Africa
European Territories established 1886-1890
(Modern country names in brackets)

Zanzibar. So, advised by Kirk, Barghash tolerated Salme's presence. He did not arrest her, but offered no hospitality, nor did he meet her.

Barghash sent his formal recognition of the German Protectorate to Carl Paschen and two months later, in response to the German action, the British government arranged for a joint commission between Britain, Germany and France to establish their own boundaries in the mainland territories that still 'belonged' to the sultan of Zanzibar.

After lengthy discussions the first Anglo-German agreement was signed by Germany and Britain in late 1886. Barghash's lands were reduced to Zanzibar, Pemba, Mafia, Lamu and a ten mile (16km) wide coastal strip stretching around 1,200km (750 miles) from the Tana River, near Lamu, to the Rovuma River, near Cape Delgado. The rest of the mainland, east of Lake Victoria and Lake Tanganyika, was divided between Britain and Germany. Britain took the northern portion, between the Tana and Umba

Rivers, which became British East Africa, later Kenya. Germany took the southern portion, between the Umba and Rovuma Rivers. This became German East Africa, later Tanganyika, with Dar es Salaam as the capital. At first it was intended that Kilimanjaro should lie in the British sector, but it was 'given' to the German Emperor, Kaiser Wilhelm, when he requested it directly. (See *Zanzibar and East Africa European Territories* map, opposite.)

Given no option Barghash agreed to this treaty in December 1886 and the French government signed it a few days later. In June 1887 Barghash leased the northern section of his coastal strip (between the Tana and Umba Rivers) to the British East African Association (BEAA), which had been formed by William Mackinnon in May the same year. Meanwhile the Germans and Portuguese met in Barghash's absence to discuss their own border, and Portugal gained more of Barghash's land in the south.

In February 1888 Barghash sailed to Muscat, to visit the healing Bushire Springs on the Persian coast, to recuperate from tuberculosis and elephantiasis. Barghash returned to Zanzibar on March 26, arriving at 8.00pm. He died five hours later, on March 27, at the age of 51.

On March 29 1888 Barghash's brother Khalifa bin Said was proclaimed Sultan. In April the same year, the British East African Association became the Imperial British East Africa Company (IBEA), with its capital at Mombasa, which was beginning to take Zanzibar's place as the commercial centre for Africa. Without the income from the slave trade, Zanzibar's prosperity was in decline.

In March 1889, Karl Peters arrived back in Zanzibar as head of the German Emin Pasha Relief Expedition, to rescue his countrymen who had been cut off by the Mahdi in Equatoria in 1885. Under the guise of this expedition Karl Peters planned to travel inwards from the German-held enclave of Witu (near Lamu), north of the British territory, to seize Uganda for Germany. In August the same year the IBEA sent a British expedition into the interior, led by Sir Frederick Jackson, also to make contact with Emin Pasha.

Meanwhile, unbeknown to both the German and British expeditions, Henry Stanley (who had left Zanzibar on his own relief expedition in 1887) had already 'found' Emin Pasha on the western shore of Lake Albert in April 1888.

British Protectorate

On September 13 1889, Khalifa signed an agreement with the British government agreeing to abolish slavery in his territories. Anybody who entered the sultan's realms, and any children born, would be free. Britain and Germany were awarded a permanent right to search for slaves in Zanzibar's waters. As a sign of Britain's appreciation, Khalifa was knighted, but less than a month later he died, aged 36.

Khalifa's brother, Ali bin Said, was proclaimed sultan. Ali was the fourth and last of Said's sons to become Sultan of Zanzibar. On August 1 1890 Ali signed an anti-slavery treaty forbidding the purchase and sale of slaves. With the end of the slave trade, the only viable export from the interior was ivory, by now a rapidly waning asset.

Meanwhile in the interior Karl Peters entered Uganda in February 1890 and claimed the territory for Germany, just ahead of Sir Frederick Jackson from England. But Britain was unhappy about Germany's claims; the British politician Lord Robert Salisbury realised that control of the Upper Nile could lead indirectly to the control of the Suez Canal and thus the trade route to India. So Germany was persuaded to renounce any claims over Uganda in return for British support of the Kaiser against France and Russia.

By the second Anglo-German agreement (The Treaty of Zanzibar) of July 1 1890, Germany agreed to recognise a British Protectorate over the Sultanate of Zanzibar, and to abandon any claim to Witu and the country inland as far as the Upper Nile. Germany also abandoned any claim to the west of Lake Nyasa but, in return, gained sovereignty over the coast of German East Africa, later to become Tanganyika. The British-German border was continued westwards across Lake Victoria to the boundary of the Belgian territory of Congo, thus securing Uganda for Britain. The British coastal strip (which still belonged to the Sultan of Zanzibar) was removed from the control of the British East Africa Company and administered by the British East Africa Protectorate, later to become Kenya and Uganda.

In exchange for these thousands of square miles of East African territory, including the islands of Zanzibar (Unguja and Pemba), Germany also gained Heligoland, a small island off the German coast which lay near the mouth of the Kiel Canal. This was of strategic importance to Germany, but Karl Peters was disgusted and wrote that 'two kingdoms had been bartered for a bath-tub in the North Sea'.

In 1891 a Constitutional Government was established in Zanzibar, with General Sir Lloyd Mathews as First Minister. But although Zanzibar enjoyed the status of a British Protectorate, the island's importance as a commercial centre was declining further in favour of Mombasa.

The British now controlled Zanzibar so when Sultan Ali died in March 1893, without making a will, they proclaimed as sultan Hamad, son of Thuwaini (the former Sultan of Oman), even though there were two other claimants: Khaled bin Barghash and Hamoud bin Mahomed bin Said, a nephew of Thuwaini.

During Hamad's reign, in November 1895, Zanzibar issued its first stamps. (From about 1875 the island had been using Indian stamps with 'Zanzibar' overprinted.) Then a newspaper, *The Gazette for Zanzibar and East Africa,* was produced. It was followed by others in English, Arabic, Swahili and Urdu.

Also in 1895, the Mazrui made a final attempt to break away from Zanzibar and rule Mombasa themselves. A year later, defeated, their leaders fled from British held Mombasa into German territory where they were taken to Dar es Salaam and imprisoned.

Sultan Hamad became ill in 1896. He summoned his nephew, Khalifa bin Harub bin Thuwaini bin Said, from Muscat to Zanzibar to be his companion and died in August that year. The British recommended Hamoud, a cousin of Hamad, as sultan.

Barghash's son, Khaled, who had already tried to seize power from Hamad, made a second attempt at snatching the throne. He was briefly successful this time but was ousted by the British, after 'the shortest war in history'. Khaled escaped to Dar es Salaam, in German territory. (See *The Shortest War in History*, page 118.)

On August 27 1896 Hamoud was conducted into the Customs House and proclaimed Sultan of Zanzibar, amidst the salute of the ships. The new sultan supported the British government and on April 5 1897 he signed a treaty to abolish the legal status of slavery in Zanzibar and Pemba. Shortly after this Queen Victoria awarded him the Grand Cross of the Most Distinguished Order of St Michael and St George. Hamoud sent his son Ali to school at Harrow in England where he represented his father at the coronation of King Edward VII.

Sultan Hamoud died on July 18 1902 and the British proclaimed the 18-year-old Ali as the new sultan. From his school days he spoke English fluently, and continued to travel in Europe during his reign. He often received medical treatment in Switzerland and Germany and also visited Paris and Constantinople. In May 1911 Ali and his brother-in-law Khalifa bin Harub attended the coronation of King George V in England. While in Europe Ali's health deteriorated and he abdicated in December 1911. He spent the last seven years of his life in Europe, and died in Paris in December 1918. Khalifa bin Harub, a cousin of Ali, became Sultan Khalifa II on December 16 1911.

Zanzibar enters the 20th century

Sultan Khalifa bin Harub proved to be a moderate but influential ruler, and proceeded to guide Zanzibar through the first half of the turbulent 20th century with skill and diplomacy.

Soon after Khalifa gained power, changes were made to the British way of overseeing their interests in Zanzibar. In July 1913 responsibility for Zanzibar was transferred from the Foreign Office to the Colonial Office. The post of British Consul became British Resident, subject to the control of the governor of the British East Africa Protectorate. At the same time a Protectorate Council was established. This was an advisory body with the sultan as president and the British Resident as vice-president.

During World War I the German and British armies, with conscripted African soldiers, were involved in several campaigns on the mainland. The war did not affect Zanzibar directly except for one incident when the British ship *Pegasus* was bombarded and sunk by the German ship *Königsberg* in Zanzibar Town harbour. Graves marking the bodies of sailors killed in this incident can still be seen on Grave Island. (Visitors with a particular interest in this often forgotten event should consult the series of booklets published by historian Kevin Patience, listed in *Further Reading* on page 213.)

Towards the end of the war, in 1917, the British army drove the Germans out of their territory and marched into Dar es Salaam. Khaled, who had tried to seize the throne of Zanzibar during 'the shortest war' in 1896, was still there and was captured. He was exiled to the Seychelles, then allowed to return to Mombasa in 1925 where he lived quietly until 1927.

After the war, the German East African territory was administered by Britain under a League of Nations mandate and called Tanganyika. Later, in 1920, the British East Africa Protectorate became known as the Kenya Colony.

In 1925 the British Resident on Zanzibar was made directly responsible to the Colonial Office in London, and a new Legislative Council was established. The ten mile (16km) wide strip of land along the coast of Kenya, including Mombasa, which had been leased to Kenya in 1895 was still technically 'owned' by the sultan of Zanzibar and the new Kenyan government continued to pay the lease of £11,000 per year.

During World War II, Zanzibar was not involved in any military action. The war's main effect was to interrupt the supply of rice, a staple food for the Asian and African people, that had until then been imported from Burma.

After the war Britain gradually allowed the local people of Zanzibar to become involved in the island's government. Several local political parties were formed and Zanzibar's first elections were held in July 1957. The Afro-Shirazi Union (which later became the Afro-Shirazi Party – ASP) defeated the Zanzibar Nationalist Party (ZNP). Broadly speaking, the ASP was dominated by Africans, the ZNP by Arabs.

In October 1960 Sultan Khalifa died, after ruling for 49 years, and was succeeded by his only son, Abdullah bin Khalifa. In November the same year Zanzibar was granted a new constitution which allowed for the elections of the members of the Legislative Council. Elections took place in January 1961, producing no clear result, and again in June 1961, but these were marked by serious inter-racial rioting. Nevertheless the ZNP, along with the aligned Zanzibar and Pemba People's Party, won 13 of the seats on the council, while the ASP won ten.

Britain realised that internal self-government for Zanzibar was inevitable, and this was finally granted in June 1963. In July that year Sultan Abdullah died. Throughout his short reign he had suffered from severe pains in his legs, which had eventually been amputated. Abdullah was succeeded by his eldest son Jamshid.

On December 10 1963, Zanzibar became an independent sultanate, and the coastal strip was finally ceded to Kenya, which also became independent two days later. Zanzibar was made a full member of the British Commonwealth and on December 16 became a member of the United Nations. But the new sultanate was short-lived: on January 12 1964 the

Zanzibar government was overthrown in a violent revolution.

Revolutionary Zanzibar

The leader of Zanzibar's revolution was a Ugandan called John Okello who had been living in Pemba. The local African population supported Okello with great enthusiasm, and went on a rampage through the islands, in which more than 17,000 Arabs and Indians were killed in one night. The leader of the Afro-Shirazi Party, Sheik Abied Amani Karume, was installed as president of the newly proclaimed People's Republic of Zanzibar and Pemba.

Karume and other prominent ASP members formed the Revolutionary Government of Zanzibar (*Serikali ya Mapinduzi ya Zanzibar*, or SMZ). Most of Zanzibar's Asian and Indian people left the islands; their property was confiscated and their land nationalised. (On the mainland Sultan Jamshid was given temporary asylum in Dar es Salaam, then went to Britain where he lives in exile in a town on the south coast.)

Meanwhile, Tanganyika had also become independent in December 1961, with Julius Nyerere elected as president the following year. Nyerere had known and supported Karume since the mid-1950s but the Zanzibar Revolution created problems in Tanganyika, inspiring an attempted coup in Dar es Salaam only a few days later. (To suppress this coup Nyerere received help from Britain in the form of a battalion of commandos.)

Once Nyerere had regained control he approached Karume to discuss a political union. Karume agreed, and on April 24 1964 the two countries joined to form the United Republic of Tanganyika and Zanzibar. In October the same year the country was renamed Tanzania. Nyerere became the president of the new state while Karume became vice-president. The SMZ was to control all local affairs on the islands of Unguja and Pemba, while foreign affairs would be handled by the Tanzanian government.

(During the negotiations John Okello had gone to the mainland to meet Nyerere. On his return to Zanzibar in March 1964 security forces immediately sent him back to Dar es Salaam. He made no further public appearances.)

Despite the so-called union Karume kept Zanzibar separate from the rest of Tanzania in many respects. The clove plantations on Unguja and Pemba were developed and the earnings from exports continued to increase, but this revenue was not shared with mainland Tanzania.

After the revolution almost all the European and Asian residents had left Zanzibar. To fill the vacuum left by the departure of these skilled people Karume attracted technical and military assistance from Cuba, China and the then Eastern bloc countries of East Germany, Bulgaria and the Soviet Union. Engineers from East Germany designed and built new blocks of flats in Zanzibar Town, and in 'new towns' elsewhere on the islands of Unguja and Pemba.

In 1970 Karume's government was accused of human rights violations against political opponents. Nyerere spoke out strongly against this but it seemed to have little effect.

On April 7 1972 Karume was assassinated whilst playing cards in the ASP headquarters in Zanzibar Town. Aboud Jumbe Mwinyi, who had been a member of the ASP since before independence, became the new leader of the Revolutionary Government. Mwinyi was less hard-line than Karume and introduced several reforms. He was also more sympathetic towards Nyerere and mainland Tanzania. On February 5 1977 the ASP united with Nyerere's party, the Tanzania African National Union (TANU), to form the Chama Cha Mapinduzi (Party of the Revolution).

After this unification, both leaders began to relax some of their policies on nationalised industries and state financial control. Relations with some Western nations, including Britain, slowly improved. In July 1979, as a sign that Tanzania was regaining some international respect, Queen Elizabeth II of the UK visited Zanzibar. She was shown a tree that had been planted by her sister, Princess Margaret, in 1956.

The 1980s

In 1980 the first presidential elections took place, and Aboud Jumbe Mwinyi was officially elected as president of Zanzibar. In 1984 Ali Hassan Mwinyi was elected president. A year later he became president of Tanzania, following Julius Nyerere's resignation. Idris Abdul Wakil was then elected president of Zanzibar.

On the economic front, Zanzibar was in trouble. During the 1980s there was a drastic decline in the world market price for cloves, dropping to US$1,000 per ton from almost ten times that amount in the 1960s. Zanzibar was unable to pay its full annual contribution to the government of Tanzania and had to look for alternative ways of generating income. Gradually, the government of Zanzibar started to encourage private-sector (rather than state controlled) operation of the economy.

In 1989, seaweed farming was introduced on the East Coast of Unguja (Zanzibar Island) and has since become a vital source of income for coastal villagers. The seaweed is planted and tended on beach areas between the high and low water marks (see box page 80). It is harvested and dried, collected in Zanzibar Town, and then exported to several countries in Europe and Asia for use as a food thickener or stabiliser. Seaweed is now a valuable addition to Zanzibar's traditional exports of coconuts, cloves and other spices. (For details on cloves and coconuts see boxes, pages 68 and 66.)

Despite the success with seaweed, exports are limited, and Zanzibar imports many basic foodstuffs, including rice (from Pakistan, Thailand, Vietnam, Indonesia, India, China and the USA), maize (from mainland Tanzania), cooking oil (from Kenya, Tanzania, Singapore and Dubai), sugar (from Brazil), and wheat and flour (from France, Germany and the USA). Other imports include mineral water (from the Gulf states) and beer (from Denmark).

The 1990s

In 1990, Dr Salmin Amour was elected president with an overwhelming majority. His government continued to actively encourage private-sector economic investment. In 1992, the government announced a major project to make Fumba, about 20km south of Zanzibar Town, into an Economic Free Zone (EFZ) with factories, warehouses and a jetty to bring in raw materials more easily. Potential investors were offered a range of incentives including exemption from import and export duties, and it was envisaged that Fumba would become a manufacturing centre for a wide range of products which could then be exported to Africa, the Gulf and elsewhere in the region. A similar EFZ was also planned for Micheweni on Pemba. By 1997, although the plans had not been officially shelved, there was no sign of development at either Fumba or Micheweni. However, if all goes to plan, history will have turned full circle, and Zanzibar will once again be a major player in the Indian Ocean trade block.

The first half of the 1990s also saw a dramatic increase in the development of another Zanzibar industry – tourism. The Zanzibar Commission for Tourism was founded in 1987 to promote Zanzibar as a tourist destination. The drive was further strengthened in 1992 with the creation of the Zanzibar Investment Promotion Agency to encourage overseas investment, particularly in tourism projects.

By 1995, over 50,000 visitors were arriving in Zanzibar each year. While still way below the figures recorded by many other popular East African tourist destinations, this is a significant growth since the lows of the early 1980s. There was a corresponding growth in hotel construction, and by 1994 most of the best coastal sites had been allocated for hotels and related schemes, mainly to European developers. By 1996, construction was in progress or near completion on more than 20 new hotels around the islands. However, observers claim that the frequent use of saline beach sand and coral blocks for building the hotels may lead to structural weaknesses in the not-too-distant future. Of more cause for concern are the reports about huge amounts of sand being taken from beaches for construction, causing erosion that is now a major problem; in some areas the coast is believed to be receding at a rate of one metre per year. Also, as the number of hotels has increased, the supplies of fresh ground water are being depleted. In recent years many wells, used for generations by villagers, have become saline or dry.

Despite these potential problems, development continues rapidly on Zanzibar Island, and is now beginning to take hold on Pemba. Of the many major projects announced, one of the largest was a multi-million dollar joint venture between the Zanzibar government and a British development company which involves converting 50km² of the Nungwi area in the northern part of Zanzibar Island into a complex of luxury resort hotels, complete with golf course and pleasure-boat marina.

In the face of such development, although tourism undoubtedly creates local jobs and is a healthy opportunity for overseas investors, some observers point out that local Zanzibaris could suffer as their culture, land, traditional livelihoods and even their water supplies are destroyed. Additionally, rapid development could spoil the natural beauty of the islands and thereby stem the flow of vital tourist-dollars. Officially, the government recognises this problem, and in 1992 introduced a National Environmental Policy for Zanzibar, stressing that the quality of life of the Zanzibaris should not be harmed by the destruction of their environment, and that cultural and biological diversity should be preserved. In the words of President Salmin Amour, 'unchecked development could soon become unsustainable for our people and our small islands'. Fine sentiments, but building and development was already rampant on many parts of Zanzibar's coast by the time the policy was introduced, and more than five years later still appears to be growing.

Latest developments

On the political front, Tanzania (with Zanzibar) ceased to be a one-party state in 1992. For the first time in almost 20 years, Chama Cha Mapinduzi (CCM) was faced with several new opposition groups, which quickly coalesced into parties. The Civic United Front (CUF) led by Seif Sherif Hamad, from Pemba, became the major opposition party for Zanzibar. Elections were not held immediately, but planned for October 1995. All parties agreed that a gradual transition to a multi-party political system would be beneficial. Salmin Amour remained Zanzibar's president and CCM leader, while on the mainland the CCM chose a new president, Benjamin Mkapa, in July 1995.

Elections were duly held in Zanzibar on October 22 1995, a week before the mainland vote. It was a simple two-horse race between Salmin Amour and Seif Sherif Hamad for president of Zanzibar, and between CCM and CUF candidates in the islands' parliament. There was a very high turn-out (over 95% of registered voters) and voting itself passed peacefully, but the counting took much longer than expected (three days for just over 300,000 votes).

As is common in politics, particularly in many parts of Africa, the ruling party's control of the government structure gave them an in-built advantage, but despite this headstart it soon transpired that the CUF were polling strongly. After two days, when reports surfaced that the candidates were running neck and neck, the CCM protested that the election process was flawed. Later they withdrew these comments when it transpired that Amour had won with 50.2% of the vote. Then the CUF picked up the claim of unfair procedures. International observers from the United Nations agreed that there was evidence of serious irregularities, but the nominally independent Zanzibar Electoral Commission refused to hold a re-count or to compare their figures with some of those recorded by the UN.

On the mainland, a divided opposition and an even more shambolic election, not to mention the possibility of vote-rigging (the count took almost a month), meant that CCM and President Mkapa stayed in power.

Some international aid donors protested about the irregularities, but after a while the dust settled, and little real action was taken. Former president Julius Nyerere called for a government of national unity, to reflect the equal support enjoyed by both parties, but this was ignored. Amour's two-seat majority in the Zanzibar parliament was boosted by an additional nine CCM MPs, appointments he was allowed to make according to rules in the national constitution. The CUF brought a high-profile legal case against the CCM on the grounds that the results and the whole election process were not representative of the wishes of the people, but this was bogged down in the courts and still unresolved by mid 1997.

Meanwhile, in Zanzibar, President Amour and the CCM remain firmly in power. There is still considerable support for CUF, but the strong Pemba following this party enjoys means that differences which are ostensibly political stand a danger of degenerating into inter-island (or 'ethnic') conflicts. This sense of grievance also translates into separatist aspirations; the desire of many Zanzibaris to be independent of mainland Tanzania is stronger than it has been for many years.

The next elections are due in the year 2000. While Tanzania and Zanzibar remain stable, the future for the islands and their peoples remains far from certain.

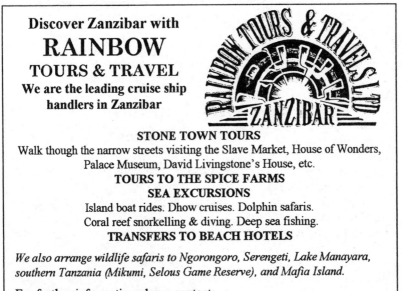

Chapter Three

Planning and Preparations

WHEN TO GO

Zanzibar has two wet seasons and two dry seasons each year. In the wet seasons rainfall is heavy and the air is humid. The best time to visit Zanzibar is during the dry seasons, from December to February and June to October. However, you should remember that Zanzibar is by the ocean and subject to unpredictable weather patterns at any time of year. Even during the 'dry' seasons, afternoon showers are not unknown, although they tend to be short and have a pleasant cooling effect.

It is also possible to visit Zanzibar during the rainy season. At this period, there are fewer visitors and you are more likely to get good bargains on hotel rooms, car and bike hire, boat trips, and so on. Rain is heavy, but not constant. Travel can be more difficult at this time, as roads can be damaged and buses delayed, but most places can still be reached eventually.

At holiday times, such as Christmas and Easter, Zanzibar is a popular short-break destination for expatriate workers from Dar es Salaam and Nairobi. This can mean fully booked flights and surcharges in some hotels.

During the Islamic fasting period of Ramadan many restaurants, snack bars and shops are closed during the day, and life on the island runs at a generally slower pace. (For details on Ramadan and other important dates in Zanzibar, see the *Public Holidays* section in *Chapter Four*.)

GETTING TO ZANZIBAR

From Europe
By air

There are no non-stop flights to Zanzibar from Europe or North America. At present (1997) all flights have at least one stop-over requiring a change of plane. However, the choice of routes and airlines is increasing every year, and reaching Zanzibar is now more straightforward than it's ever been.

Airlines flying from Europe to Zanzibar include Kenya Airways (changing planes in Nairobi or Mombasa); Gulf Air (changing in Abu Dhabi or Dubai); and Oman Air (changing in Muscat). From London to Zanzibar, return flights in the low season start at UK£400 (about US$600), and are about UK£500–600 in the high season, although by shopping around and buying long in advance you can get some good bargains. Several specialist agents offer Gulf Air flights at very reasonable fares.

It is also possible to use a airline flying from Europe to reach Mombasa or Dar es Salaam (such as British Airways, Alliance, Sabena or KLM) then a regional service (such as Kenya Airways and Air Tanzania) or private charter plane to fly to Zanzibar. (Details on these options are given under *Getting to Zanzibar from mainland Tanzania/Kenya*, pages 44 and 48.

As an alternative to flying all the way to Zanzibar, once you've flown into Dar es Salaam or Mombasa, you can travel on to Zanzibar by ship (details are given on page 44).

Another alternative is to fly from Europe (or from North America, Australasia or elsewhere in Africa, if you're coming from that direction) into Nairobi, then go by air or rail to Mombasa or Dar es Salaam and take a plane or a ship to Zanzibar from there.

If you want to fly straight to Zanzibar (without spending any time in Nairobi, Mombasa or Dar es Salaam) it may be possible to plan your international flight to tie in directly with a regional flight to Zanzibar. A good specialist travel agent will be able to help you with these arrangements.

For visitors from Europe (especially the UK and Italy), a cheap way of getting to Mombasa is on a charter flight. These are often advertised in the travel pages of national newspapers or in travel agents' windows. Charter deals are usually only valid for a two- or three-week stay, but this still gives you plenty of time to visit Zanzibar. There are also weekly charter

---

ZANZIBAR DIVING AND FISHING SEASONS

If you are coming to Zanzibar specifically for scuba diving, there are some points you need to know. Diving is possible at any time of year, although most people avoid the main rainy season from March to May, and divers visit different parts of the archipelago according to conditions. For example, the southern coasts are best from November to February, when the winds come from the north. The northern coasts are better from July to October, and at their absolute best from August to October. The east coast areas are exposed to the Indian Ocean swell and, although conditions for diving are good, with some good beginners' learning areas and exciting options for experienced divers, the west coast areas are more sheltered, with impressive reefs and top-quality diving conditions. However, most dive centres are based on the east coast of Zanzibar Island as this area has better beaches and a wider choice of hotels so is favoured by visitors. Several dive centres are based in Zanzibar Town, and are close to good sites, while some of the smarter hotels and dive centres on the east coast use boats to take divers round to the west side of the island, or to other sites nearby according to conditions such as tide and wind which affect visibility, anchorages, the chances of encountering large fish or dolphins, and many other factors. More details on dive centres, rates, equipment hire etc are given in *Chapter Five*, and hotels with attached dive centres are listed in *Chapter Six*.

If you're seriously into game fishing, the best time is October to March, although conditions are reasonable July to September also. More details on companies organising game fishing are given in *Chapter Five*.

flights from Europe (particularly Italy and France) straight into Zanzibar, although by 1997 there were none from the UK. It can only be a matter of time, so keep your eye on the travel press or contact a good agent.

London is one of the cheapest places in Europe to buy scheduled flights to Zanzibar, Mombasa, Nairobi or Dar. Specialist travel agencies here can also arrange onward flights to Zanzibar, and make other arrangements if you need them, such as hotel and train bookings. Some also sell charters, so can offer you a whole range of flights and deals.

There are a great many travel companies selling cheap flights to various parts of the world, including East Africa and Zanzibar. You can find these by looking at the advertisements in any travel magazine or newspaper supplement, simply comparing prices and giving them a call to check availability and other details. Prices tend to vary widely, and usually reflect the quality of airline, the flight duration and the number of stops en route.

Travel agents and tour companies

If you're travelling from the UK, the following travel agents and tour companies are worth a particular mention. The travel agents will sell flights to Zanzibar and many other parts of Africa, even if you want to make all your other arrangements yourself. The tour companies run tours which are either scheduled (ie: you join a group and keep to pre-set departure dates and itineraries) or tailor-made (prepared to fit in exactly with what you want to do). Some agents can also plan you a tailor-made itinerary, and offer a range of scheduled tours.

An organised tour is ideal if you don't have the time and inclination to travel to and around Zanzibar making your own arrangements. Several tour companies include Zanzibar in their Tanzania or East Africa itineraries, and a few offer dedicated trips to Zanzibar alone. The main advantage of this kind of tour is its all-inclusive nature – you pay one price which includes your flight, transfers, accommodation, meals, excursions and the services of a guide or tour leader. Once your plane takes off you can sit back and enjoy the trip; there's nothing more to plan or arrange. The main disadvantage is, of course, the fixed itinerary; you cannot change your plans to spend more or less time at a particular place.

Organised tours range from the very luxurious to the very simple, catering for various interests (such as diving, history, cultural experiences or simply relaxing), and may be based either at a hotel on the beach or in Zanzibar Town. Prices and lengths of stay vary too. The best way to find a trip that suits your own interest and pocket is to phone the companies direct and ask for a brochure. Some companies run their own trips; others are agents for various operators. Those listed below are all based in Britain, but those marked with an asterisk (*) are also represented in the USA and in various other countries, by local specialist travel agencies. Alternatively, from outside Britain, the companies can be contacted direct.

Abercrombie and Kent, Sloane Square House, Holbein Place, London SW1W 8NS, tel: 0171 730 9600, fax: 0171 730 9376.*

Africa Travel Centre, 21 Leigh St, London WC1H 9QX, tel: 0171 388 4163, fax: 0171 383 7512, email: africatravel@easynet.co.uk

Art of Travel, 268 Lavender Hill, London SW11 1LJ, tel: 0171 738 2038, fax: 0171 738 1893.

Explore Worldwide, 1 Frederick St, Aldershot, Hampshire GU11 1LQ, tel: 01252 319448, fax: 01252 343170, email: info@explore.co.uk*

Footloose Adventure Travel, 105 Leeds Rd, Ilkley LS26 8EG, tel: 01943 604030, fax: 01943 604070, email: footrv@globalnet.co.uk

Gane and Marshall International, 98 Crescent Rd, New Barnet, Hertfordshire EN4 9RJ, tel: 0181 441 9592, fax: 0181 441 7376, email: gmtours@compuserve.com

Hayes and Jarvis, 152 King St, London W6 0QU, tel: 0181 748 5050, fax: 0181 741 0299.*

Okavango Tours and Safaris, Gadd House, Arcadia Ave, London N3 2TJ, tel: 0181 343 3283, fax: 0181 343 3287, email: tours@okavango.com *

Kilimanjaro Wildlife Holidays, Croft House, Brampton, Cumbria CA8 1SG, tel/fax: 016977 3172.

Somak Holidays, Somak House, Harrovian Village, Bessborough Rd, Harrow-on the-Hill, Middlesex HA1 3EX, tel: 0181 423 3000, fax: 0181 423 7700.*

Travelbag Adventures, 15 Turk St, Alton GU34 1AG, tel: 01420 541007, fax: 01420 541022, email: mail@travelbag-adventures.co.uk

From the USA, South Africa and elsewhere

There are no direct flights to Zanzibar from the USA. You must fly to Europe and then take one of the flights mentioned above.

From South Africa there are no direct flights, but several airlines, notably Alliance (a partnership of South Africa Airways, Air Tanzania and Uganda Airways), fly between Johannesburg and Dar es Salaam, from where you can take a plane or ship to Zanzibar. Another option to consider is the Gulf Air flight from Durban to Dar es Salaam.

If you want to reach Zanzibar from somewhere in the world other than the countries mentioned above, it is usual to fly to Europe, East Africa, or the Gulf states and pick up a connecting flight from there. For example, from many parts of Asia you could fly on Gulf Air to Abu Dhabi or Dubai then take another plane to Zanzibar or Dar es Salaam.

The runway at Zanzibar Airport was extended in 1994. As tourism continues to grow, it is likely that an increasing number of large aircraft direct from Europe, Asia and the islands of the Indian Ocean will start arriving in the future.

From mainland Tanzania
By air

Air Tanzania Corporation (ATC) flies five times per week between Dar es Salaam (often shortened to Dar) and Zanzibar. Fares are $43 one-way, $86 return, and flights take about 30 minutes. The service is not very reliable (with frequent delays and cancelled reservations), although it is improving gradually. The ATC reservations desk is in ATC House, a large building on Ohio Street in central Dar. It is unfortunate that this smart new building is not matched by an equally impressive service.

If you don't want to chance your luck with ATC, a number of private regional air companies offer regular flights from Dar to Zanzibar. These include: **Coastal Travels** (tel: Dar es Salaam (051) 31216, mobile: 0811 325673), with Zanzibar-Dar flights at $44, and other flights between Zanzibar and the Selous and Ruaha wildlife reserves, and to/from Mafia Island; and **Precision Air Flight Services** (tel: Arusha (057) 6903, 2818, fax: 8204, tel: Dar es Salaam (051) 30800), with a modern fleet and daily flights between Zanzibar and Dar or Kilimanjaro International Airport (with road connections to Arusha), plus many other destinations all over East Africa. Fares to Zanzibar are $55 from Dar and $146 from Kilimanjaro International. More details on all the above services between Zanzibar and mainland Tanzania are given in *Chapter Five* on page 106.

Another option is the thrice-weekly scheduled service is operated by **Air Zanzibar**, a charter company based in Zanzibar Town. The fare is $44. You can contact Air Zanzibar direct (their numbers are listed under *Air charter companies*, page 107) or get any travel agent in Dar to make arrangements for you.

If you're in a hurry, or all the scheduled flights are full, you can charter your own aircraft. The main local players are **Air Zanzibar** and **ZanAir**. Rates for a six-seater plane between Dar and Zanzibar start at about $250. You can contact the companies direct – see page 107. Alternatively, visit any travel agent in Dar, Arusha or Moshi and they will make the arrangements for you, usually at little extra cost.

By ship

Several passenger ships travel between Dar es Salaam and Zanzibar. There is a wide choice of vessels, and many departures each day. Some ships have different class decks or lounges. Generally, fares are the same for all ships, although occasionally there are differences – cost usually reflects the comfort and speed of the ship.

In Dar, all the ship booking offices are at the main passenger port, very near the city centre. Schedules and prices are chalked up on boards outside each office. You can buy tickets on the spot very easily. Reservations are not essential, but if you are in Dar a day or two (or even an hour or two) before you want to travel, you should buy a ticket in advance to make sure. Non-Tanzanians usually have to pay in US dollars and prices are quoted in this currency. Tanzanian residents can pay in TSh.

Note that all non-Tanzanian passengers leaving Dar must pay a port departure tax of $5. The departure tax office is near the ship booking offices, and tickets are carefully checked before you board.

Beware of hustlers who loiter around the passenger port, offering to help you buy tickets and port tax, carry luggage, or simply show you the way. It's best politely to decline assistance, as some of these men are experts at currency con-tricks or simply run off with your bag.

The main ships used by visitors are:

Flying Horse This is a large catamaran, with a capacity of more than 400 passengers, operated by the Africa Shipping Corporation, running once every day in each direction between Zanzibar and Dar, taking about three hours. All seats cost $30, except on the night service which is $15. The seating areas are air-conditioned, and an in-flight video is usually shown. The ship also has a small bar and restaurant. You can also travel on the deck, which has a few seats and an awning to keep off the sun but little else; tourists are still charged $30 to sit here. However, it is a very pleasant way to travel, especially when you come into Zanzibar port at sunset. *Flying Horse* also plans to be serving Mombasa sometime in the future.

Sea Express This is the name of four large hydrofoils, run by a company of the same name, each with a capacity of 150 passengers, travelling between Dar and Zanzibar around five times per day in each direction. The journey takes about 70 minutes. A seat in first class costs $35, and in second class $30, one way. There is no deck-space. These boats are reported to be unsteady in rough seas, and seasick-bags are not provided! A new Sea Express service, linking Zanzibar to Mombasa, is planned.

Condor and *Muungano* Two large ferries operated by Azam Marine Ltd, running daily with journey time about four hours and costing $30 for all seats. The *Muungano* used to run between Athens and the Aegean islands; all signs and notices are in Greek, and even the subtitles on the video shown in the bar are in Greek.

Talieh and *Sepideh* Two fast boats run by a company called Mega Speed Liners. *Talieh* goes twice daily between Zanzibar and Dar, while *Sepideh* goes between Dar es Salaam and Zanzibar daily, with a service to and from Pemba five times weekly and Mombasa and Tanga twice weekly with plans to extend the service to Lamu.

For times and fares see *Chapter Five*, page 108. Other ships on the Dar to Zanzibar route, less frequently used by tourists, are:

Mapinduzi and *Maendeleo* These two old cargo ships are operated by Zanzibar Shipping Corporation (ZSC), the state-owned line, running between Dar and Zanzibar, and also between Zanzibar and Pemba. The service is used by local people as it is cheap: about $3, payable in TSh. Some travellers on a tight budget also use it. The boats are supposed to go once a week, but the service is notoriously unreliable. Even the booking clerks in the ZSC office advise visitors to take one of the other ships. See also *Chapter Five*, page 109.

Lingen Another cargo boat used mainly by locals running between Dar, Zanzibar and Pemba with cheap fares ($6) but an unfathomable schedule.

Canadian Spirit This is a large roll-on-roll-off ferry which steams up and down the Tanzanian coast, between Mtwara and Dar, calling in at Zanzibar officially once a week (but seemingly at random). It also goes to Tanga, Pemba and Mafia Island, and sometimes to Mombasa. Deck space for passengers is reportedly cheap, but tying in your travel plans with this boat's timetable is hard. It's only worth using it if you are coming from the far south of Tanzania, and want to avoid the cost of flying or the horrors of the bus journey.

By dhow

Up until the end of the 1980s, for anyone who couldn't afford the air fare, the usual way to reach Zanzibar from Dar was to go by dhow, one of the traditional wooden boats widely used around the coasts of Arabia and East Africa. This was a romantic and very authentic way to travel, although most of the boats had motors rather than sails. Unfortunately, it is now illegal for tourists to travel between Dar and Zanzibar in this way, although we have heard from a few intrepid travellers who find dhow captains willing to take them from Zanzibar back to Dar (but not going out from Dar, as the port police are strict). Details are given in *Chapter Five*.

However, if you really want to go by dhow, it's possible to reach Zanzibar by sailing from Tanga, a port on the mainland about 200km north of Dar. Some dhows also occasionally go from Bagamoyo, in between Dar and Tanga. Many dhows actually go to Pemba Island, rather than Zanzibar Island (more correctly called Unguja), but once on Pemba you can easily reach Unguja.

Whichever way you go, if you are searching for that authentic East African sailing-boat experience, this is where you find it. Tourists are not allowed on any dhow travelling under sail, so only boats with motors carry passengers. This may shatter your illusions but, for many people, 'the dhow experience' is still a bit *too* authentic. It may appear to be a romantic way to travel but, in reality, these voyages are not for the faint-hearted. The dhows tend to be dangerously overloaded, and a small boat riding low in a rough sea can be very frightening. The roll is considerable and seasickness is not at all uncommon. Motors are installed with no exhaust outlet pipes, and the stench of fumes coming up through the floorboards doesn't do much to calm weak stomachs. And, for when things get really bad, the toilet is a 'captain's chair' hanging out over the rail, usually in full view of the rest of the passengers. Journeys between Tanga and Zanzibar are supposed to take about 12 hours, but can take more than two days. You need to bring all your own food and water. Horror stories, involving leaky boats, engine failures, drunken sailors and even shipwrecks, are regularly told on the travellers' grapevine.

It is also possible to reach Zanzibar by dhow from Mombasa (see page 110).

From Kenya
By air
Air Kenya flies three times a week in each direction between Mombasa and Zanzibar. This service is reliable, and the number of flights is likely to increase in the future. The flights take 35 minutes and economy tickets are about $40. It is also possible to fly between Nairobi and Zanzibar (via Mombasa); the one-way cost is about $90. Tickets can be bought in any travel agent in Mombasa or Nairobi, and it may be worth shopping around to compare prices. Details on flying from Zanzibar to Kenya are given in *Chapter Five*.

Your other option is a flight on **Eagle Aviation**, a Kenya-based company, with regular flights between Nairobi, Mombasa and Zanzibar. The Mombasa–Zanzibar service operates on the days when Kenya Airways doesn't. Fares are around $55. You can also use Eagle services to reach Zanzibar from several of Kenya's national parks (via Nairobi). For details contact Eagle in Mombasa (tel: 01 43402) or any agents in Mombasa and Nairobi. In Zanzibar, several agents listed in *Chapter Five* sell Eagle flights.

Your other option is private charter. Several of the local air companies listed in *Chapter Five* offer services to Zanzibar from Mombasa, Nairobi or the national parks. Rates for a five-seater plane between Mombasa and Zanzibar start at about $700. A travel agent in Mombasa or elsewhere can make the arrangements for you, usually at little extra cost.

By ship
The *Sepideh,* run by Mega Speed Liners, speeds up and down the coast of East Africa between Dar es Salaam and Mombasa, via Zanzibar, Pemba and Tanga. For details see page 109. For travellers coming from Kenya, this service is ideal: the Mombasa–Pemba fare is $30 one way, the Mombasa–Zanzibar fare is $45. In Dar or Mombasa you can buy their tickets from most travel agents.

At some time, new services on the *Sea Express* and the *Flying Horse* are planned for the Mombasa to Zanzibar route. (More information on these boats is given on page 45.) When these services become established, tickets will be available from travel agents in Mombasa. Again, it may be worth shopping around to compare prices.

By dhow
While tourists cannot legally travel by dhow from Dar to Zanzibar, it is still permitted from Mombasa, although dhows going from Kenya to Zanzibar Island are rare. Dhows go more frequently between Mombasa and Pemba (more details in *Chapter Seven*), and some travellers go to Pemba first then travel on to Zanzibar Island from there. Before deciding to travel by dhow, read the section above on travelling from Tanga. If that doesn't put you off, you can find a dhow from Mombasa to Zanzibar by asking around in the old port area of Mombasa. There is usually a boat

twice a week, going either to Zanzibar Town or to Wete or Mkoani on Pemba, although times and days are variable. A one-way trip costs about $10 to $15, payable in Kenyan shillings or hard currency.

ARRIVING AND LEAVING
Arrival at Zanzibar
If you fly into Zanzibar, the main airport is on the outskirts of Zanzibar Town. If you travel by ship from Dar you arrive at the main port in Zanzibar Town. The customs and immigration officials on Zanzibar used to have a reputation for toughness. Today, at the airport and main port, arrival formalities are fairly quick and not too strenuous, although they are somewhat disorganised. You will be required to complete an immigration card and show your visa, even if you have arrived from mainland Tanzania. (Remember that Zanzibar is a separate state within Tanzania.) If you arrive from Pemba Island (which is part of the state of Zanzibar) from Kenya or mainland Tanzania you will also be required to complete these formalities.

You will be asked how long you want to stay (two to four weeks is usual, and creates no problem), and then given a Zanzibar stamp in your passport. The customs officials may want to check your bag, but a detailed search is unlikely. You are not allowed to import or export Tanzanian shillings, unless you are travelling to or from mainland Tanzania. There are no other currency regulations at present, which means you can import or export as much foreign ('hard') currency as you like. (It is possible that this rule could change, which means you may have to complete a declaration form saying how much foreign currency you have. This will be used to record all the hard currency you change, and will be checked again when you leave.)

Leaving Zanzibar
To leave Zanzibar by air, your options include flights to Dar on Air Tanzania, to Mombasa on Kenya Airways, or further afield on an international flight. Tickets can be bought from travel agents or from the airlines' own offices in Zanzibar Town. You can also go with one of the regional or local air companies which fly regularly to Dar, Mombasa, and other destinations such as Nairobi or Arusha. They advertise spare seats in travel agents and large hotels around town, or you can visit their offices to see what they have available. To leave Zanzibar Island by ship, most of the companies have booking offices at the main port in Zanzibar Town. You can also arrange a ticket through a travel agent. (All air and ship office addresses are given in *Chapter Five*.)

If you are including Pemba in your visit, you can travel back to Mombasa or Tanga by ship or dhow from there, without having to come back to Zanzibar Island. (For more details, see the sections above and *Chapter Seven*.)

When you leave Zanzibar Town, by air or sea, formalities at the airport and port are fairly straightforward. You will be given a departure card, which you need to fill in, even if you are going to mainland Tanzania. You also show your passport to prove you have not overstayed, and maybe have your bags checked. (If currency restrictions are reintroduced you may have to hand back your declaration form and show some bank receipts to prove you have changed money legally.)

If you're leaving Zanzibar for Kenya, or elsewhere beyond Tanzania, the airport has a restaurant and café-bar where you can spend the last of your Tanzanian shillings.

Departure taxes

All passengers have to pay a departure tax of $20 (payable in dollars) when flying out of Zanzibar Airport on international flights. Tanzanian shillings are not acceptable. For flights from Zanzibar to Dar or Pemba the airport tax is $2, payable in TSh.

Even ship passengers cannot escape departure tax! All tourists leaving by boat from Zanzibar are charged a $5 'seaport departure service charge'. This is also payable in dollars only.

BEFORE YOU GO

Entry regulations

All non-Tanzanian visitors to Zanzibar need a passport, valid for the duration of their stay. Zanzibar is part of Tanzania and most foreigners entering the country need a visa or visitor's pass, depending on their own nationality. Visas and visitor's passes cannot always be issued at a point of entry, so you may need to apply in advance to your nearest Tanzanian Embassy or High Commission. A charge is usually made for issuing a visa. Costs range from $20 to $50 depending on your nationality. If you are planning to reach Zanzibar via Nairobi or Mombasa, you may also need a visa or visitor's pass for Kenya. Again, this depends on your own nationality.

Arriving by air at Zanzibar, Dar es Salaam, Mombasa or Nairobi, you may need to show certificates to prove you have been vaccinated against yellow fever (and cholera if you are coming from an endemic area). You may also need a return ticket out of Tanzania or Kenya, or be required to show that you have sufficient funds to cover your stay. (Other currency regulations are covered in *Chapter Five,* page 120.)

Entry regulations are always liable to change, so you should make enquiries at your nearest Tanzania diplomatic representative (embassy or high commission) or tourist office before you leave. As visas can take several weeks to issue, you should do this well in advance of your planned travel date.

Visitors from the UK can make enquiries at:

Tanzania High Commission, 43 Hertford St, London W1Y 7FF, tel: 0171 491 3600 or 0171 499 8951.

Tanzania Tourist Office, 78-80 Borough High St, London SE1 1LL, tel: 0171 407 0566.

Visitors from the USA should contact:
Tanzanian Embassy, 2139 R St, NW, Washington DC 20008, tel: (202) 232 0501.
Tanzania Tourist Office, 210 E 42nd St, New York, NY 10017, tel: (212) 972 9160.

Visitors coming from Kenya should contact:
Tanzania High Commission, Continental House, corner of Harambee Ave and Uhuru Highway, Nairobi, tel: 331056.

Medical regulations and advice

All visitors to Tanzania (including Zanzibar) must be vaccinated against yellow fever. You will be required to show a yellow fever certificate when you enter the country. Vaccinations for typhoid, tetanus, meningitis and hepatitis A are also generally recommended. You should visit your own doctor to discuss your requirements a few months before you plan to travel, as some vaccinations need to be administered in separate doses with gaps of several weeks in between.

It is also essential to be protected against malaria during your visit to Zanzibar. You cannot be vaccinated against this disease, but there are several different types of drug available for malaria prevention. Recommendations vary in different parts of the world, and as the malaria parasites become immune to some preventative treatments, so your doctor will advise you on required drugs and doses.

If your doctor is not sure about the current recommendations concerning vaccinations and malaria prevention for Zanzibar and the coast of East Africa, you should contact a specialist information centre to get detailed and up-to-date advice. In the UK, these include the Malaria Reference Laboratory at the London School of Tropical Medicine (tel: 0171 636 7921), and the chain of British Airways Travel Clinics in several towns and cities around the country (tel: 0171 831 5333 for details of your nearest clinic). In the USA, contact the Centers for Disease Control, Atlanta, Georgia, tel: (404) 332 4559. For more details on how to stay healthy during your visit, see *Health and Safety* in *Chapter Four*. You can also consult one of the health books listed in the *Further Reading* section.

Zanzibar's hospitals and medical centres are listed on page 124.

Teeth

It's a good idea to have a dental check-up before you go, as local dentists can be painful, expensive, or both.

Insurance

You should have a good travel insurance policy to cover your stay. Conditions in local hospitals are often poor, and private hospitals can be expensive. Your policy should cover all medical costs, including emergency air evacuation from Zanzibar to the Tanzanian mainland, to Kenya, or back to your own country. Several insurance companies offer policies for independent travel overseas. Costs vary widely, and depend on how risky the insurance company regards a visit to Zanzibar or East Africa, so it is well worth shopping around. A specialist travel agency will be able to advise you.

Money

Tanzania's unit of currency is the Tanzania shilling (TSh), and this is used throughout Zanzibar. Foreign ('hard') currency can be exchanged for TSh at banks or change bureaux in Dar es Salaam or in Zanzibar Town. (Rates of exchange are given on page 4.) Exchange rates are likely to fluctuate, and prices generally are likely to increase as Zanzibar becomes a more popular tourist destination and the number of visitors to the island grows.

Non-Tanzanians in Zanzibar have to pay for some items, such as air flights, ship tickets and hotels, in foreign currency. US dollars are most readily accepted and the easiest to deal with. The prices of many other items, such as tours or rental cars, are often quoted in dollars, although these are also payable in TSh at the current rate. In this book, the prices of many items are quoted in US dollars, as these prices are less likely to become out of date. VAT (Value Added Tax) at 20% may be introduced in 1998 or 1999. This will obviously have a marked effect on prices.

For visitors to Zanzibar, the most convenient currency to use is US dollars (as it is in most parts of eastern or southern Africa). This should be carried in a combination of cash and travellers cheques (TCs), and a mix of high and low denominations. Cash is handy as it can be used almost anywhere. TCs are more secure, and can be replaced if stolen. Well-known brands of TC are more readily accepted and tend to be processed faster.

In Zanzibar, money can be changed at the main branch of the People's Bank of Zanzibar in Zanzibar Town (although not at branches of the Commercial Bank of Zanzibar), or at one of the many privately run bureaux de change (also called 'forex bureaux') around the town. (More details on banks and bureaux are given in *Chapter Five*.) Several hotels and tour companies are also licensed to change money. If you have time, it is worth shopping around between the bank and a few forex bureaux to compare rates. Generally, the bank offers better rates for TCs and the private bureaux offer better rates for cash, particularly for large denomination bills.

Credit cards

You can pay for many items such as tours, hotels and air tickets with a credit card, but you may be charged a high commission (around 20%). Drawing cash may also be possible, but once again high commissions are charged. This is technically not allowed, so many hotels and companies get around it by quoting you a price in TSh, then converting to dollars or pounds at a poor rate (ie: favourable to them). The official reason for the charges is that Zanzibar is not hooked up to any international electronic card validation process, and staff have physically to make telephone calls (sometimes to the card's country of origin) to get authorisation before the card can be accepted. In reality, it's because plastic is pretty new on Zanzibar, and most people still prefer to deal in tangible cash!

The black market
It is possible to change money on the black market, ie: unofficially. There used to be a very high demand for US dollars in Zanzibar, and visitors could get several times more than the official bank rate by changing 'on the black'. However, since currency forms were abolished and free market exchange rates introduced, the black market demand has diminished considerably, and almost disappeared, although some black market dealers will still give you slightly more than the bank or bureau rate.

If you do decide to change on the black market, remember that you are depriving a developing country of its income. More important, remember that unofficial dealing is dangerous and highly illegal. Never change in the open, and beware of con-artists and police informers.

Costs
The cost of a visit to Zanzibar depends very much on your standard of travel. At the bottom line, the cheapest hotels cost between $5 and $10 a night, per person. If you have meals in local eating-houses, supplemented by lunches of fruit and bread from the market, plus tea or soft drinks, food will cost another $5 to $10 a day. Hotels in the middle range cost between $20 and $50 a double, and meals in smarter restaurants cost the equivalent of around $10 per person. Towards the top of the range, good quality hotels are upwards of $60 to $100 for a double, with meals in the best establishments from around $20.

You also need to take into account the costs of getting around. Buses are very cheap, costing the equivalent of only a few dollars to cross the island. For independent travel, you can hire bicycles for around $5 per day, motor-scooters for $25 or cars from around $40.

Organised tours of the spice plantations or boat trips out to the smaller islands start from about $10 per person for a small group. If you want a vehicle or boat to yourself this can go up to about $50 for a day's outing. Entry to most of the historical sites and ruins on the island is free, as is lying on the beach!

Reading up
A very important part of your preparation for a visit should be to find out as much as you can about the history, geography and culture of Zanzibar before you arrive. If text books and encyclopaedias put you off, read a few novels or travelogues to get yourself in the mood, or dip into some of the early explorers' accounts (see *Further Reading*). Also, scan the foreign pages of newspapers, or magazines specialising in developing countries, to familiarise yourself with politics and current affairs. You could even try

learning a few phrases of Swahili. All this will make your trip much more rewarding.

WHAT TO TAKE

Clothing

You are unlikely to experience great extremes of temperature on Zanzibar, although days can be very warm and nights chilly. Clothing should be light and loose-fitting for daytime, and you'll need something slightly more substantial for evenings. Even in the dry seasons, a rain jacket is essential and an umbrella (available locally) highly recommended. You'll need a good pair of shoes for 'doing' the sights, and a pair of sandals for relaxing. A hat to keep off sun and rain completes the outfit.

Plastic beach shoes, or something similar to avoid the spiky sea-urchins, are useful for walking out into the sea across old coral beds. (Remember, though, never to tread on live coral. In a few seconds you can break off chunks which will take several decades to re-grow.)

Dress codes are relaxed, even in the smartest hotels and restaurants, so you won't need black tie or ball gown. However, for wandering around towns and villages you should be aware of local Muslim sensibilities and not expose too much bare flesh. As visitors, we have absolutely no right to impose our attitudes on the local people, who are always dressed modestly. Remember that walking around a Zanzibar town with your shoulders and most of your legs bare is almost like being naked in your own high street back home.

Of course, tourists don't need to don robes, veils and turbans but around town it is important for women to have knees and shoulders covered. This is recommended for men too. Therefore, for men and women, long trousers are better than shorts, although baggy surf-shorts or culottes are acceptable. Many women find skirts more comfortable than trousers. For men and women, long-sleeved shirts and blouses are better than vests and skimpy T-shirts. For the beach, normal swimming gear is fine, although going into local fishing villages in briefs or bikinis shows a complete lack of sensitivity.

Equipment

Unless you're planning to base yourself in one place during your stay, it is usually easier to carry all your clothing and equipment in a **rucksack** rather than in a suitcase. Old-fashioned rucksacks with external frames are bulky, and liable to break on planes and buses, and thus not recommended. Much better are rucksacks with internal frames, or the type of rucksacks that turn neatly into travel bags, with a zipped flap to enclose the straps and waist-belt. These convertible bags are ideal if you've got to carry your kit for any distance, but also look smart enough to be acceptable in up-market hotels. Another advantage: with the straps zipped away, they don't get damaged on bus roof-racks or airport carousels.

If you're staying in the cheaper hotels, sheets are not always very clean, so a light **sleeping bag** is useful. A sheet sleeping bag liner is also suitable for this purpose.

It is important to protect yourself from mosquitoes, to avoid getting malaria. Most hotels provide nets over the beds, but some are in bad condition, with holes big enough to let small birds through, let alone the odd mosquito. Either take your own **mosquito net** (some excellent portable models are available in good outdoor equipment shops – those impregnated with a repellent are best), or take safety pins or needle and cotton to make running repairs. For more protection take a roll-on insect repellent or use mosquito coils (available locally) in your room at night. Remember, it only takes one pesky mozzie to spoil your night's sleep and maybe spoil your whole holiday by giving you malaria.

Some travellers carry a small **stove** and set of pots and plates. This is a good idea if you're planning to spend a few days (or longer) on the beaches, where fresh fish and vegetables can sometimes be bought, or if you fancy a break from local fare. Petrol stoves are probably the most versatile as this fuel is usually available in towns, although it is sometimes dirty. Gas cartridges can occasionally be bought in Zanzibar Town, but supplies seem erratic. Methylated spirit, suitable for Trangia-type stoves, is available from chemists in Zanzibar Town.

A tent is not essential for a visit to Zanzibar. There are a few official places for camping and putting up a tent. Camping is possible on the beaches, near the low budget hotels, but this is not the general practice as the hotels are cheap anyway and security cannot always be guaranteed.

Personal items include a towel, wash-kit, lipsalve, sun protection cream, sunglasses and a small first-aid kit. Soap, toothpaste and basic medicines can be bought locally if you run out. Suncream is sometimes available, but it's expensive, so bring all you need.

Your **first-aid kit** should include sticking plasters (some waterproof), antiseptic cream, tubi-grip bandages, aspirin or paracetamol and anti-diarrhoea pills. Oil of cloves for toothache is useful, or you can just chew on a local clove bud. More elaborate medicines, if you need them, are available from the private hospitals in Zanzibar (listed on page 124). Remember to bring adequate supplies of any personal medication you may need. Many travellers also carry an 'anti-AIDS' kit (a pack of needles, syringes and other items which come into contact with blood) for use in an emergency. Your doctor or a vaccination centre can provide more information.

Other useful items to take include the following:

Torch/flashlight Power cuts are not infrequent in the towns, and the beach hotels have generators that only run for a few hours each night. A supply of candles would also be useful.

Water bottle, water filter and purification tablets Water supplies in towns are not always drinkable, and wells at the beach and in rural areas are shallow and can often be contaminated. (Purification works more effectively if you filter the water first.)

Universal sink plug Plugs always seem to be missing from all but the best hotels.

Rubber wedge or **small padlock** These are useful for securing doors. Theft from rooms is not a major problem in Zanzibar, but it pays to be careful at all times in the cheaper hotels where locks are sometimes broken or missing.

Snorkelling gear Some readers have written to us complaining about the expense of hiring snorkelling gear, and about the poor quality of many of the masks available. If you're keen on snorkelling (and Zanzibar offers some of the best in the world) it might be worth taking your own mask, or a full set of gear, with you.

In the UK, small travel gadgets and a whole range of items specially designed for tropical travellers are available mail order from SafariQuip, The Stones, Castleton, Hope Valley S33 8ZZ, tel: 01433 620320. They also supply a good range of water purifiers and filters, and can provide an information sheet about water purification.

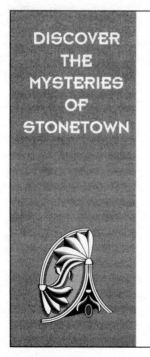

Chapter Four

Facts about Zanzibar

This chapter gives a general overview of various items relevant to visitors in Zanzibar. For more specific details on towns, villages, places to stay and places to visit, see Chapter Five *Zanzibar Town*, Chapter Six *Zanzibar Island* and Chapter Seven *Pemba Island*.

ACCOMMODATION, FOOD AND TRANSPORT

For independent travellers, the accommodation, food and transport available in Zanzibar are probably the three most important aspects of a visit. This section describes briefly what you can expect, and will give you a general impression. However, at the time of writing (1997), Zanzibar is going through a period of great change so these three aspects, more than any others, are likely to be different by the time you arrive. Several more hotels will have been built, new cafés and restaurants opened, roads repaired, and much more. Be ready for these changes when using information from this book and your visit will go more smoothly.

Accommodation
Zanzibar Town
At the upper end of the range, Zanzibar Town's only large, international-standard hotel is the Serena Inn, part of a chain with other properties in Tanzania and Kenya, completed in 1997. Several grand old buildings in Zanzibar Town have been renovated and opened as hotels combining good quality with a local atmosphere. Prices range from $75 to $150 for a double room. In this price bracket, most hotels offer air-conditioned rooms, fridges, TVs and telephones; however, some of the more interesting places make a deliberate selling point of the fact that they offer *none* of these!

Zanzibar Town has a wide choice of mid-range hotels, costing between $20 and $50 for a double, where rooms are en suite, clean and comfortable, but may not be air-conditioned.

At the lower end of the price range there are several small hotels and guesthouses which offer good-value service for between $5 and $10 per person. Rooms may not be spotless, and are not usually en suite, but these smaller places are generally friendly, and popular with independent travellers on a tight budget.

Several hotels have been opened on the outer edges of Zanzibar Town, around 5km from the centre, on the south side of town nearer the airport, and on the north side of town towards the village of Bububu. These range from top-quality hotels to basic guesthouses.

All hotels in Zanzibar include breakfast in the room price, unless otherwise stated.

Zanzibar Island

On Zanzibar Island many hotels are on the coast, mostly in the north and east, near the reefs and beaches. There are several different kinds of place to stay here, ranging from large, modern 'club resorts', through modest but comfortable bungalows and lodges, to small guesthouses run by local families.

On Pemba Island there is very little in the way of tourist accommodation. Each of the three main towns has a ZTC hotel (these are plain, dilapidated and somewhat overpriced), and a couple of local guesthouses which are less impersonal and better value.

As yet, there are no official campsites in Zanzibar. Camping is permitted in the grounds of some budget hotels on the coast, but this is not usual as the hotels are so cheap anyway. However, during very busy periods, some of the popular beach hotels can be full, and then camping is the only option. Unfortunately, on the most popular beaches, there have been occasional incidents of theft from unoccupied tents.

Food
Restaurants

In Zanzibar Town, there are several good restaurants catering specifically for the tourist trade, specialising in local dishes, sea-food or curries (remember that Zanzibar is on the shores of the Indian Ocean). The town also has restaurants where meals and snacks are less elaborate and prices are more reasonable. There are also some small eating-houses catering mainly for local people where you can eat very cheaply. They usually only have one or two types of food available, such as stew and rice, but they also serve chapatis, samosas and other snacks.

Outside Zanzibar Town, in the smaller towns and villages, there are very few places to eat. Local people tend to eat in their own houses and there are not enough tourists around yet to create a market for cafés and restaurants.

On the coast, hotels and guesthouses usually have restaurants attached, where food and service generally reflect the overall standard of the accommodation. A few small restaurants have opened by the most popular beaches, catering for the growing influx of visitors.

On Pemba, Chake Chake and Wete have a couple of local restaurants, but there is little else in the other towns on the island.

Self-catering
If you plan to provide for yourself, in Zanzibar Town there are several shops selling locally produced bread and cakes, plus a reasonable choice of food in tins and packets imported from Kenya or other parts of the world. Zanzibar Town has a very good market where you can buy all sorts of fruit and vegetables, plus fresh meat and fish if you have a way of cooking it. Other towns on Zanzibar and Pemba also have small markets where you can buy meat, fish, fruit and vegetables, and shops with a limited but adequate supply of tinned food.

THE PORTUGUESE LEGACY

Zanzibar was occupied by the Portuguese in the 16th and 17th centuries. They introduced many new foods, brought from their colonies in other parts of the world, and the Swahili words used today are borrowed directly from the Portuguese language. Cassava or manioc is *muhogo* in Swahili (from the Portuguese *mandioca*) and the cashew nut is *mbibo* (from *bibo*), both plants were originally grown in Brazil. Avocado is *mpea* and guava is *mpera*, both from the Portuguese word *pera*. The Portuguese also introduced the use of dung (Swahili: *mboleo*, Portuguese: *boleo*) for cultivation, and the iron nail (Swahili: *parafujo*, Portuguese: *parafuso*) for boat-building.

Source: A History of East Africa, Oliver Roland and Mathew Gervase. Oxford University Press, London, 1963

Transport
For independent travellers, local buses link Zanzibar Town with several of the smaller towns and villages around the island. On Pemba, buses link Chake Chake to the other towns of Wete and Mkoani. Both islands also have small pick-up vans called *dala-dalas* which serve areas around the main towns, or complement the bus services. Fares are cheap, around $1 to cross the island, and the same on buses or dala-dalas, although dala-dalas are quicker.

Buses and dalas from outlying villages heading for Zanzibar Town tend to leave very early in the morning but, apart from that, there are no fixed timetables; most buses and dalas simply leave when they're full. At any bus or dala-dala station, don't expect an information board: you will need to ask around to find the transport you need.

Most independent travellers go from Zanzibar Town to one of the beaches in a minibus organised by the *papaasi* (touts) who meet incoming ships and lurk at budget hotels looking for custom. A ride in one of these vehicles is much quicker than the bus and costs $3 to $5. They normally pick you up from your hotel and drop you at any of the hotels on the southern part of the East Coast, or at Nungwi. As other parts of the coast become more popular, similar services may start operating there.

If dealing with the *papaasi* is not your scene, most tour companies can arrange transfer from Zanzibar Town to any point on the island. Rates start at about $50 for a car or minibus.

It is possible to tour Zanzibar Island by rented car or motor-scooter: there are several hotels and agencies in Zanzibar Town where this can be arranged. Bicycles can also be hired in Zanzibar Town, on the East Coast beaches and in a few places on Pemba.

HEALTH AND SAFETY

'What with bad water and worse liquor, the Briton finds it hard to live on Zanzibar.'

Richard Burton, British explorer (1857)

Health

When travelling around Zanzibar or East Africa, the different climatic and social conditions mean visitors are exposed to diseases not normally encountered at home. Although you will have received all the vaccinations recommended in the *Before you go* section (see page 50), this does not mean you will be free of all illness during your travels: certain precautions still have to be taken.

You should read a good book on travel medicine (see *Further Reading*) and be aware of the causes, symptoms and treatments of the more serious diseases. But don't let these colourful descriptions put you off – with a little care and attention most of these illnesses can be avoided.

The easiest way to avoid sickness is by taking care with what you eat and drink: many diseases (including cholera, dysentery and hepatitis A) are transmitted through unclean food and water. (Experienced travellers say: 'Peel it, boil it, cook it or forget it'!) contaminated plates, cups and cutlery can also be a cause. To cut the chances of contracting anything you should make sure your drinking water is clean and safe. As the supplies in Zanzibar are not always reliable this means you should use purifying tablets or solutions, and/or a filter bag. These are not available in Zanzibar and should be bought from a good outdoor shop before you leave.

Imported bottled spring-water is available in some shops in Zanzibar Town. Most of this is reliable, although you should check the seal around the cap as it is not unknown for discarded bottles to be filled with tap water and sold again. (Don't become nervous and avoid drinking all together. It is very important to keep up your liquid intake in the hot climate to avoid the headaches caused by mild dehydration.)

In restaurants and cafés you should eat freshly cooked meals if you can, rather than food which may have been kept warm or inadequately re-heated. Check that meat and fish has been well-cooked right through. Uncooked food, such as salads or peeled fruit, should be avoided unless you know for sure it's been properly prepared; it may have been washed in dirty water, if it's been washed at all. To keep up your intake of fresh foods you should peel your own fruit or prepare your own picnic salads with vegetables you have cleaned yourself.

To stay healthy it is particularly important to maintain a high standard of personal hygiene: wash your hands after going to the toilet and before eating. It's a good idea to carry a few antiseptic wipes for the times when water or soap may be hard to find.

Visitors to Zanzibar are also exposed to malaria, which is caused by a blood parasite transmitted by the bite of an infected mosquito. As with other vector-borne diseases, the chances of contracting malaria can be reduced if you take proper preventative steps. No vaccination is available, so an anti-malaria drug needs to be taken (see *Before you go*). Keep to the advised dose for a week before you reach the malarial area, throughout your visit, and for a period of four to six weeks after your return.

Anti-malaria drugs do not provide complete protection, so you should also take steps to avoid being bitten by a mosquito initially: in the evening when mosquitoes are active wear long-sleeved shirts and long trousers, covering wrists and ankles; use a repellent to rub on exposed skin; and consider using an insect spray for your bedroom or bathroom at night. Most hotels have mosquito nets and these should always be used. In cheaper hotels some nets may be broken, so a needle and thread for quick repairs is useful. Alternatively, to avoid worrying, you could carry your own net; see the *Equipment* section on page 55 for more details.

Insect sprays and mosquito coils, which burn slowly through the night, can be bought in shops in Zanzibar Town, but the tubes of repellent to rub on your skin (which tend to be very effective) are not available.

If you need medical attention, there are several hospitals and medical centres in Zanzibar Town. These are listed in *Chapter Five.*

Safety

Crime of any sort is rare in the rural areas of Zanzibar Island and on Pemba Island, but unfortunately it is on the increase in some parts of Zanzibar Town. A few pickpockets operate in the main market, and some tourists have had bags and cameras snatched while walking around the narrow streets of the Old Town. (For more specific details on places to be careful, see *Chapter Five.*) There have also been attacks and robberies on some of the beaches around Zanzibar Town and on the East Coast beaches popular with travellers. It is better not to go to the beach alone, especially at night.

There will always be a large financial gap between tourists and local people, but you can reduce the chances of having anything stolen by not displaying your wealth. Keep your valuables secure and out of sight in a pouch under your shirt or inside your trousers. Keep most of your money there too, and do not peel off notes from a huge wad for every small purchase. Wandering around the town with a camera or personal stereo casually slung over your shoulder is insensitive and simply asking for trouble. A simple, dull-looking bag is much less attractive than something brightly coloured and fashionable.

As in many other places around the world, thieves see women, especially lone women, as easy prey. If you are a woman travelling alone, this should not put you off going to Zanzibar, but you must use common sense and not make yourself a target (eg: avoid dark back streets at night). Touts selling souvenirs, tours or postcards may also tend to hassle women more initially, although anecdotal evidence suggests women can handle this without tempers breaking on either side, whereas men tend to get confrontational, which simply leads to unpleasantness.

Theft from hotel rooms is unusual. Most hotels have safes, where valuables can be stored, but in a few small hotels there have been reports of stuff disappearing even from the safe. For more details see *Chapter Five.*

THINGS TO BUY

Zanzibar Town has several curio shops selling antiques, all sorts of hand-crafted pieces, and a lot of genuine junk. Some of the antique items have been brought to the islands by Arab or Indian traders in the last couple of centuries. The unique Zanzibar clocks, originally used by Zanzibar merchants, are often bought by collectors. Carpets, rugs and mats, made in the Persian or Arab style, are sold in some shops. Most curio shops also sell wood carvings: boxes inlaid with shells, or decorated with hammered brass, are very popular.

Traditional Zanzibar furniture, such as tables, beds and wardrobes decorated with stained glass and mirrors, can be found but these are hard to carry in a rucksack! More portable are the small baskets and bowls made from woven palm leaves, local paintings (on canvas or wooden boards), or the mobiles of dhows, turtles and dolphins made from coconut shells. In the market, and various shops, you can also buy some of the many different

---

THINGS TO AVOID

Some shops sell shells and coral, taken from the reefs and beaches around the islands. This trade encourages local people to catch live molluscs, rather than simply collect empty shells from the beach, and to break off live coral from a reef which will take many years (or even decades) to re-grow. If you buy any of these items you are helping to degrade, and eventually destroy, the islands' fascinating marine life.

You may see turtle shells, or items made from turtle-shell such as bracelets or earrings, but you should avoid buying these things as turtles are an endangered species in Zanzibar. (For more details, see *Sea Turtles,* page 74.) You should also avoid buying carvings and other products made from ivory; in this part of the world it's likely to have come from a poached elephant. In an effort to sell their wares, some traders will tell you turtle-shell or ivory products are made from horn or bone, but if you're in any doubt – don't buy.

sorts of aromatic spices that make Zanzibar so famous. (For more details see *Food shooping*, page 104 and *Shopping*, page 117.)

BUSINESS HOURS, PUBLIC HOLIDAYS AND FESTIVALS

Business hours

Most shops and travel company offices in Zanzibar Town are open every day, although some close on Fridays, the Muslim holy day, or on Sundays, the official day off. Normal business hours are from between 08.00 and 09.00 until noon, then from 13.00 or 14.00 until 17.00 or 18.00. Some private shops and tour agencies take a longer break at midday and stay open later in the evening. Government offices and banks are closed on Saturdays and Sundays. Post offices are closed on Saturday afternoons and Sundays.

Public holidays

Zanzibar shares most public holidays with the rest of Tanzania. Offices and businesses are usually closed on these days, although some tour companies remain open. Public holidays are:

January 12	Mapinduzi (Revolution) Day
February 5	Chapa Cha Mapinduzi Day (this may be discontinued now CCM is no longer the sole political party)
May 1	Workers' Day
July 7	Peasants' and Farmers' Day (also called *Saba Saba* – Seven Seven).

Christmas Day and New Year's Day are also public holidays, although many tour companies stay open, and celebrations are low-key on this largely Muslim island.

Muslim feasts and holy days are celebrated by many people and are effectively public holidays. These are Idd il Fitri – the end of Ramadan, Idd il Maulidi (also called Maulidi ya Mtume) – Mohamed's birthday and Idd il Hajj – to celebrate the pilgrimage to Mecca. Dates of these holidays depend on the lunar calendar, and fall 11 or 12 days earlier every year. In 1997, Ramadan was from January 12 to February 8, Idd il Fitri was March 9, Idd il Hajj was April 18 and Idd il Maulidi was July 18.

Festivals

As well as the religious (Christian and Muslim) feasts mentioned above, there are some other festivals to look out for.

The **Zanzibar Music Festival** is a week-long event held every July, with musicians and dancers from Zanzibar, Africa, Arabia, Asia and Europe and a range of performances, seminars and workshops. For most visitors this is their only chance of seeing traditional *Taarab* and *Ngoma* performances (see page 64). Many shows take place in the new open-air theatre at the Arab Fort in Zanzibar Town, but there are several other smaller venues.

For more details, ask at the Fort or try contacting the Ministry of Information, Culture, Youth and Tourism, PO Box 772, Zanzibar, tel: 32321, fax: 33448.

The festival of **Mwaka Kogwa** is held every year in several villages around Zanzibar, but most famously and most flamboyantly at the village of Makunduchi, in the south of Zanzibar Island. The festival originated in Persia and celebrates the arrival of the New Year according to the Shirazi calendar. It occurred on July 24 in 1994 and 1995. According to some tour companies it is likely to be on July 23 until 1999, but it would be better to check this locally as changes are possible. For more details on the festival itself see page 176.

MUSIC AND DANCE
Thanks to Fiona Clark and Jim Boggs for their valuable contributions to this section

Zanzibar's history is rich and fascinating, but the customs and activities of the people are not lodged permanently in the past. Zanzibar has a thriving tradition of music and dance that is vibrant and very active today.

Taarab
Taarab is the most popular form of music in Zanzibar. It's a mixture of influences from Africa, India and Arabia, and its name comes from an Arab word, defined as 'joy, pleasure and entertainment brought about by an artistic combination of lyrics, poems and music'. Although developed on the coast of East Africa, it has spread inland and is now popular in mainland Tanzania, Kenya, Burundi and Mozambique. It is also popular in the Gulf States of Oman and Dubai.

For Western visitors, this music may be an acquired taste, but as an event a Taarab concert is worth seeing. The band contains at least one singer and about 40 or 50 musicians in full evening suits, playing a range of instruments from violins to traditional drums. They are impressive, but it is the audience that makes the event. The men in the audience dress in their best clothes and the women wear the most colourful and outrageous *gowni* (Taarab frocks) – the more frills the better!

Most of the songs are about love, and members of the audience can 'buy' lines from the song that pertains to their own situation. The technique involves flouncing down to the stage (showing off your clothes to best advantage) and giving some money to the singer, drawing out the giving for as long as you can, perhaps holding an imaginary microphone and miming to a verse or two.

The most popular Taarab bands in Zanzibar are Culture Musical Club and Malindi Music Club. The best places to see a show are the Bwawani Hotel, Haile Selassie School (on Creek Road) or the theatre in the Arab Fort in Zanzibar Town (with several shows each week during the tourist season).

Ngoma

Ngoma is traditional drumming and dance, almost totally African in influence, which probably originally came to Zanzibar from the mainland. All Ngoma troupes perform dances from Zanzibar Island and Pemba, and from the mainland (including the Makonde region of southern Tanzania). Most of the dances were originally performed at celebrations (weddings, harvest festivals, circumcision ceremonies, etc), and many are also accompanied by songs, sung by the dancers, or tunes on the clarinet-like *zumari*. Ngomas are performed in rural villages, and can also be seen at the Zanzibar Dance Studio at the Arab Fort in Zanzibar Town (more details in *Chapter Five*). Troupes to look out for include JICU, Mafunzo, and Amaani.

Other types of music and dance you might come across include *kidumbaki*, an unrefined type of Taarab, which is very popular at rural weddings; *beni*, a local brass band originally introduced in colonial times to accompany military parades, and *fensi*, a colourful, though rarely seen, street-dance believed to have been introduced by the Portuguese.

Perhaps one of the best times to experience all these types of Zanzibari music and dance is at the annual Music Festival. More details are given in the *Festivals* section, page 63.

GEOLOGY AND SOILS

The islands of Pemba and Unguja (usually called Zanzibar Island) were formed about 27 million years ago and 7 million years ago respectively. The main rock type is coral limestone. The eastern sides of the islands have a thin, calcareous sandstone soil, and receive less rain than the western sides of the islands which are characterised by a deep, red, iron-rich fertile soil. The western sides of the islands are where most of the cloves and other spices are grown.

VEGETATION

The indigenous vegetation of Zanzibar has been determined largely by the topography and soil types found on the island, and then altered greatly by clearance and cultivation.

On the eastern side of Zanzibar Island, and in parts of the northern and southern areas, the landscape is very flat where coral rock (called 'rag') is exposed or covered by a thin layer of soil, which supports low scrubby bush, quite dense in some areas. The western and central parts of the island are slightly more undulating, with a deeper and more fertile soil cover; this area used to be covered in forest, similar in most respects to the low coastal forest which existed on the East African mainland. Today, unfortunately, very little of Zanzibar's indigenous natural forest remains.

The earliest peoples on Zanzibar are thought to have been hunter-gatherers who made little impact on the natural vegetation. However, the first Bantu

COCONUTS

Coconuts are the second-most important crop on Zanzibar after cloves. They grow on a certain species of palm tree which is generally planted where clove trees cannnot survive, although as diversification is encouraged it is not uncommon today to see coconut palms and clove trees on the same plantation.

Coconuts are picked throughout the year. The pickers skilfully climb up the palm trunks using only a short loop of rope, then drop the nuts to the ground. The outer husks of the coconuts are removed by striking them on to a sharp stick or metal bar fixed in the ground. This is also a skilful process. Then the coconuts are split in two and left to dry so that the white fleshy kernels can be removed from the shells. The kernels are then dried for a few more days in the sun or in a special kiln. Gangs of workers separating the husks and kernels, and small coconut kilns, can be seen in the plantation areas outside Zanzibar Town.

When the kernels are properly dried, the substance is called 'copra'. It is widely used in the food industry as a flavouring, or for decoration. Copra is also processed into an oil, which is used in some foods and in the production of soap, candles and hair-oils. In the days before aerosol foam, copra was particularly good for making shaving soap as it helped produce a good lather.

The coconut husks are not wasted: they are buried under sand on the beach for several months, which helps to soften the fibres and make them separate from the rest of the husk. They are periodically dug up, beaten on rocks to help this process, and then buried again for another few months. The fibre is called 'coir', and is used for mats and rope-making. In the areas outside Zanzibar Town you will often see local women working with coir in this way.

Large quantities of coconuts are also consumed locally as food.

settlers, who probably arrived some time in the 3rd or 4th centuries AD, started to clear patches of natural forest to plant crops such as millet and sorghum.

At some stage, plants such as bananas, coconut palms and yams were introduced, possibly by peoples from Madagascar who in turn had originally migrated from the islands of Indonesia. As these crops became more popular, more indigenous forest was cleared.

In the 16th century, Portuguese traders established bases along the East African coast, including those on Zanzibar and Pemba, and introduced plants, such as cassava and maize, from their colonies in South America. More forest was felled as the local people cleared the land required to grow these crops.

After the Omani Arabs gained control of the islands in the early 18th century, and the trade in ivory and slaves expanded, Zanzibar became an important import and export centre. Cassava was used for feeding the vast number of slaves that passed through the island's infamous market. Another major export at this time was copra (produced from coconuts) which meant more land was cleared for coconut palm plantations.

Towards the end of the 18th century cloves were introduced from the islands of Reunion (where they had been brought from the Moluccas in Indonesia by French sailors). They soon became a major export crop. Other spices, such as vanilla and cardamom, were also grown and yet more forest was cleared for plantations.

Throughout the 19th century, the powerful nations of Europe put pressure on the sultans of Zanzibar to restrict the trade in slaves. As this was reduced, the trade in cloves and other spices became even more important.

During the colonial period, plantations continued to be developed and the natural forest continued to be reduced. A Department of Forestry was established to exploit the forests' timber supplies.

Apparently, in the 1950s it came to the attention of the Forestry Department that there was very little indigenous forest left on the island of Zanzibar. The largest remaining area, called Jozani Forest, to the southeast of Zanzibar Town, was purchased from an Arab landowner by the Department and the felling of trees was restricted. In 1960, Jozani was declared a protected nature reserve. This went some way to ensuring the survival of several species of forest animal whose habitat was being drastically reduced by forest felling in other parts of the island.

Today, Jozani is a forest reserve, and the only significant area of natural forest remaining on Zanzibar Island, although small patches do exist elsewhere. On Pembe Island, significant areas of natural forest include the reserves at Ngezi and Ras Kiuyu. The water-table around Jozani is particularly high (during the rainy season the water can be over one metre above the ground) and the trees are mainly moisture-loving species including several different types of palm and fig. These trees, along with the high water-table and humid air, give the forest a very 'tropical' feel. For more details on Jozani, see page 184.

Despite the establishment of forest reserves such as Jozani, Ngezi on Pemba, and the newly created Chumbe Island Reserve, Zanzibar's forests continue to be cut down at an alarming rate. Timber is used for boat and furniture building, charcoal burning and fuel wood, both for domestic purposes and to burn coral to produce lime for building construction. (This latter use has grown particularly quickly as the number of hotels in Zanzibar has increased.)

Mangrove wood from coastal areas is also being cut at an unsustainable rate. Forestry Department figures show that in 1992 10 million poles were cut in Chwaka Bay Forest, compared to 2.5 million in 1990. This wood is used for fuel and furniture, and in the construction and repair of buildings, but unfortunately the cutting of poles in the mangrove swamps leads to beach erosion and the destruction of habitats for fish and other marine life.

To replace some of the disappearing forest, the Zanzibar Forestry Department is currently planting acacia, casuarina and eucalyptus trees in Unguja and Pemba, as well as orange, coffee and cinnamon plants in Pemba. Another scheme, called the Zanzibar Cash Crop Farming System Project (ZCCFSP), is discouraging farmers from cutting clove trees for firewood. All logging, and even the removal of deadwood, has officially been stopped in the Jozani and Ngezi reserves, although how carefully this new rule will be policed remains to be seen. (The Forestry Department has been supported

CLOVES

During the second half of the 19th century the islands of Zanzibar produced more than 90% of the world's supply of cloves. The power and wealth of Zanzibar was based largely on this trade. Today, agricultural diversification is encouraged but Zanzibar is still a major exporter of cloves and clove products, with revenue earned amounting to between 50% and 75% of the total value of all exports.

Cloves are the buds of a tree which, when dried, produce a pleasant taste and smell. Their name comes from the French word 'clou' meaning nail, which the buds resemble. Clove oil was originally a highly prized ingredient used in cooking and preserving. Today it is also important in the cosmetic and pharmaceutical industries.

Cloves were introduced to Zanzibar in the early 19th century from the French colonies of Seychelles and Ile de France (now Mauritius). Sultan Said (sultan from 1804 to 1856) recognised their value and encouraged the setting up of plantations on Zanzibar and Pemba. Today, many of the plantations remain. About 75% of the islands' total produce comes from Pemba as growing conditions there are superior to those on Zanzibar Island.

Clove trees (their scientific name is *Eugenia aromatica* or *Eugena caryophyllata*) grow to a height of around 10m to 15m and can produce crops for over 50 years. In the first eight years of growth the buds are not picked, and turn into colourful pink flowers. When a tree reaches maturity the buds are picked by hand before they open (normally the harvest period is between July and January, with a break during the November rainy season), then separated from their stems. Buds and stems are dried in the sun on palm-leaf mats or on a special stone platform called a *sakufu*. Cloves are green when picked but turn brown during the drying process.

The stems are sent to Zanzibar Town where they are processed into oil in the distillery near the port. This oil is used mainly as a flavouring device in foods such as cakes, pickles, cooked meats and ready-made mixes. It is also used in some antiseptic solutions, such as mouthwashes and in mild painkillers for toothache. Its other major use is in cosmetics, where it gives a sweet-spicy note to many different kinds of perfumes.

The best quality dried buds are kept separate and used whole in cooking, pickling or the making of spiced wines and liqueurs. These buds are also distilled into a high-grade oil for use in particularly fine perfumes. In the cosmetic industry the oil from good Zanzibar clove buds is reckoned to be the best in the world.

by the Finnish International Development Agency since 1980, and the ZCCFSP is supported by the British Overseas Development Agency.)

Other trees occurring on Zanzibar include mango, which is used for its fruit and as timber for boat-building, and kapok (capoc), which produces a substance similar to cotton, traditionally used to make stuffing for mattresses and pillows. Other fruit-producing trees, grown in plantations or singly around local villages, include guava, breadfruit, orange and pomegranate.

As well as the famous clove trees, other spice plants found on Zanzibar and Pemba include black pepper, cinnamon, cardamom, jasmin, chilli and henna. The main crops grown by local people for their own consumption include maize, cassava, bananas and pumpkins.

WILDLIFE

Mammals

As described above, much of Zanzibar's indigenous forested areas have been cleared, so natural habitats for all wild animals are severely restricted. Probably the best places to see indigenous mammals are the Jozani Forest Reserve on Zanzibar Island and the Ngezi Forest Reserve on Pemba Island.

In this section, scientific names of species are given according to information provided by Jozani Forest Reserve and Ngezi Forest Reserve. Other authorities disagree on some classifications and nomenclature, especially regarding subspecies, but this is unlikely to be important for most visitors.

Jozani Forest Reserve is well-known for its population of **red colobus monkey**. This animal is found elsewhere in Africa, but those on Zanzibar form a distinct species, called Kirk's red colobus (*Procolobus kirkii*), endemic to the island and one of the rarest primates in Africa. There are only around 500 red colobus in Jozani itself, with another 1,000 elsewhere on the island (some were translocated to Ngezi on Pemba in the 1970s). Although rare, the monkeys in Jozani are fairly used to humans so you are quite likely to spot some if you visit. They are mainly reddish-brown in colour, with a darker back and 'cap', and a paler forehead patch. On closer inspection, particularly of facial areas, you will notice that each monkey has slightly different coat patterns and colourings.

In Jozani and some other patches of forest you are likely to see the **blue monkey**, also called Sykes' monkey, mitis monkey or the Zanzibar white-throated guenon (*Cercopithecus mitis albogularis*), which on Zanzibar is bluish-grey, or even a greenish-grey, with a distinct white throat-patch. Although the two types of monkey compete for some food items, they are often seen foraging peacefully in mixed groups. The Swahili word for monkey is *kima*. On Zanzibar, the blue monkey is more commonly given this name. When distinguishing between the two, the blue money is called *kima mweusi,* and the red colobus *kima punju* – 'poison monkey' (probably because the colobus has a stronger smell than other monkeys, and is reputed to have an evil influence on trees where it feeds).

A local species of **vervet monkey** (*Cercopithecus aethiops nesiotes*) occurs on Pemba, but not on Zanzibar Island. This monkey is smaller than the red colobus and the blue monkey, generally greyish with a dark, rusty brown back and black feet.

Other mammals found on Zanzibar, mainly in forested areas, include **bush pig** (*Potamochoerus porcus*), although its numbers are reported to be greatly reduced; **Zanzibar tree hyrax** (*Dendrohyrax arboreus neumanni*), a rodent-like animal the size of a rabbit (this subspecies is endemic), with hoofed feet and rounded ears, and a loud piercing scream when threatened; **Aders' duiker** (*Cephalophus adersi*), a species of small antelope found only on Zanzibar and some parts of the Kenyan coast; and **Zanzibar suni** (*Nesotragus moschatu moschatus*), another endemic subspecies of antelope

LEOPARDS IN ZANZIBAR

The Zanzibar leopard (*Panthera pardus adersi*) is a local sub-species. Two different types are thought to exist: the Kisutu, which is similar to the mainland leopard, but with a more compact spot pattern and lighter background; and the Konge, which is larger than the Kisutu with dark fur and faint spot pattern. Both are shy, mainly active at night, and only very occasionally sighted.

Perhaps because of their elusive, nocturnal habits, leopards have traditionally been considered unlucky by local people, and are often associated with witchcraft. They were also hunted for their skins and by 1980 were believed to be extinct in Zanzibar.

However, in 1994 an American researcher called Scott Marshall found evidence of three leopards on Unguja (Zanzibar Island), including prints, droppings and a suspected den near Chwaka. In his report, Marshall suggests that these leopards were trapped and 'domesticated' at a young age and are now used in ceremonies by local witch-doctors or traditional healers. He also suggests that there may be several more leopards similarly kept in captivity at other villages in Zanzibar.

which is even smaller than the duiker. The endemic **Pemba blue duiker** (*Cephalophus monticola pembae*) occurs at Ngezi Forest. All these animals are nocturnal or extremely shy and are unlikely to be seen.

Leopard (*panthera pardus adersi*, or *chui* in Swahili) have been recorded in Jozani, and elsewhere in Zanzibar. Again, this is an endemic sub-species, smaller than the mainland version and with finer markings, and also very unlikely to be sighted. (For more details see the box about *Leopards in Zanzibar* above.)

Greater and lesser **galagos** or **bushbabies** (*Otolemur garnetiti garnettii* and *Galago senegalensis zanzibaricus*) both occur in Zanzibar. The greater galago (*komba* in Swahili) is about the size of a rabbit, generally brown, with very distinctive large eyes and ears, and a large bushy tail. The lesser galago (*komba ndogo*) also has large eyes and ears, but it is smaller (about half the size of the greater galago) and grey in colour. Both animals are nocturnal, especially active at dawn and dusk, and have distinctive cries – sometimes like a child crying (hence their name), other times loud and shrill, and positively spine-chilling. They are known to be inquisitive and will forage around huts and villages at night. They are attracted to bowls of locally brewed palm wine, and often get captured when intoxicated and incapable of escape. A local saying *'mlevi kama komba'* means 'as drunk as a bushbaby'!

Also found in Zanzibar is the **African civet** (*Viverra civetta schwarzi*, *ngawa* in Swahili), which looks like a very large cat with a stocky body and thick tail, with black, white and grey markings which form rough stripes. The **Javan civet** (*Viverricula indica rasse*) occurs on Pemba, probably introduced by South-East Asian traders.

Smaller mammals include the Zanzibar **slender mongoose** (*Herpestes sanguineus rufescens*), most often seen running across roads with its tail vertical, and the **bushy-tailed mongoose** (*Bdeogale crassicauda tenuis*) –

rarely seen anywhere. The **marsh mongoose** (*Atilax paludinosus rubescens*) occurs only on Pemba and may be seen at Ngezi Forest. The **banded mongoose** is a non-indigenous species, introduced to Zanzibar Island.

Populations of rats, mice, shrews and bats occur on both Zanzibar and Pemba Islands. Those worthy of note include the **Zanzibar four-toed elephant shrew** (*Petrodromus tetradactylus zanzibaricus*) with distinctive long slender legs and trunk-like snout for eating insects, and the **Pemba flying fox** (*Pteropus voeltzkowi*), a species of bat with a rufus fox-like face, which is found only in Ngezi Forest on Pemba.

Reptiles and amphibians

Of all the reptiles on Zanzibar, undoubtedly the easiest to spot are the **giant tortoises** that inhabit Prison Island, a few kilometres offshore from Zanzibar Town, and also live in the garden of the Peace Memorial Museum. They were introduced here from the island of Aldabra in the Seychelles Archipelago, it is thought sometime in the 18th century.

If you visit Jozani, you'll see some of the forest's population of tiny black and gold frogs. In the rainy season, when the ground floods, you'll see their tadpoles too. Chameleons can also be seen in Jozani and other parts of the island. Like the mongoose, they are often seen crossing roads, but often very slowly, and *very* precariously. Other reptiles include snakes (rarely seen) and geckos (frequently seen on the inside walls of buildings – particularly the budget hotels in Zanzibar Town – although this is no cause for concern as they're small, timid and harmless).

Birds

Zanzibar is not noted as a major bird-watching area, but over 100 species of bird have been recorded on the islands. Additionally, Zanzibar is visited by various long-distance migrants and seabirds.

On inlets and lagoons, birds you can see include black crake, jacana or lilytrotter, white-faced whistling duck, purple heron, grey heron, little grebe, little egret, Hottentot and red-billed teal, and moorhen. Kingfishers (mangrove, pied and malachite) are also seen. Inland, especially in patches of woodland on the edge of areas which have been cleared for farming, you may see various palm-weavers, coucals, sunbirds and bulbuls.

A good area for keen birders, particularly if you visit early or late in the day, is Jozani Forest Reserve, although the birds here typically hide themselves in the undergrowth or high canopies. Birds occurring here include the olive sunbird, the little greenbul and the crowned hornbill. Local 'specials' include the East Coast akalat and Fischer's touraco.

On Pemba Island, Ngezi Forest is also good. Birds recorded here include palm-nut vulture, African goshawk, scops owl and the endemic Pemba white-eye.

In the towns and rural areas you are also likely to see the Indian house crow, identified by its grey head which distinguishes it from the (less common) pied crow, which has a white neck-patch. The Indian house crow was introduced into Zanzibar the 1890s; the idea was that it would help reduce the domestic waste building up in the Stone Town at the time. Although the Indian house crow did consume some of this rubbish, it is by nature an aggressive bird and it began to attack many of the island's smaller bird species. By the 1940s it had spread throughout Zanzibar Island, and by the 1970s its population had increased to such an extent that most of the small birds were rarely seen. By the 1980s the very existence of many of the smaller birds was reported to be threatened. However, since the early 1990s, local bird enthusiasts, under the direction of Tony Archer, and with help from the Zanzibar government and FINNIDA (the Finnish aid organisation), have started to fight back. Traps have been set in some areas, and local people encouraged to capture and destroy crow eggs and chicks.

An article in the newsletter of the Wildlife Conservation Society of Tanzania by Dudley Iles, the Environmental Club's co-ordinator for Zanzibar, reported that this project had been largely successful; by 1994 the crow population had been reduced by about 90%, although the situation still needs careful monitoring to avoid once again getting out of control.

Dudley Iles also reports that, since the decline of the Indian house crow, a good place for birding in Zanzibar Town is the People's Gardens (formerly Victoria Gardens), where mannikins, African reed warblers, coucals and sunbirds can now be easily seen. It seems that many of these smaller birds are beginning to breed successfully again, and hopefully this will continue in the future.

Further information

Some field guides are listed in the *Further Reading* section (page 213). For keen zoologists, the natural history section of the National Museum in Zanzibar Town has exhibits and more information about all the animals and birds found on the islands of Zanzibar.

THE SEAS AND SHORES OF ZANZIBAR

Matt Richmond

For anyone visiting the islands of Zanzibar, or Mafia Island or any other part of the mainland coast of Tanzania, the diversity of marine life in these shallow waters may not be obvious immediately. In fact, the main marine habitats (mangroves, coral reefs and seagrass beds) are part of an extremely diverse, productive and vitally important marine ecosystem. The species of plants and animals which make up these habitats are mostly the same throughout the western Indian Ocean (eg: Mozambique, Madagascar, Mauritius and Seychelles), though slightly different from those in similar habitats as far away as southeast Asia, Australia and the South Pacific islands. Some species of fish and other creatures do, however, span this entire Indo-Pacific region.

Beaches and cliffs

Around Zanzibar, many shores are fringed by either coconut-lined coral-sand beaches, where ghost crabs scamper, or rocky limestone cliffs – remains of ancient reefs once below the sea over two million years ago – now undercut and battered by high tide waves. The cliffs provide a home to the brilliant red-yellow grapsid rock crabs and the bizarre eight-plated chiton snail, plus numerous other small snails, rock oysters and rock-skipper fish.

Mangroves

In sheltered bays and inlets, where wave action is reduced, mangrove stands and forests are commonplace. The eight species of mangrove trees are specially adapted to survive in the sea and at high tide attract numerous species of fish, crabs and shrimps which depend on the forests as nursery grounds for their young. At low tide, red-clawed fiddler crabs carry out their formal challenges when not sifting the mud for food, while mud-skippers flip from pool to pool, or from branch to branch when the tide is in.

Seagrass beds and lagoons

Further down the shore, the intertidal flats, which may extend 2km out to the low water mark, provide a habitat for thousands of molluscs, crabs, sea-cucumbers, seaweeds and several species of seagrasses, which are themselves food for fish at high tide. Along the East Coast of Unguja (and the east coasts of the other islands and the mainland) shallow lagoons occur, extending to the reef crest. The lagoons support assorted coral, seagrass and seaweed communities and often great selections of starfish and beautiful nudibranch (sea hares and their relatives).

Coral reefs

On the east coasts, classic fringeing coral reefs are marked by a continuous line of surf. At low tide the reef crest dries out revealing pink algal-rock and boulders – the coral itself usually only becoming prolific on the seaward slope below 5m. The coral-covered reef-slopes dip down to about 20m, after which a fairly bare sandy seabed continues down a further 4km to the ocean bottom. On the more sheltered west coasts of the Zanzibar Channel smaller, isolated patch reefs with sandbars, and island reefs (around Chapwani, Changuu, Bawe and Chumbi islands), provide coral gardens in the relatively shallow waters. In contrast, parts of the reef around Pemba Island drop down over 50m or more offering spectacular vertical coral walls. On any of these coral reefs you will immediately note the amazing variety of colourful fish of all sizes and shapes, incredible in their patterns and forms: butterfly-fish, parrot-fish, surgeonfish, damselfish, emperors, goatfish, pufferfish, angel-fish, triggerfish, groupers and grunts to name a few. Most of these typical coral reef fish are territorial and reside over small areas of reef, rarely leaving their patch and aggressively protecting it

SEA TURTLES

Fiona Clark

Five types of sea turtle occur in the western Indian Ocean: the green turtle (*Chelonia mydas*), the hawksbill turtle (*Erctmochelys imbricata*), the loggerhead turtle (*Caretta caretta*), the olive ridley turtle (*lepidochelys olivacea*) and the leatherback turtle (*Dermochhelys coriacea*). All are endangered species. The most commonly found turtle in Zanzibar is the green turtle, followed by the hawksbill. Both nest in Zanzibar. Loggerhead are sometimes seen, but don't nest. Leatherback and ridley are very occasional visitors.

Zanzibar is not a major turtle nesting site, but appears to be a feeding ground for sea turtles from other areas. Conservationists have recovered tags from captured turtles showing that green turtles come to Zanzibar from Aldabra Island, in the Seychelles, and from Europa and Tromelin islands. Loggerheads that nest in Natal (South Africa) also feed in Tanzania – one loggerhead was captured in Tanzania just 66 days after being tagged in Natal.

The bad news

The sea turtle population is decreasing. The number of nesting sites has been reduced, and the turtles are hunted and trapped by more efficient means.

Local fishermen tell how, 20 or 30 years ago, some beaches would contain 100 or more turtle nests every year. But these days the same beaches only contain two or three nests. Places where more nests are still found include Mnemba Island, the beaches north of Matemwe Bungalows, and around Kizimkazi. On Pemba, turtles nest on Mesali Island, at Ras Kiyuyu and on the beaches near Ngezi Forest. Few of these nests are successful; many eggs are lost to people, while others are lost to the sea since erosion has formed steps on some beaches making them unsuitable for nesting as the turtle cannot pass the high water mark.

Turtle hunting in Zanzibar only became illegal in October 1993. Although penalties are quite severe (a 20,000 TSh to 40,000 TSh fine, or two years in prison, or both) enforcement of the new law is unlikely. The Fisheries Department is under-resourced and has many other problems to deal with (such as dynamite fishing).

Turtles are usually captured with gill nets, which are set on the sea bed, while others are caught with spear guns. They are brought ashore and have their flippers and shell removed, often while still alive. The number of turtles caught increased dramatically in the 1960s when gill nets, snorkelling gear and spear guns were introduced. Some local fishermen claim that their increased catch proves the population is increasing too, but the same fishermen also agree that nesting turtles have all but disappeared.

The good news

In 1992, the Zanzibari Departments of Environment and Fisheries, with support from FINNIDA (the Finnish international aid organisation) instigated several small-scale turtle protection projects. These include the following:

• A Swahili-language education package for schools and other youth groups,

from others of their own species. Some, like the butterflyfish, pair up for life and occupy a patch the size of a tennis court; others, such as the blue-lined yellow snappers, roam around the reefs in schools of a few hundred.

Corals themselves are usually pink or pale brown in colour, though emphasising the plight of sea turtles, and their need to be protected. A poster carrying the same message has also been produced both in English, aimed at visitors, and in Swahili, aimed at locals.

• A nest protection scheme, run by Matemwe Bungalows, a hotel on the east coast, and supervised by the tireless Shirocco, the hotel cook. Local villagers are paid 3,000 TSh if they report an intact nest, and a further 50 TSh for each successful hatchling. To avoid the problems of beach erosion, some nests are moved to safer sites.

• A survey and protection scheme carried out by the management of the exclusive lodge on the private Mnemba Island. This is an ideal site for turtles, with safe beaches (no local fishermen are allowed to land) and deep water access. Although the lodge was a controversial development, the island is possibly the only protected turtle nesting site in Zanzibar and probably the whole of Tanzania.

Turtle-shell products

Zanzibar used to be a major centre for turtle-shell, usually called 'tortoiseshell', and at the height of the trade (the early 1900s) some 3,300kg were exported every year from the the islands and nearby mainland coast. Demand dropped, but has recently been revived by the growth of tourism. A recent survey showed that the amount of turtle-shell jewellery had gone up five times between early 1993 and late 1994. Less than half the tourists who bought turtle-shell items knew what it was, or that turtles were endangered. However, local conservationists and aware tourists have complained to such a degree that many shops now refuse to stock turtle-shell products. Participating shop-keepers are being awarded 'turtle-friendly' certificates. Tourists are asked to boycott any shops that continue to sell turtle products.

Local police and customs officials are now also aware that turtle-shell products are illegal. In 1995, a tourist who bought a whole shell from a hawker on the east coast was stopped at a road block on the way back to Zanzibar Town after hotel staff tipped off the police. The tourist was reprimanded, and the shell was confiscated.

Local perspectives

Lest we get too self-righteous about all this, we should perhaps remember that Zanzibar is a poor country and that a large sea turtle is worth about a month's wages for an office worker, and considerably more than that to a fisherman or farmer. Stopping the local people from catching turtles will inevitably make some of them poorer, yet if the turtle hunting continues there will soon be none left anyway. But many Zanzibaris can't afford the luxury of thinking ahead. Life is hand to mouth and the 'if I don't catch it someone else will' attitude is of course reasonable.

So, sea turtle conservation is more about a slow change of attitudes, and this will take a long time. Perhaps the most important step is to keep turtle hunting a subsistence activity. It was in danger of becoming big business, and that, more than anything else, would have ensured that the turtle remained one of the world's rare and endangered species.

individual colonies vary in shape and size. Hard coral species such as the commonly known varieties – staghorns, plate or table corals and brain corals – are abundant in shallow water. The coloration is due to the vital plant pigments found in coral tissues, which trap the sunlight needed to power the chemical reactions which produce calcium carbonate – the white coral skeleton characteristic of dead colonies. At night-time on a reef, most hard coral species are busy with their many-tentacled polyps extended to catch planktonic foods. Soft corals, on the other hand, are far more colourful but also require light to build the tiny crystal fibres embedded in their soft pink, lilac or cream-coloured tissues. The day-time feeding of the eight-tentacled polyps, a feature of this group, is clearly visible on soft corals which can, in places, dominate underwater scenes.

Because of the rich diversity of life forms, coral reefs have been compared to tropical rainforests. With Zanzibar's waters containing more than 700 fish species associated with coral reefs, over 100 species of hard corals, 150-odd species of seaweed and 200 plus species of seashells, to mention just a few of the more obvious sea creatures, the comparison is certainly a valid one. Then there are sponges, anemones, brittlestars, sea-squirts, feather stars and crustaceans, all forming a seemingly chaotic, mind-boggling complexity which has fascinated scientists since Darwin's time.

For the visitor, access to good snorkelling or dive sites is easily gained from Zanzibar Town. Full information is given in *Chapter Five*. East Coast and Pemba Island snorkelling is also possible by negotiating with local fishermen, though equipment may not always be available.

Open waters

The open waters, though mostly empty at first glance, can be very busy at times. They are home to vast schools of small, plankton-feeding, pelagic fish species such as sardines, silver-sides and Indian mackerel, continuously on the move and relentlessly pursued by larger pelagic fish, like skipjack, yellowfin tuna, kingfish, sailfish and marlin. Out at sea, in the Channel or off the east coast, flocks of hundreds of white terns identify tuna feeding frenzies as they dart into the shoals of small pelagic fish forced up to the surface by the tuna below.

Also feeding out at sea for most of their lives are turtles, coming into shallow waters when looking for a mate. Green and hawksbill turtles are the most common. (See *Sea turtles,* page 74.)

Both the friendly bottlenose dolphin and the less bold humpback dolphin can be seen in small groups, or pods, quite close to the shore. Around Unguja there appear to be a few pods of 10–15 members, each with its own territory. One area where they are commonly seen is off Kizimikazi in southwest Unguja (viewing is easily arranged with a local boat), or around Mnemba Island in the northeast, or, with a bit of luck, even off Town. (Watching dolphins is especially enjoyable if you're also sipping a cool beer on Africa House Hotel terrace at sunset.) Less common are whales, though humpback whales have been spotted several times around October-November in the Zanzibar Channel and off Nungwi in the north, leading their recently born young back to the summer feeding grounds in Antarctica.

Weather

Prevailing weather influences sea conditions and travellers should be aware of the main seasons. There are two main wind seasons, the same winds which drove the Arabian traders and others up and down the eastern African shores over 2,000 years ago. During the northeast monsoon (*Kaskazi*), between December and March, the seas are warmest (28°C) but can be rough, and access to exposed reefs impossible, thus it is a good time to be down in the sheltered southwest part of any island. This season is also the main mango time on Zanzibar and no boat trip, on the frequent calmer days, should leave shore without them. From March to mid-June it's the wet season (*masika*) during which the weather can change, in less than an hour, from beautifully calm and sunny to full-blown tropical rainstorms, reducing visibility on the surface to a few hundred metres, so keep a weather eye out and prepare for the worst. Sunsets during the wet season are magnificent on the west coast and pineapples are in season. July through to September witnesses the coolest part of the year and the steady though occasionally strong southwest monsoon winds (*Kusi*) can rough up the Zanzibar Channel, hence it is better to be on the east and north coasts. Oranges are in abundance then.

Tides

Tides, the daily rise and fall of sea level, are a noticeable feature along this coast of Africa. Tides are dictated mostly by the moon (and to a lesser extent the sun) and there are two main types. The smaller tides, known as neap tides, occur during the half-moon phases and result in a tidal range (the difference between high and low water) of only a metre and a half. From these lunar days onwards the tidal range increases, until when at full or new moon, ie: every two weeks, spring tides follow. These result in the largest tidal range, of about four metres, with low water occurring at around 10.00–11.00 and high water six hours earlier and six hours later. During spring low tides the low water mark can be a couple of kilometres out and these days are ideal for walking out on the intertidal flats and reef crest to explore the kaleidoscope of life. Take care to avoid trampling on living coral and on sea-urchins or blue-spotted stingrays. Good footwear (trainers, plastic sandals or neoprene booties) are strongly recommended. Even the tiniest cut or graze can flare up into a nasty tropical ulcer which will keep the victim out of the sea for days recovering. Be aware, also, of the speed with which the tide comes in and don't be caught out on the reef crest of the east coast with the incoming tide around your waist – you'll have an exhausting swim back to the beach if you do. And remember, tidal currents are strongest during spring tides so be careful not to swim too far out, or into tidal channels.

Local people and marine life

It won't take long to realise that a great number of Zanzibaris are dependent on the surrounding seas and shallows for their variety of foods. Various

THE UNDERWATER WORLD

Matt Richmond

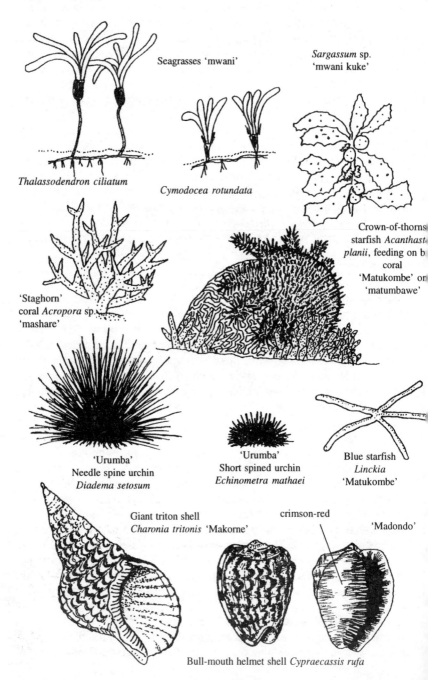

Seagrasses 'mwani'

Sargassum sp. 'mwani kuke'

Thalassodendron ciliatum

Cymodocea rotundata

Crown-of-thorns starfish *Acanthast planii*, feeding on b coral 'Matukombe' or 'matumbawe'

'Staghorn' coral *Acropora* sp. 'mashare'

'Urumba' Needle spine urchin *Diadema setosum*

'Urumba' Short spined urchin *Echinometra mathaei*

Blue starfish *Linckia* 'Matukombe'

Giant triton shell *Charonia tritonis* 'Makorne'

crimson-red

'Madondo'

Bull-mouth helmet shell *Cypraecassis rufa*

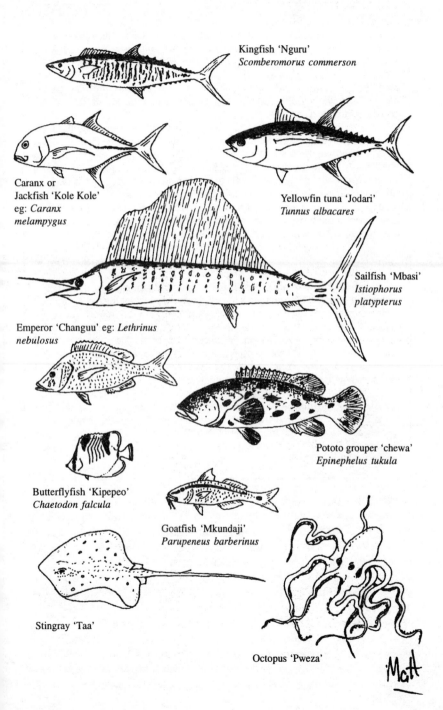

Kingfish 'Nguru'
Scomberomorus commerson

Caranx or
Jackfish 'Kole Kole'
eg: *Caranx
melampygus*

Yellowfin tuna 'Jodari'
Tunnus albacares

Sailfish 'Mbasi'
*Istiophorus
platypterus*

Emperor 'Changuu' eg: *Lethrinus
nebulosus*

Pototo grouper 'chewa'
Epinephelus tukula

Butterflyfish 'Kipepeo'
Chaetodon falcula

Goatfish 'Mkundaji'
Parupeneus barberinus

Stingray 'Taa'

Octopus 'Pweza'

SEAWEED FARMING

Seaweed farming was introduced to Zanzibar in 1989. One of the main farming areas is around Paje, on the east coast of Unguja (Zanzibar Island). The seaweed species are *Euchema spinosum* and *E. cottoni* and seaweed plots can be recognised by rectangular patterns of sticks in the sand, just below the low tide mark. Young seaweed cuttings are tied on to strings which run between the sticks. Each plot has up to 50 rows of strings between 25cm and 35cm apart, and each string carries 10 to 15 cuttings.

The seaweed grows at a rate of 7% per day. Plots are tended by the local villagers, who remove algae from the strings to prevent the seaweed from breaking off. After two weeks the cuttings have increased ten-fold in weight and are harvested. The wet seaweed is laid out in the sun to dry, and loses 80% of its weight. It is then sold to dealers who export the seaweed to countries such as Denmark and the Philippines, where it is used as a thickening agent in cosmetics, medicines, food (including ice-cream) and even beer. Each plot yields about five to seven kilos per harvest, which earns the farmer 70 TSh (about US7¢) per kilo in Zanzibar, but sells for 2,000 to 2,500 TSh ($4 to $5) on the world market.

Despite the relatively low prices that the villagers receive, the additional income from seaweed farming has improved their standard of living considerably. In common with many other parts of Africa, farming has been traditionally regarded as women's work, and this is the case with seaweed farming on Zanzibar. The drying and selling is also women's responsibility, so much of the money earned from the seaweed stays in their hands. Normally, rural women would not have their own source of income, so the advent of seaweed farming has given them a certain degree of freedom and empowerment. Money is used for house improvements, kitchenware or even luxuries like radios and cassette players. Many people use the money to pay for school fees, and in 1991 the villagers of Paje built two day-care centres for their children.

The success and growth of seaweed farming has led to conflict on the east coast between the villagers and the owners of hotels. The latter claim that seaweed farms are unsightly (somewhat unfair, considering the size and style of some hotels), and deter tourists from swimming. This may be true, but it is also worth remembering that the local people may benefit more from a beach full of seaweed than a beach full of hotels.

fishing methods are used to catch this vital source of protein which contributes over 70% of the needs of the local population. On dark new-moon nights in the Zanzibar Channel, sardine boats with lights attract and net vast shoals; on the same nights gill-netting boats, with 15cm-mesh nets, are after the large pelagic species (tuna, kingfish and billfish) in the southern Pemba Channel, operating mostly from Nungwi. Conventional hook-and-line fishing and passive fish-trapping using baited basket-traps (*madema*) are still practised all around the islands.

During the low spring tides thousands of women and children collect octopus, shells, sea-cucumbers and moray eels from the intertidal flats, whilst other women tend to their seaweed (*mwani*) farm patches in the lagoons on the East Coast. The lines of sticks protruding out of the water at low tide can't be missed (see above). The mangroves are also harvested:

the wood has been used for building poles for hundreds of years. However, the rapid increase in demand over the last few years, with overcutting in places, has led to deterioration of the forests and the marine life which relies on them. Recently, the felling of planted *Casuarina* (Australian pine, though not actually a true pine) has produced, so far, acceptable insect-resistant poles, easing some of the pressure on the mangroves.

Conservation

Unfortunately, due to the rapid increase in population (at present doubling every 20 years), the availability of new fishing materials and the inability of the government to enforce fisheries regulations, the development of a number of destructive fishing methods is beginning to destroy the delicate balance of life in the shallow seas. Spear-fishing is on the increase and due to its effectiveness can quickly strip the reefs of the larger fish, and even of small species such as butterfly-fish. Not only does it reduce fish numbers and make them wary of snorkellers, such as around the shallow reefs close to Zanzibar Town or in the lagoon on the east, but by removing these vital predators the balance within the ecosystem is being lost. Netting around reefs, and the *Kijani* fishing where corals are broken deliberately to force fish out into the surrounding net, are also practised and extremely destructive, whilst dynamite-fishing is mostly restricted to the mainland coast. Also restricted to the mainland and Mafia coasts, fortunately for Zanzibar, is the collecting of shallow live coral (mainly of the genus *Porites*) for baking on open kilns into lime. On Unguja at least, quarried coral rock is used instead.

Careless anchoring of boats on coral reefs can also, over a short time, cause considerable localised damage. In 1994 a project funded by the Dutch Embassy of Dar es Salaam through the Institute of Marine Sciences established, in conjunction with the tourist boat operators who use the reefs, 15 permanent moorings for the islands and reefs close to Zanzibar Town, thus reducing tourism-related damage.

The local demand for marine curios (shells, dead coral and turtle products) has increased with the growing number of tourists, further adding to the over-exploitation of the marine resources. The collection of large, attractive mollusc shells like the Giant Triton (*Charonia tritonis*) and the Bull-mouth helmet shell (*Cypraecassis rufa*) have secondary effects which are not that obvious. These feed on the Crown-of-thorns starfish (*Acanthaster planci*) and sea-urchins respectively. Absence of the molluscs again upsets the balance and populations of these echinoderms can increase alarmingly, furthering the destruction of the coral reefs. Collection of live hard corals is, of course, extremely damaging to the reef ecosystem. A colony the size of a football can take over 20 years to grow and the implications of mass removal for sale to tourists or export needs no further explanation. Don't buy the stuff!

Some steps are being taken to try and address the problems. With the support of donor organisations and bodies like WWF, the Department of the Environment, together with the Commission of Fisheries and the Institute of Marine Sciences on Zanzibar, are beginning to develop protected areas (both in the sea and on land) with the involvement of local communities – which is encouraging. So far only Chumbi Island has a marine park and also a programme to develop a small eco-tourism-type hotel with an education centre promoting environmental awareness for local schoolchildren and tourists. Further developments of this sort will help arrest destruction of this unique and valuable resource. Sales of locally made 'Survival Zanzibar' T-shirts promoting turtle and reef protection provide some funds for the much-needed conservation and awareness projects. Tourism development, now a rapidly growing industry, also has a role to play. By acknowledging that the marine resources on which it depends are finite and also vital to the neighbouring coastal villages, and by attempting to come up with methods which assist all the users, tourism can contribute to a healthy future for all concerned. Survival of both may be in the balance.

So, when bobbing around over a coral garden, or simply sitting on the seabed, ten metres down, watching the coral reef world around you for ten minutes or so, or wading through the dark mud in a mangrove forest, think about it ... and enjoy it. There's a whole lot going on: between individuals, between species, between habitats and between the ecosystem and the people who use it. This section has touched on some of the more salient issues and examples of life in the seas and on the shores of Zanzibar – many more exist to be discovered and pondered upon; whilst doing so, the following are a few points to remember:

• Don't touch living coral. There's no need to – it is more sensitive than it looks. Be careful when reef walking and snorkelling or diving. Be aware of what your flippers are doing and avoid landing on coral when entering into the water. Maintain good buoyancy control at all times.

• Help prevent anchor damage. Insist on the use of permanent moorings, if available, or anchor only in sand.

• Don't buy shells, turtle products or corals.

• Spread the word. Explain what you now know about the local marine ecosystems to other visitors and locals.

Adventure Afloat

African Boat Safaris

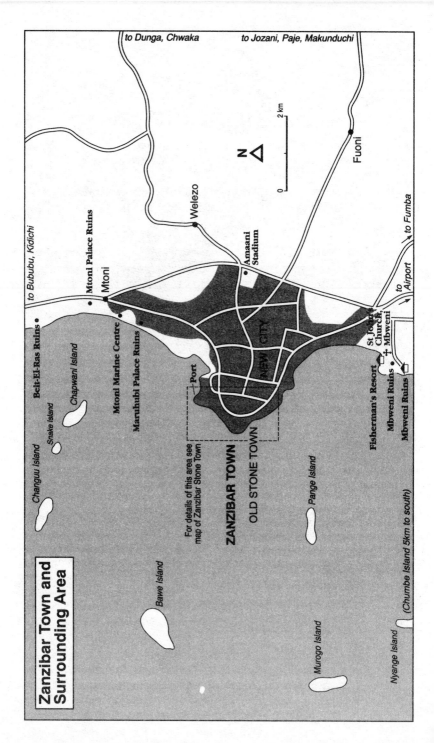

Zanzibar Town and Surrounding Area

to Dunga, Chwaka

to Jozani, Paje, Makunduchi

N

0   2 km

Fuoni

Welezo

to Bububu, Kidichi

Mtoni Palace Ruins ●

Mtoni

Amaani Stadium

Beit-El-Ras Ruins ●

Changu Island

Snake Island

Chapwani Island

Mtoni Marine Centre

Maruhubi Palace Ruins

Port

NEW CITY

to Airport

to Fumba

St John's Church

Mbweni

Fisherman's Resort

Mbweni Ruins ●

Mbweni Ruins

For details of this area see
map of Zanzibar Stone Town

ZANZIBAR TOWN

OLD STONE TOWN

Bawe Island

Pange Island

Murogo Island

Nyange Island

(Chumbe Island 5km to south)

Chapter Five

Zanzibar Town

'The streets are, as they should be under such a sky, deep and winding alleys, hardly twenty feet broad, and travellers compare them to the threads of a tangled skein.'

Richard Burton, British explorer (1857)

Zanzibar Town (sometimes called Zanzibar City) is situated about halfway along the west coast of Zanzibar Island. It has a population estimated at more than 100,000 which makes it by far the largest settlement on the islands of Zanzibar, and one of the five largest in Tanzania. Before the development of towns such as Dar es Salaam, Nairobi and Mombasa during the colonial period, Zanzibar Town was the largest settlement in the whole of East Africa.

Zanzibar Town is divided into two sections by Creek Road. (The creek itself has now been reclaimed.) On the west side lies the 'heart' of Zanzibar Town: the old quarter, usually called the Stone Town. This is the most interesting section for visitors: most of the buildings here were constructed during the 19th century (although some date from before this time), when Zanzibar was a major trading centre and at the height of its power. The trade passing through the port of Zanzibar created wealth which in turn led to the construction of palaces, mosques and many fine houses. Between the buildings of the Stone Town winds a tortuous maze of narrow streets and alleyways. This is the area described by Burton in the quote above.

On the east side of Creek Road is the part of town which used to be called Ng'ambo (literally 'the other side') but is now called Michenzani, or the 'New City'. This is an extended area of mainly one-storey houses and other buildings, covering a much wider area than the Stone Town. This used to be where the poorer African and Swahili people lived, while more wealthy Arabs, Indians and Europeans lived in the Stone Town. To a large extent this rich-poor division still exists today. Some attempt has been made to 'modernise' this area: at the centre of Michenzani are some ugly blocks of flats (apartment buildings) which were built in the late 1960s by East German engineers as part of an international aid scheme.

Few visitors go to this eastern part of Zanzibar Town, as there is little in the way of 'sights'. But it helps to broaden your perception if you realise that outside the 'touristy' areas of the Stone Town is a place where many thousands of real people live and work in much less exotic, but no less authentic, surroundings. To help you get your bearings, it is useful to think of the Stone Town as a triangle, bounded on two sides by sea, and along the third by Creek Road (see map). If you get lost, it is always possible to aim in one direction until you reach the outer edge of the town where you should find a recognisable landmark.

Most of the streets in the Stone Town are too narrow for cars, but you should watch out for bikes and scooters being ridden around at breakneck speed! (Streets which are wide enough for cars are usually called roads. Hence, you can drive along New Mkunazini Road or Kenyatta Road, but to visit a place on Kiponda Street or Mkunazini Street you have to walk.)

When looking for hotels or places of interest, you should note that most areas of the Stone Town are named after the main street in that area. But sometimes the area is referred to as Kiponda Street or Malindi Street, instead of simply Kiponda or Malindi. This can be confusing, as you may not be on the street of that name. But don't worry: at least you're near!

TRAVEL AROUND ZANZIBAR TOWN

Most visitors and locals get around the town on foot (and in the Stone Town this is the best way), but there are other means of transport available.

Taxis

Taxis for journeys around town are available from the taxi rank near the BP petrol station on Creek Road, from the area around the Port Gates or from the small car park beside the House of Wonders. You should check the fare with the driver before starting your journey. Minimum fare is $2. Across town costs about $3. From town to the airport is between $6 and $10. If there is a petrol shortage, taxi fares go up.

From the airport into town, taxi drivers may quote fares of $20 or higher, but the standard price should be around $10. (If there are no taxis at the airport when you arrive, there is also a *dala-dala* service between town and the airport. See below for details.)

Dala-dalas

Pick-up vans called *dala-dalas* (or *dalas* for short) carry passengers on local runs around town and to outlying suburbs. All routes start at the Darajani Bus Station on Creek Road. The most useful routes for visitors are:

Route A   to Amaani Stadium and the eastern part of the New Town, via the main post office
Route B   along the coast road north of Zanzibar Town, to Bububu, near Fuji Beach;
Route U   along the main road south of Zanzibar Town, to the airport (Uwanje ya Ndege).

If you go the whole way, dala-dala fares are about $0.30 on Route A, and about $0.50 on Routes B and U. If you travel only part of the route, the fare is slightly cheaper.

Bicycle hire

For getting around Zanzibar Town and the surrounding area, a bike can be very handy. Bikes can be hired from several of the tour companies listed in this chapter. They are either sturdy steel Chinese-made models, or more

---

GUIDES AND THE *PAPAASI*

Nearly every tourist who comes to Zanzibar Town uses the services of a guide at some stage during their visit. If you come on an all-inclusive package, this will of course include the services of a guide. Even if you arrange something simple through a tour company, like a trip to the spice plantations, the price always includes a guide to show you around. Guides from reputable companies have to be registered with the Tourism Commission, and those who are carry identity cards.

There are also many other guides in Zanzibar who are not registered. Most of these are not really guides at all, but touts and hustlers who make their money showing tourists to hotels, arranging transport or boat rides. These touts are known locally as *papaasi* – literally meaning 'ticks' (ie: parasites or irritating blood-suckers).

When a ship comes into Zanzibar from Dar, there is usually a group of *papaasi* on the dockside. Some can be quite aggressive, but others are not too unpleasant and will help you find a place to stay (which may be useful, as the labyrinth of alleys in the Stone Town is disorientating at first). Tell them exactly what you want in terms of standard and price. It should not cost you any more money (the *papaasi* get a commission from the hotel) and could save you a lot of walking.

Unfortunately, this plan does not always work, as some hotels pay more commission than others, and some do not pay at all, so the *papaasi* will only take you to the places where they get a decent cut. We have heard from several travellers who arrived on Zanzibar aiming to stay in a certain hotel who were told by the *papaasi* that it was 'full' or 'closed', or even 'burnt down'. If you're in any doubt, it is best to be polite but firm with the *papaasi* (or simply ignore them completely) and find your own hotel. Even better, make a phone call from Dar es Salaam and reserve a room in advance. (Some hotels even give discounts for advance bookings.)

After arranging your hotel, most *papaasi* will want to be your 'guide', offering to show you around the sights or souvenir shops of the Stone Town, find companions for dive trips or boat excursions, or arrange transport to the East Coast. Use these services if you need them, but be prepared to pay if necessary, or be aware that the owners of the souvenir shops, boats and dive centres will have to pay commission to the *papaasi*, a charge which will of course be passed on to you.

Although reputable guides have identity cards, some *papaasi* have managed to get some too (they could be fakes, or simply stolen – it's hard to tell). This of course is confusing for tourists. There is a need for legitimate guides on Zanzibar, who can help tourists without hassling them, and it is hoped that the government departments responsible for tourism will apply itself to this matter in the near future.

WARNING

As the number of visitors to Zanzibar increases, the number of robberies in Zanzibar Town has increased also. Some tourists have had bags or cameras snatched while walking round the market or narrow streets; the obvious way to avoid this is not carry a bag or camera in the first place, or to have it secure, rather than dangling loosely over one shoulder.

More serious robberies have occurred on the beaches in and around Zanzibar Town. You should not walk here alone, particularly after dark. Other notorious parts of town include the port, and the areas around the Tarambata Club and the Bottom's Up Bar, especially late at night when drunken youths wander the streets looking for kicks (just as they do in many other parts of the world).

We've also heard from some readers of a scam played by staff in one of the less reputable hotels in Zanzibar Town. Apparently, they left a small bag of valuables (passport, air tickets, money, etc) in the hotel safe, only to find items missing when they returned to collect it. It seems that a member of staff had a duplicate key to the safe and removed a few $20 bills in the hope that the theft wouldn't be noticed. The only way to prevent this happening to you is to store your valuables in a lockable bag or pouch, to prevent tampering when it's out of your hands, or count and write down everything you have in the presence of the receptionist (although this can be embarrassing and possibly even a bit too tempting...). The other alternatives are to stay in reputable hotels, or keep your stuff securely on you at all times.

Don't let these warnings worry you too much and spoil your visit to Zanzibar. Trouble can usually be avoided. Take care, use your common sense, and you should have no problems. (For more details, see the general *Safety* section in *Chapter Four*.)

---

modern looking (though almost as heavy) mountain bikes. Prices for Chinese bikes start at about $1 per hour, or $5 per day (payable in TSh). Mountain bikes are $10 per day. A deposit of around $50 may be required.

Car and motorbike hire

A car or motorbike is not really necessary for getting around Zanzibar Town as distances are short, but they can be hired from various tour companies listed in this chapter. Prices vary, but are generally around $15 to $25 per day for a scooter, $30 per day for a motorbike, and between $40 and $60 per day for a small car (eg: Suzuki 'jeep') and around $100 per day for a larger car (eg: Landcruiser). Petrol costs about $0.80 per litre. For more details on car hire see page 161.

HOTELS AND GUESTHOUSES

This is a selection of places to stay in and around Zanzibar Town. Details of hotels elsewhere on Zanzibar Island are given in *Chapter Six*. Pemba Island is covered in *Chapter Seven*. The list is not complete, as the number of hotels increases every year, and there are frequent name and location changes, but it indicates the range of accommodation available.

If you arrive by air you can get to town by dala-dala, or take a taxi. If you don't have a reservation, be firm about which hotel you want to go to, otherwise the taxi driver will take you to a place where he gets the best commission. Also, remember that many hotels cannot be reached by vehicle, and you may have to walk some distance through the narrow streets and alleys. If the driver shows you the way, he'll expect a good tip.

The same applies if you come in to Zanzibar Town by ship and get a taxi from the port to your hotel, although this may not be necessary as several hotels are within easy walking distance of the port.

All non-Tanzanian visitors must pay hotel bills in hard currency, usually US dollars, so all prices are quoted in this currency. In larger hotels you can pay with travellers cheques; in smaller hotels they only accept cash. Some of the hotels, mostly in the $50-plus bracket, accept credit cards – mainly Visa and American Express. Some of the smaller places accept cards too. Residents and citizens are charged lower rates (between 50% and 80% of the visitor rate), and can usually pay in TSh.

Double room prices are mostly given here, with some single and triple rates. Where only double rates are given, some hotels also do single rooms for about 60% to 75% of the double room price, or triple rooms for about 125% of the double room price. All hotels on Zanzibar include breakfast in the room price, unless otherwise stated.

Throughout this chapter, all prices quoted for hotels are high-season rates. You can normally get discounts of 25% to 50% in the low season, and there may be additional premiums at the Christmas and New Year peaks. At any time of year, rates may be negotiable if you're in a small group, or plan to stay several nights. All places include breakfast, unless otherwise stated.

If you intend staying in one of the cheaper places it is usually possible simply to arrive and get a room on the spot. However, advance reservations may be necessary for some of the smarter hotels, or at very busy periods. You can book a room in advance by phone or fax (see box below for details), although connections are sometimes hard to make. Several hotels also have an email address. Or you can use good old-fashioned post and write direct to the hotel. Include the PO Box number in the address and allow between three and five weeks for a reply. Whichever method you use, if you can't book in advance, don't worry – except at seasonal peaks (Christmas and Easter) you're very unlikely to get completely stuck with owhere to stay.

TELEPHONING ZANZIBAR

The area code for Zanzibar (Zanzibar Island and Pemba Island) is 054, if you are calling from elsewhere in Tanzania, or from Kenya or Uganda. For calls from other countries, the international code for Tanzania is +255, then 54 for Zanzibar.

ELECTRICITY IN ZANZIBAR

Zanzibar Town gets frequent cuts in the electrical supply. To overcome this, most of the larger hotels have generators, but some of the small ones don't, which can mean no lights and no fans. If the lights go out, kerosene lamps may be provided but it's best to have a torch or candles handy just in case. When the fans stop working there's not much you can do, and inside rooms can get unbearable during Zanzibar's hot season. Bear this in mind when choosing a place to stay. Hotels that have been built recently rely on a constant electrical supply to work the fans or air-conditioning. Older hotels have been built to withstand the hot weather using designs that date from before the invention of electricity. If you can't find a genuine old hotel, look for one built in traditional style – with large windows, thick walls, high ceilings, courtyards, wide verandas and even a double roof, not just a pseudo-oriental facade. If all the new hotels were built using genuine traditional designs, fans and air-conditioning would be unnecessary, Zanzibar would not need to burn so much imported oil, and tourists would be more comfortable during power cuts!

Hotels in Zanzibar Town

Many hotels are in, or very near, Stone Town, and this is the best area for atmosphere and ease of getting around. The places to stay are arranged in this section roughly in descending order of price and standard (ie: the best or most expensive first, the cheapest last) although you should note that some of the more costly hotels may be overpriced, while some of the cheaper guesthouses offer remarkably good value for money.

Zanzibar Serena Inn (tel: 32277/31015, fax: 33019, mobile: 0811 321077) Part of the internationally renowned Serena chain, with hotels and lodges all over East Africa, this hotel opened in 1997, the first of its kind in Zanzibar. Two historic buildings in the Shangani part of the Stone Town, overlooking the sea, have been restored at great expense and converted into the hotel. (See box opposite for whole story.) All rooms are en-suite and air-conditioned, with all the facilities visitors expect of an international class hotel, including a large pool and fine restaurant with à la carte and table d'hôte menus. A coffee shop is planned, with light meals, snacks and ice-creams. If you happen not to be on holiday here, there's a business centre with fax, photocopy and email services, and conference facilities. The bed and breakfast rates for walk-in visitors are $130.00 per single, $180.00 per double. Half board is an extra $28 per person. Full board is an extra $42. The hotel also has state, executive, honeymoon and business rooms. Generous discounts are available in the low season and sometimes also during quiet midweek periods. Cheaper rates are also sometimes available if you book through a travel agent rather than direct. Outside Zanzibar you can use Serena central reservations in Tanzania on Arusha (057) 8175, or in Kenya on Nairobi (02) 711077.

Tembo Hotel (PO Box 3974, tel: 33005) This hotel was opened in 1994, in a grand old house on Shangani Street, near Forodhani Gardens. It has recently been extended, so that there's now a new wing and old wing, both overlooking the ocean and decorated in a mixture of traditional and modern styles. A notable feature is the upstairs lounge area separated from a balcony by a huge stained-glass window which fills the room with coloured light. All rooms are en-suite, with air-conditioning, fridge, telephone and TV. Most rooms have a sea view, or overlook the swimming pool. Doubles cost between $75 and $100, including breakfast, plus $35 for full board. Alcohol is not served in this hotel.

Emerson's House (PO Box 4044, tel: 32153/30609, fax: 33135) In the Mkunazini area, not far from the market, this hotel was once the house of the brother of Sultan Barghash, and then home to a wealthy Indian family, before being abandoned after the revolution. Now run by Emerson Skeens, it has been completely restored and tastefully decorated, with antique Zanzibar furniture and carpets, and has a peaceful and slightly bohemian atmosphere. It was listed by the British *Sunday Times* newspaper as one of the 'great little hotels of the world'. Double rooms range from $60 to $85 per night. On the roof is a tea-house, which becomes a stylish restaurant at night serving dinner for $15. Downstairs is a small café, serving snacks, locally made cakes, coffee and fresh fruit juices.

Emerson's & Green (PO Box 4044, tel: 32153/30609, fax: 33135) This hotel is in the Hurumzi area. It is closely allied to Emerson's House (listed above) with the additional talents of Tom Green, and even more stylish decor. There are seven rooms, each different in character, including the vast Ball Room and the airy island South Room – reached by a small bridge! All rooms cost $120 (single or double), with an extra bed $10. Just like Emerson's, each room has no phone, no TV and no fridge. Some rooms have air-conditioning, others rely on natural cooling – shutters, shades, deep balconies and a sea breeze. Dating from the 1840 to 1870 period, the building

SERENA INN

The Zanzibar Serena Inn is in the Shangani part of Stone Town. The main building was originally the External Communications ('Extelcoms') headquarters, built in the early 20th century by the British colonial administration. The house next door is much older and was originally known as the 'Chinese Doctor's Residence'. The explorer David Livingstone stayed here before one of his journeys to the African mainland. It later became the private home of the British Consul.

The Extelcoms Building had been empty for many years, and the Chinese Doctor's Residence had fallen into a bad state of repair. Restoration of these two buildings, and their conversion into a hotel, has been sensitive and appropriate. The design reflects Zanzibar's mixed heritage, and includes Indian, Arabic and colonial styles. Restoration was completed in 1997. Big 'chain' hotels of this nature often appear bland and anonymous, but the architects and local craftsmen who worked here have done a very good job.

The walls of the hotel are decorated with historic prints and some contemporary paintings, but perhaps the most interesting 'decorations' are the old telecommunications equipment that were discovered in the basement, where they'd been dumped and forgotten by colonial staff almost a hundred years ago. Most of this equipment was hand-made in wood and brass, and several items have also been restored to their original condition.

The Serena's restoration goes beyond façades and decorations. It is the first hotel in Zanzibar to install a sewage plant, so that waste discharges are treated to international standards. (Most other waste from the Stone Town gets pumped out to sea in its raw state.) Although dumping sewage at sea, in whatever state, is never an ideal solution, the hotel owners should be congratulated for this positive step.

was once the home of a prominent Ismaili Indian merchant called Tharia Topan who also built the Dispensary (listed in *Places to See*). As financial advisor to Sultan Barghash, and the second wealthiest man on Zanzibar at the time, his house was the second highest in town, lower only than the House of Wonders. The hotel's 'Tower Top Restaurant' makes full use of this vantage point and has some of the finest views on the whole island, with top-quality evening meals for $20 (reservations essential).

Mazsons Hotel (PO Box 3367, tel: 33694, fax: 33695) This hotel in the Shangani area has an interesting history: old records show it was built in the mid-1800s by one Said bin Dhanin, who is thought to have settled here about the time Sultan Said moved his court to Zanzibar from Muscat. Ownership changed hands several times, and during the early part of the 20th century the building was a Greek-run hotel before becoming a private dwelling once again. After the revolution the house, along with many others, fell into disrepair. Today, it is once more a hotel. The lounge and lobby area are furnished in traditional style, but some of the rooms, although self-contained, air-conditioned and well-appointed, are a little soulless. A 'moderate' single is $36. Standard singles are $48, while doubles range from $64 to $90. The hotel has a good restaurant, satellite TV, a business centre and bureau de change. Although power supplies are pretty good on Zanzibar these days, this hotel has its own generator in case of cuts – so big it supplies many surrounding buildings as well!

Baghani House Hotel (PO Box 609, tel: 20165, fax: 31816) In the Shangani area, this is a small friendly place with double rooms with television and air-conditioning from $40 to $70, including full breakfast and afternoon tea. The hotel has a restaurant, and the street-front Livingstone Bar is popular with tourists and expats. This bar is furnished with camp chairs and contemporary prints of the great explorer; placed next to the large TV showing CNN, they're a striking reminder of how the world has shrunk in the last 100 years.

Dhow Palace Hotel (PO Box 3974, tel: 33012, fax: 33008) Almost next door to the Baghani House Hotel (listed above), the Dhow Palace is a very pleasant hotel, in a renovated old house built around a cool central courtyard, complete with tinkling fountain. Rooms (complete with Persian baths) lead off long balconies which overlook the courtyard and the whole atmosphere is very tranquil. It lacks only sea views. Single rooms are $50, and doubles range from $65 to $80.

Bwawani Plaza International Hotel (PO Box 670, tel: 30200, fax/tel: 30202) Just to the north of the Stone Town, overlooking the sea, this was once the island's premier government-run hotel. It has been taken over by private management, but some lingering government interference meant that despite the grand title the hotel still remains a fairly drab grey concrete building. However, great improvements are expected so the hotel might be worth checking. A double room, air-conditioned and en-suite, costs $65, plus 15% tax. Singles, suites and full-board rates are also available. The hotel has squash and tennis courts, swimming pool, bar, bakery and a restaurant serving à la carte meals. The weekend discos are popular.

Karwan Sarai (PO Box 145, tel/fax: 33524, 33186) An alternative spelling of *caravanserai*, a traditional resthouse for travellers in the Arab world, this hotel in the Kokoni area (between Malindi Street and Creek Road) is built in local style, with modern facilities and tasteful en-suite doubles from $60. The roof-top lounge has great views across the Stone Town.

Shangani Hotel (PO Box 4222, tel: 33524, tel/fax: 33688) This new hotel, on

Kenyatta Rd near the old post office, is a good choice in the middle range. En-suite doubles are $55 ($40 with shared bathroom) and triples $65. Rooms have air-conditioning, fridge, telephone and satellite TV. Breakfast is included. Other meals in the roof-top restaurant are $12.

Hotel International (PO Box 3784, tel: 33182, fax: 30052) In the Ukatani area, this hotel is a large old house, built around a central roofed courtyard. It has been completely renovated and re-fitted with new furniture rather than original antiques. The hotel has a range of rooms, all air-conditioned and completely self-contained, each with its own bathroom, lounge and dining area, fridge, satellite TV and video, starting at $55 for a double, although some there are some cheaper rooms on the ground floor. The hotel also has an efficient bureau de change.

Spice Inn (PO Box 1029, tel: 30728) This is one of the town's oldest hotels, with a very impressive facade of balconies overlooking a small square. Inside, on the stairway and in the lounge, are several antique pieces of furniture, and the place has a feel of faded elegance, although some of the rooms are quite plain. Double en-suite rooms range from $30 to $50. Smaller rooms with shared facilities are $25. The hotel's 'Curry Pot' Restaurant and 'Spicer's' street café are both popular.

THE BWAWANI HOTEL

The Bwawani Hotel was built in 1972, on a narrow piece of land between the sea and the creek on the edge of Zanzibar Town. Abeid Karume, President of Zanzibar after the 1964 revolution, wanted a luxurious hotel to impress foreign dignitaries. Modern mythology has it that once the frame of the hotel was up, Karume realised he had forgotten to include a kitchen and dining room, so these were built as a separate block. (Disgruntled guests have said that this might explain why orders took so long and why meals were so cold when they arrived.)

The hotel was meant to be open for January 1974, the tenth anniversary of the revolution, but in October 1973 it was no more than a shell. An Indian hotel chain was asked to manage the hotel and it was opened on the required date, although it was still only partly finished.

The hotel was finally completed in October 1976. It was full for the first time when scientists, journalists and tourists filled the 125 rooms to watch a full eclipse of the sun, scheduled for October 23. Most of the visitors checked in the evening before the eclipse but when they turned on the lights and air-conditioners the hotel's main transformer, located outside under a huge bronze statue of Karume, suddenly exploded. The hotel was without electricity and, to cap it all, when many of the guests opened their windows for ventilation, they were besieged by mosquitoes from the creek.

Another story about the Bwawani Hotel concerns two Indian elephants, called Indirani and Govindon, who were presented to the government of Zanzibar and used by the Bwawani Hotel in 1976. The hotel sold elephant rides for 15 shillings each, although very few Zanzibaris could afford them. Every morning two attendants walked the elephants from their enclosure near the Maharubi Palace to the kitchen area of the hotel where the staff fed them on leftover food.

Source: *Zanzibar: Tradition and Revolution*, E B Martin, Hamish Hamilton, London 1978

Blue Ocean Hotel (PO Box 4052, tel: 33566) Just off Kenyatta Road, near the Dolphin Restaurant, this hotel is pleasant enough but nothing special and a touch expensive at $20 per person for en-suite double rooms, although rates may be negotiable. The best room (which *is* worth the $20) is the Seaview Room, right at the top of the house, with views in all directions over the whole of the Stone Town and out across the bay towards the islands.

Narrow Street Hotel Annex II (PO Box 3784, tel: 33006, fax: 30052) The Narrow Street Hotel itself was temporarily closed when this book was being researched, but it may re-open. Meanwhile the hotel's 'Annex II' continues to thrive, with small clean, en-suite double rooms, with fridge, air-conditioning and Zanzibar-style beds, for $40. (There's also an Annex I, where rates are cheaper.)

Hotel Kiponda (PO Box 3446, tel: 33052, fax: 33020) On Nyumba ya Moto Street, in the Kiponda area, not far from the main seafront, this is a small, quiet hotel in a building which used to house part of a sultan's harem. It has been renovated in local style and still has an original carved wooden entrance door. The Dutch-Australian-Zanzibari management team have given the place a relaxed and friendly atmosphere: we've received several letters from travellers recommending this hotel. Single rooms are $18, doubles $35, and triples $45. En-suite doubles are $45. All prices are discountable for long stays and for groups, with extra reductions in low season. There's a roof-top restaurant specialising in Zanzibari and seafood dishes. The hotel also has good connections with the local Kenya Airways office and can help with flights and reservations. They also offer a phone and fax service; international calls are $10 per minute (minimum). Credit cards accepted.

Africa House Hotel (PO Box 216, tel: 30708) This was the English Club in colonial days, and the building still has a marble floor, panelled rooms and dusty old hunting trophies on the walls. The hotel was taken over by the Zanzibar Tourist Corporation after the revolution and, it seems, run completely into the ground. (The Committee Room, which contained the library, was apparently locked when the British left. It has been disused, and seldom entered, ever since.) Despite its grand history, this hotel is now shabby and dirty, and rooms are vastly overpriced at $30 a double. The restaurant gets mixed reports; the food may sometimes be good, but the waits can be endless. However, the terrace bar overlooking the sea is a popular place for sun-downers (see the section on *Bars*, page 105) although a large crowd and a small fridge mean the beer isn't always cold.

There are plans to privatise and completely renovate the hotel, so it may have been restored to its former glory by the time you read this – in which case the drinks in the bar will no doubt have increased in price, although the views from the terrace will still be just as good.

Stone Town Inn (PO Box 3530, tel: 33101, fax: 33060) In the Shangani area, next to the Fisherman Restaurant, with clean, straightforward rooms for $15 per person, or en-suite doubles with air-conditioning and hot shower for $50.

Coco de Mer Hotel (PO Box 2363, tel: 30852) In Shangani, off Kenyatta Road, this is a clean and friendly place with rooms set around an airy courtyard, decorated with potted plants. En-suite singles are $25, doubles $35 and triples $45. The restaurant does good-value food, with seafood specials at $5.

Zanzibar Hotel (PO Box 216, tel: 30708) This is a state-run ZTC hotel, very near the Africa House, but not quite so dilapidated (although it's a close-run thing). Double en-suite rooms are $30, or $45 with air-conditioning. This place is poor value, but worth trying in busy periods when everything else is full.

Malindi Annex Guesthouse Connected to the Malindi Guesthouse (listed below) but more pricy at $15 a single and $20 a double, due to the central location (near Ciné Afrique and the Port Gates) and air-conditioning. Other features include old photographs of past Zanzibari presidents.

Malindi Guesthouse (PO Box 609, tel: 30165) In the northern part of the Stone Town, near the port, this place has been consistently popular with travellers for many years. It's clean and nicely decorated, with a lot of character. There's a bar and restaurant. There are singles, doubles and triples all for $10 per person.

Pyramid Hotel (PO Box 254, tel: 33000, fax: 30045) On Kokoni Street, between the Malindi and Kiponda areas, this long-standing hotel is just behind the Ijumaa Mosque near the seafront. It's been a budget travellers' favourite for many years,

---

MEMORIES OF THE ENGLISH CLUB

We received these reminiscences from a former member of the English Club (now the Africa House Hotel) who served in the colonial government before Zanzibar's independence:

'The English Club, Zanzibar, was the oldest expatriate club in East Africa. The Rules and Regulations of 1888 – the year of its foundation – state that "it is established for the association of an unlimited number of English Residents, together with officers of the Royal Navy stationed in these waters". At this date the RN officers from no less than six warships outnumbered the other members.

By the 1950s eligibility for membership was widened to include "any British subject or American citizen of European extraction". Extraordinary members could also be elected from other residents such as the representatives of European trading companies. Honorary membership was extended to resident members of the Universities Mission to Central Africa, the Catholic Mission to Zanzibar, Armed Forces officers, Officers of any British Cable or Merchant Ship or Civil Aircraft, and so on. There was also reciprocity with similar clubs in Nairobi, Dar es Salaam and Mombasa, which was a bonus when travelling in East Africa.

Bedrooms were available for visitors, and for use by members when departing or arriving from home leave. A Dining Room provided meals for single members, if required, and was popular for entertaining. After garages were built at ground level, their roof formed an attractive outdoor dining area – which is apparently still in use. There was a Billiard Room and a quite extensive Library. Sporting facilities were available at a separate site at the far end of Mnazi Mmoja Road, where tennis and golf were popular, together with squash, cricket and hockey.

In the latter years of the Club's existence, the fancy dress dance on New Year's Eve was a well-attended event. Among the other communities it was known that the "wazungu" (Europeans) would be walking through Stone Town, or arriving by car at the Club about 8.00pm, dressed in weird costumes, and there was always a sizeable gathering of local people to watch with amusement at these strange antics.

The reader may be of the opinion that this all smacked of a monopoly of club life, but this was not so. There were Goan, Parsee, Bohora, Hindu, Ismaili, Ithnashery and other clubs, each used by a single community, whilst preserving an easy-going and relaxed contact among the various communities resident in the Island.'

with single, double and triple rooms all for $10 per person. There are also some smarter en-suite rooms for $15 per person. The staff are very friendly, and the roof-top restaurant does good food. If you crave the small screen, the hotel has a lounge with TV and video player: you can hire a video from a shop in the town centre (full of Indian soap-dramas and American action movies) and enjoy a great evening in front of the box!

St Monica's Hostel Very near the Anglican Cathedral, on New Mkunazini Road, this hostel is mainly for church guests, but it is also open to the public. The hostel was built in the 1890s and formerly housed teachers and nurses working at the UMCA mission. Rooms are very clean, costing $12 per person including breakfast. In the same building is a restaurant, with simple good-value meals. No alcohol is allowed. On the upper floor is a small art workshop where you can buy paintings and hand-printed T-shirts.

Victoria Guesthouse (tel: 32861) Near the People's Gardens, this place is old (in fact, in the early 1980s it was just about the only budget option on the island) and is nothing special, but it's in a nice position and worth checking in case of improvements. The official charge is $10 per person, but this is reported to be negotiable.

Jambo Guesthouse (PO Box 635, tel: 33779) In the Mkunazini area, near the Anglican Cathedral, this straightforward place has a range of rooms: doubles cost $16, or $18 with air-conditioning; singles cost $10. There are also some triples. Meals are available at the nearby Green Garden Restaurant (see page 103).

Haven Hotel (PO Box 3746, tel: 33454) Several budget travellers have written to recommend this place, which is clean, with hot showers, single rooms at $10 and double rooms at $16.

Riverman Hotel (PO Box 1805, tel: 33188) This place, behind the market and near the Empire Cinema, is highly recommended by budget travellers; with good showers, fans, nets, laundry facilities and clean rooms for $10 per person including breakfast.

Warere Guesthouse (PO Box 1298, tel: 31187) In the northern part of the town, very near the port, this place is popular with budget travellers, with singles and doubles at $7 per person. It's plain but reasonable for the price.

Karibu Inn (PO Box 3428, tel: 33058) In the Shangani part of town, with clean but basic double rooms for $20 ($25 en-suite), and small dorms for four at $10 per person or for six at $8 per person.

Flamingo Guest House (PO Box 4279, tel: 32850) On Mkunazini Street, off New Mkunazini Road, this is a friendly place, popular with budget travellers. Facilities include TV and video lounge, book-swap service and sale of cold drinks. Clean double rooms cost $7 per person ($10 for en-suite rooms).

Manch Lodge Near the Flamingo Guest House, this friendly budget lodge charges $8 per person in singles, doubles or triples ($9 for en-suite), with extra discounts for stays of over two nights.

Florida Guesthouse Set back from Vuga Rd, this is another popular budget place, charging $10 per person.

Garden Lodge (PO Box 3413, tel: 33298, fax: 31619) Near the People's Gardens and the main hospital, spartan but clean, with double rooms from $16.

Bottoms Up Guesthouse Attached to the somewhat disreputable bar of the same name, this place is hard to find in the narrow alleys between the Spice Inn and the House of Wonders. However, it's popular with budget travellers as rooms are $7 per person. There's a lounge with TV and a book-swap service, and a restaurant is planned. The bar is also cheap, and frequented by low-life locals and off-duty tour touts seriously spending their ill-gotten gains, but the atmosphere is lively and not too unpleasant, although the noise makes an early night impossible.

Hotels near Zanzibar Town

The hotels in the outer suburbs of Zanzibar Town are harder to reach, and inconvenient for sightseeing, shopping or visiting restaurants unless you hire a car or bike, or are happy waiting for taxis. However, they are generally quieter, often with gardens, and may be the only places with rooms during very busy times, such as Christmas or Easter.

South side

About 2km south of the town, at Kilimani, on the road towards the airport, is **Island View Hotel** (tel: 32666, mobile: 0811 333147). This new place is clean and friendly, with doubles at $22. Tea and coffee are available all day free of charge. Some rooms are still to be finished. When complete all will have air-conditioning, TV and telephone. This place is loosely linked with Chit-Chat Restaurant (see page 102), and if you eat at the restaurant you get a discount at the hotel.

Further away from town, in the Mbweni area, a few kilometres off the airport road, is the **Mbweni Ruins Hotel** (PO Box 2542, tel: 31832, fax: 30536, mobile: 0811 320855, email: mbweni-ruins@twiga.com). As the name suggests, this hotel is in the grounds of Mbweni Ruins, originally built in the 1870s as a school for the children of freed slaves. The ruins are currently being renovated, and a small museum is planned. Also close is St John's Anglican Church (see page 147). The hotel is tastefully decorated, and set in extensive well-maintained grounds with a lush botanical garden and nature trail, with a small private beach and swimming pool. There are only 12 rooms (all en-suite suites with air-conditioning) and the hotel is proud of its personalised service. Bed and breakfast is $90 per person. Full board is an extra $25 per person. The food in the terrace restaurant overlooking the sea is recommended with many visitors staying in Zanzibar Town coming here for dinner; a full meal is around $15. There is a free shuttle service to and from town, and transfers to/from the port or airport cost $10 for four people. Nearby mangroves provide good birding, and the hotel has its own bird list. They also have a boat which can be hired for trips to islands or nearby beaches. Another interesting feature is the Natural Health Centre where aromatherapy and shiatsu massage are available.

Nearby is the **Inn By The Sea Hotel**, in an old house once the grand home of Miss Caroline Thackeray (see page 148) but now a rather gloomy place with double en-suite rooms at $30. It is however a very quiet and relaxing place, except on Friday nights when the giant thatched dance hall hosts a popular disco.

Further away (about 7km) from Zanzibar Town and 3km from the airport, in an area called Mazizini, is the smart **Fisherman's Resort** (PO Box 2586, tel: 30208, fax: 30556). This hotel (formerly the Zanzibar Reef) has 57 en-suite rooms in traditional-style buildings, set in landscaped grounds overlooking the sea. Double rooms start at $150, or $180 for a sea view, although groups get more reasonable rates. Rates include breakfast; half board is an extra $10 per person; full board is an extra $20 per person. The hotel has a restaurant, bar and disco, squash court, sauna, gym, swimming pool, conference room, and facilities for fishing and watersports.

North side

On the north side of Zanzibar Town, about 4km from the port, is the **Mtoni Sunset Beach Guesthouse**. Rooms are basic, but this is a popular place with budget travellers. Rooms cost $7 per person and prices are sometimes negotiable. Dala-dalas on Route B run regularly between Bububu village and Zanzibar Town, past the hotel.

Also in Mtoni is **Mtoni Marine Centre** (PO Box 992, tel/fax: 32540, fax: 865692, mobile: 0811 323226, email: mmc@twiga.com), set in extensive grounds with a large stretch of beach. This place is efficiently run but relaxed and friendly. They have smart bungalows and suites costing $38 per person sharing a double, or $58 for a single. Standard rooms are $23 per double. These prices include a transfer from the airport, if you book in advance and arrive by air. Cheaper room-only rates are available for walk-in guests, and some good value half-board and full-board rates are also on offer. The food in the restaurant is reported to be very good – many people come to eat here even if they're not staying – the beach buffet barbecues ($14) are particularly popular. The staff can also arrange tours, car hire, boat trips and so on. Mtoni Marine are also the official Visa International assistance agent for Zanzibar, and the only place which reliably gives cash on a Visa credit card.

In the area of Kibweni, about 3km from Mtoni, is **Kibweni Beach Villa** (PO Box 1689, tel/fax: 33496), with en-suite doubles for $30. The hotel has a free transfer service into town, and is on a dala-dala route.

Further north, in Bububu village, about 5km beyond Mtoni, is the **Bububu Guesthouse** (PO Box 1929, tel: 30308), a simple place but clean, friendly and good value charging from $8 per person. It's near Fuji Beach (more details on page 155), which has a bar and restaurant, and the guesthouse can arrange spice tours. They have a pick-up to transfer guests into town, or you can catch a dala-dala from the terminus on the main road nearby.

Even further north, near the village of Chuini, about 20km outside the Stone Town, is the **Mawimbini Club Village** (PO Box 4281, tel: 31163). This is an international-style resort complex, part of the VentaClub chain, catering almost exclusively for fly-in package tourists. It was the first hotel of its kind on the island, but there are now many other similar places all round the coast, with more being built. The hotel consists of bungalows set in a large garden around a central area with swimming pool, restaurant (with African and European chefs) and bar. A theatre has regular dancing and cabaret shows. Doubles cost between $100 and $200 per person, full board, depending on the season. To stay here, it is easier to make arrangements through one of the tour companies in Zanzibar Town, as they can phone and check availability for you.

Offshore

Also outside Zanzibar Town, about 5km offshore on Changuu Island (more commonly called Prison Island), is the small **Changuu Island Guesthouse**, a group of wooden bungalows set back from the main beach. The island can only be reached by boat, and many people go there just for the day (see page 156), but this is a nice place to stay for a night or two. The guesthouse is run by ZTC (book in advance at the ZTC office on Creek Road, or at Livingstone House). En-suite rooms are $16 single, $20 double, with breakfast. Camping is also permitted here. Other meals are available from the island restaurant, or you can bring picnic food from Zanzibar Town, or more elaborate supplies and a stove if you have one.

On Chapwani Island (more commonly called Grave Island), between Changuu and Zanzibar Town, the **Chapwani Guesthouse** has small bungalows for rent, although building here seems to continue sporadically. You can get more information from a tour company in Zanzibar Town. Hotels are also under construction on Bawe Island and Nyange Island.

The most interesting offshore accommodation is on **Chumbe Island** (see also page 157), some 12km to the south of Zanzibar Town. The island and surrounding reefs are a marine sanctuary called Chumbe Island Coral Park. Day trips to the island are available (these cost $50), but visitors are encouraged to overnight in the reserve to get full appreciation of their surroundings. The bungalows are described as 'eco-friendly', and for once this term is used in a genuine manner – each is very comfortable and completely self-sufficient with solar panels to provide electricity, funnel-shaped roofs to catch and collect rainwater, even 'compost toilets' to avoid septic tanks and the pollutants they often produce. This place is unique in Zanzibar, and one of very few in the whole of Africa. Unfortunately, genuine eco-friendliness is not cheap, with rates starting at $70 per person. As the island becomes more established, demand is likely to be high, so rates may go up towards $200 for full board, guides, transfers and all activities. This is on a par with other top-notch wildlife lodges elsewhere in Africa, so if you've got the money a visit here is highly recommended. For enquiries and reservations contact Chumbe Island Coral Park (CHICOP), PO Box 3203, tel/fax: 31040, radio 156.725/ch74. Alternatively, you can make enquiries at Mbweni Ruins Hotel (see page 96) where boat trips to the island depart. Chumbe Island Coral Park is recognised internationally as a site of major significance. It is hoped that the Zanzibar government also recognise the island's importance and its potential as a tourism attraction and flagship environmental project.

New hotels

Several new hotels are planned in and around Zanzibar Town. These include some up-market establishments on the small offshore islands, and on the coast north of the town. Several new places are planned or under construction between Bububu and Mawimbini, and another new hotel is being built near Mangapwani.

Hotels are also being opened in the town itself. These include the Chavda Hotel, a grand old house now completely renovated in Indian style. The old External Telecommunications (Extelcoms) office in Shangani has now been transformed into the Serena Inn, and another international hotel group plans similarly to transform the large building between the Customs House and the Palace Museum on the main seafront near Forodhani Gardens. No doubt several smaller hotels will spring up in other parts of the town.

EATING AND DRINKING

Restaurants and cafés

Zanzibar Town has a wide choice of places to eat. Some are simple and aimed at locals; others are smarter and cater specifically for tourists, expatriates and more well-off residents. The following list, arranged loosely in order of descending price (best and most expensive first, cheaper options last), cannot hope to be complete, but it will give you an idea about the type and range of places available. All the restaurants included here are open in the evenings for dinner, and some also open for lunch. Some are open all day from early morning. At busy times reservations may be necessary in some of the smarter establishments. At least one place gives a discount if you book ahead.

Hotel restaurants

Many restaurants in Zanzibar Town are connected to hotels (see the *Hotels* section above for directions and phone numbers), but are open to all. In most of these, the quality and prices in the restaurant reflect the standard of the hotel, but a few places are worthy of special mention.

Emerson's House in Mkunazini has a splendid tea-shop on the roof, which becomes a restaurant at night serving dinner for $15. Downstairs is an atmospheric café, serving snacks, locally made cakes, coffee and fresh fruit juices. At the closely aligned **Emerson's & Green** hotel in Hurumzi there's another roof-top restaurant with a superb view, modestly claiming to be the 'best on the island'. Most visitors seem to agree that it is. At both of Emerson's places, evening meals are relaxed affairs, starting with sundowner drinks, working slowly through several courses and ending with Arabic coffee. Numbers are limited, so that guests can stay for the whole evening. Reservations are essential. Dinner is $20, plus drinks. Some nights the price is $25, but includes performances by local dancers and musicians.

Less flamboyant, but very good value, is the restaurant at the **Hotel Kiponda**, serving speciality Zanzibari and seafood dishes from $3 to $5. The restaurant at the **Narrow Street Hotel Annex II** has also been recommended. Also very good quality, but with slightly more formal surroundings, the restaurant at **Mazsons Hotel** has main courses in the $4 to $7 range. The **Spice Hotel** has a street café called 'Spicers' with straightforward decor, good coffee and cakes at very reasonable prices and is favoured for its people-watching vantage point; the upstairs Curry Pot restaurant also does good-value meals in the $3 to $5 range. The terrace restaurant at the **Tembo Hotel** is luxurious and has good seaviews, with meals between $5 and $9. The café at the **Baghani House Hotel** is in a pleasant shady courtyard, and the restaurant at the **Coco de Mer Hotel** is friendly; both offer reasonably priced meals starting at $3.

Out of town, **Mtoni Marine Centre** has a good restaurant – the thrice-weekly beach buffet barbecues ($14) are particularly popular.

Other restaurants

Of the restaurants not connected to hotels, one of the oldest is the **Sea View Indian Restaurant** (tel: 32132), with a most pleasant location on the seafront, near the People's Palace, with tables on a balcony and a beautiful view across the bay. They are open all day, for breakfasts, lunches, midday snacks and evening meals, offering spicy snacks from around $2 and good curries (including vegetarian) from about $7. Further along the seafront road (Mizingani Road), just past the Palace Museum, is the small open-air **1001 Nights Restaurant**, doing good-value meals with an Indian flavour; lunches around $5 and dinners in the $6 to $9 bracket. Nearby, in Forodhani Gardens the **Café Sea View**, on a pier jutting out above the water, serves drinks, snacks and ice-cream.

Opposite the Gardens is the **Old Arab Fort** (known locally as *Ngome Kongwe*), which was renovated in the early 1990s and is now a very impressive cultural centre, with a semi-circular open-air theatre, several smart souvenir shops, and a shady café-restaurant with interesting dishes in the $4 to $10 range, plus snacks, coffees, beers and chilled wine. This is a very good place to meet friends or take a break from sightseeing in the heat of the day.

Further west, on Shangani Road, is the **Fisherman Restaurant** (tel: 33658, 33101), decorated in hybrid Zanzibari-Mediterranean style and doing all sorts of seafood dishes in the $8 to $16 range, with specials around $20, and a three-course *menu de jour* for $14. Nearby, on Gizenga Street, just off the northern end of Kenyatta Road, is the **Luna Mare Restaurant** (tel: 31922), with a large menu containing European, Indian and Chinese dishes; main courses start at $5. In the same area is **Le Bistrot**, doing good seafood, Zanzibari, African and Indian dishes, with lunch around $2 to $3 and evening meals $5 to $12.

On Kenyatta Street is **Camlur's** (tel: 31919), serving delicious Goan specialities, such as fish and coconut curry, starting from about $5, open lunchtime and evening. Another place offering Goan food, as well as Zanzibari specialities, is the **Chit-Chat Restaurant** (tel: 32548) near St Joseph's Cathedral. This friendly, family-run place attracts a mix of locals and tourists of all budgets, with very good meals in the $4 to $8 range. Favourable reviews from various newspapers, magazines and guidebooks are proudly pasted to the wall. It's open every evening, except Mondays, 18.00 to 22.00 (6pm to 10 pm) – even during power cuts as they have a small generator. If you book a table in advance you get a discount. The owner refuses to pay *papaasi* commission, so ignore the touts who tell you this place is closed.

For good Indian food, just down the road from Camlur's is the new **Maharaja Restaurant** (tel: 30359). Also recommended for Indian food is the no-frills **Taj Restaurant**, on the northeastern side of the Stone Town, near the Hotel International, where vegetarian *talis* cost $8 (groups get a discount). There are plans for a bar.

Also on the northeastern side of the Stone Town, between the market and Kiponda Street, is the popular **House of Spices** (tel: 31264), which is a gift shop downstairs and a restaurant upstairs where the cuisine is authentic Italian and prices for lunches or evening meals start from around $8. The adjoining cocktail bar, overlooking the street, has a lively atmosphere at night and is a pleasant place to relax during the day, when snack lunches cost around $3. Another place for pizza is **Pychi's** (pronounced 'peaches') in a fine setting on the seafront, overlooking a small beach near the Big Tree and Old Dispensary. Pizzas cost from $6 to $9, sandwiches are $1.50. Next door is a smaller cheaper place, serving snacks and soft drinks.

At the far north end of town, in the port area, is the **Pagoda Chinese Restaurant** (tel: 31758). This is run by Mr Chung, who has lived on Zanzibar for many years and used to run a diving outfit, along with his son George (known to all as 'Young Chung'). The restaurant is open evenings only and highly rated by expats. Chinese agricultural technicians from projects around the island often come here – so it must be good! Single courses start at around $5, and you can have a good meal for $10 to $20.

FREDDIE MERCURY

Freddie Mercury, lead singer and front man for the rock band Queen, was born Farouk Bulsara in Zanzibar on September 5 1946. His father was an accountant working for the British government in the House of Wonders in Zanzibar Town, and his family had immigrated to Zanzibar from India but were originally of Persian extraction. The current inhabitants of various houses around Zanzibar Town will tell visitors 'Freddie lived here', but his father moved house several times so the claims could all be genuine. Local historians confirm that the Bulsara family lived in the house now occupied by Camlur's Restaurant.

The menu includes all the favourite Chinese dishes, plus a few specialities which show local influence, such as Chinese curried crab. It has to be said that the restaurant is not in the most salubrious part of town; you would be wise to get a taxi, and arrange for collection after your meal.

Particularly worthy of mention, because it's good and because there's nothing else quite like it on Zanzibar, is **Sambusa Two Tables Restaurant**, usually called simply **Two Tables** (tel: 31979). This is a small place (it really does have only two tables – although one seats about eight people), on the balcony of a private house. It's set back off Victoria Street, near the junction with Kaunda Road, but clearly signposted. The entrance is round the back. Food is cooked by husband-and-wife team Salim and Hidaya, with help from the rest of the family. It's best to phone or call in the afternoon to tell Salim you'll be coming in the evening. A full meal with a variety of local dishes costs $7.

Outside Stone Town, on the road to the airport, is the **Fisherman Restaurant–Mgombani**, connected to the place of the same name in town (with prices slightly higher), where fine-quality seafood is served on the terrace. Specialities include crayfish and 'steak sultan of Zanzibar'. (Open evenings only, reservations recommended, tel: 33658, 33101.) The same restaurant also arranges outside catering for large or small groups.

If you're leaving Zanzibar by air, the restaurant at the **airport** does a very good squid and chips for $3.

Cafés and snack bars

The long-standing **Luis' Yoghurt Parlour**, near St Joseph's Cathedral, offers snacks, lunches, fruit juices and, of course, a tasty selection of home-made yoghurt and milk drinks in clean and peaceful friendly surroundings. It's open lunchtimes only, from late morning. Also popular is the open-air **Green Garden Restaurant**, off Mkunazini Street, near the Jambo and Flamingo guesthouses, where snacks (around $3) and meals ($4 to $6) are served by friendly staff in peaceful and unpretentious surroundings.

The **Malkiya Restaurant**, near the Pyramid Guesthouse, off Mizingani Road, is run by a local women's co-operative, and has been recommended for tasty and genuine Swahili food at very good prices. Although reservations are not required, if you want a full evening meal it may be worth visiting in the afternoon, to give the staff a few hours' notice.

For very cheap eats, and a taste of local atmosphere, go to **Forodhani Gardens**, on the seafront opposite the House of Wonders. This is a gathering place for local people in the evenings and there are several stalls serving snacks and drinks, although the food stalls are sometimes prevented from opening by town officials. Alternatively, go to the street outside the Ciné Afrique Cinema in the Malindi area, or to the Majestic Cinema on Vuga Road, or the Empire Cinema near the market. As crowds gather for the evening film, stalls do a brisk trade in cakes and snacks such as chapatis and samosas. Mandazis (fried dough-balls) are also available.

Also near the Ciné Afrique are several simple eating houses, including the **Malindi Restaurant** and the **Passing Show Hotel**, serving bowls of rice, chapatis and sauce for around $1, or larger plates for up to $2. They cater mainly for local people, but visitors are always welcomed. There are some similar places around the Empire Cinema too. Round the corner from Malindi, on the north end of Creek Road is the **Al Jabry Restaurant**, a clean and friendly place with some outside seating, catering for Zanzibaris and tourists, with local-style meals from $2 to $4 and snacks for less than $1.

Other popular 'cheapies' include the **Tropicana**, next to the High Court on Kaunda Road. Near the Masumo Bookshop in the Mkunazini area, just back from the market, are several local tea-shops, also selling snacks and cakes, including the **Sinai Restaurant**, the **Utamanduni Restaurant**, the **SB Café** and **Bakan's Restaurant**. The **Café de Zenj** on Vuga Road claims to specialise in 'the selling of fast food', although we heard from some travellers who waited over an hour for hamburger and chips!

There are many other, seemingly nameless, basic eating houses which you may just stumble across as you walk around the streets of Zanzibar Town. Try the one next to the Dhow Palace Hotel, or next to the Bank of Commerce near the orphanage, or near the gates of the Bwawani Hotel, or around Soko Muhogo Street near its junction with Baghani Street. Menus are rare in the simple establishments, and some of the very small places may only have one meal available (sometimes called *chukula leo* – food of the day): you'll have to ask what they've got.

Another restaurant which caters for locals and tourists is **Kawaida**, in the new part of Zanzibar Town near the roundabout close to Michenzani flats. The Zanzibari staff serve up good Swahili food in a pleasant setting at reasonable prices, and this place has been highly recommended.

Food shopping

If you are self-catering, or just going on a picnic for the day, Zanzibar Town has a large market selling many types of fruit and vegetables, plus fresh fish and meat. You can also buy fresh bread in the market from the salesmen who ride in from the bakeries in the suburbs with large baskets on the backs of their bicycles. Dotted around the town are many small shops with a supply of basics, such as bread, biscuits, some fruit and

---

DAFU

A delicious Zanzibari snack is one of the young coconuts that can be found all over the island when they are in season. Locally they are called *dafu*. Around town, they are displayed at the side of the road or in the market, like a pile of rough, light brown footballs. You choose your coconut and the salesman will chop off its top with a knife so that you can drink the milk inside. It is very refreshing. After that, he will carve a makeshift spoon from part of the coconut shell, so that you can scoop out the fresh tender 'meat' from inside.

vegetables, and maybe a few tinned items. As these foods are mainly for local people, prices are low. For more choice go to the 'container stores' (they're built in converted shipping containers) along Creek Road or to the shops in the street near the Ciné Afrique, where you'll find a good range of food in tins and packets, imported mainly from Kenya, but also from other parts of the Indian Ocean. Most items are reasonably priced, only slightly more than if bought in Dar or Mombasa. Also worth a look if you crave imported specialities is the Zanzibar Catering Supermarket, in the same building as the Fisherman Restaurant–Mgombani, on the road to the airport. This place re-supplies passing cruise ships so the stock is of good quality. It's also a bakery and butchery, and a ships' chandler.

Bars and clubs

The number of bars in Zanzibar Town grows steadily each year as visitors continue to come in ever-increasing numbers. Some bars cater almost exclusively for tourists, others mainly for locals (generally Tanzanians who have immigrated to Zanzibar from the mainland, as most indigenous Zanzibaris are Muslim and do not drink). Most of the smarter restaurants mentioned above serve beer or wine at the table, and many of the larger hotels have separate bars. Tanzanian, Kenyan, South African and international beers and soft drinks, plus local and imported spirits, are usually available. Wines are mostly South African.

The roof-top bar at the **Africa House Hotel** (more details on page 94) in Shangani is popular for drinks at sunset, and a long-standing meeting place for travellers and locals, even though the beer often runs out and the bartender must rank as one of the surliest characters in Zanzibar. The noticeboard in the corridor by the bar is good for leaving messages, to find those friends you arranged to meet here, or perhaps to find companions for onward travels. There are also adverts for charter flights with spare seats, sailing or fishing trips with spare places, cars for sale, flats for rent, and just about anything else. Nearby is the **Oman International Club**, which also has a terrace overlooking the sea although due to an architectural oversight the setting sun is not always visible.

Also good for sun-downers is the smart **Pychi's**, which serves drinks and pizzas all day and long into the evening. In the May to September period, the angle of the sun means the sunsets are easier to appreciate here than at the Africa House (which is better October to April!). Other stylish bars include the **Livingstone Bar** and the **Stanley Bar**, both at the Baghani House Hotel, and the cocktail bar at the **House of Spices**. Even smarter is the **Baraza Bar** on Victoria Street near Victoria Gardens. These places are always open to late evening.

Bars with a more local atmosphere include the **New Happy**, next to the Africa House Hotel, and the **Cave Resort** at the end of Kenyatta Road. Also on Kenyatta Road, almost opposite Mazsons Hotel, is the **Sunrise Restaurant and Pub**, serving snacks and drinks in an open-air setting. At the other end of Kenyatta Road is **Le Pecheur Bar** (next to the Fisherman Restaurant), popular with expats and visitors, with a mostly male clientele which over the last few years has also attracted a friendly crowd of prostitutes from Dar. The atmosphere can get very hot and lively later in the evening, and may not be to everyone's taste. Next door is the even livelier **Tarambata Club**, where the music is loud and the clientele mostly local, mostly drunk and mostly unpleasant. At night, the street outside this club can be dangerous. Just 50m down Shangani Road from here is the much more peaceful **Starehe Club**, where the staff are friendly and the beers nearly always cold, although this place is due for renovation soon which might alter things. Also nearby is the pleasant bar at **Le Bistro**. In the narrow streets between the Spice Inn and the House of Wonders is the **Bottoms Up Bar**, a serious drinking den catering mainly for locals although some more intrepid visitors also go there.

In the same area, near the Hotel Kiponda, is the new **Palace Nightclub**, a European-Zanzibari enterprise combining a café, bistro and disco. There are also discos most nights at the **Bwawani Plaza** hotel, every Friday at the **Inn by the Sea**, and occasionally at **Bar Baraza**. Sometimes there are live bands as well. Look for posters around town advertising special events.

TRAVEL COMPANIES

For travel away from Zanzibar Island, to either Pemba, mainland Tanzania, or elsewhere in Africa, you have several choices, depending mainly on your budget and the way you want to go.

International airlines

Air Tanzania Corporation (PO Box 773, tel: 30297, 30213)
ATC planes fly between Zanzibar and Dar es Salaam, where you can connect to any other destination on the ATC network or transfer to a flight on another airline (see also *Getting to Zanzibar* on page 39). ATC has a reputation for being very unreliable (locals say ATC means Any Time Cancel), although the service is improving gradually. There are flights between Zanzibar and Dar five times a week, taking about half an hour and costing $43 one way. A twice-weekly flight from Zanzibar to Kilimanjaro International (between Moshi and Arusha), via Dar, costs $123. The ATC office is on Vuga Road, near its junction with Creek Road. ATC is a partner in a new airline called Alliance (with the airlines of Uganda and South Africa) and Alliance planes may operate on this route in the future, when services are likely to improve.

Kenya Airways (PO Box 3840, tel: 32041/3)
Kenya Airways planes fly between Zanzibar, Mombasa and Nairobi, from where you connect with any other airline. Kenya Airways is a global partner of KLM and shares many of its routes. You can make reservations and buy tickets on this route, and to any other destination on the Kenya Airways network in their Zanzibar office, which is set back from the seafront road (Mizingani Road), near the Big Tree. There are flights between Zanzibar and Mombasa three times a week, taking about 35 minutes. The one-way fare to Mombasa is $40; to Nairobi $90.

Gulf Air (PO Box 3197, tel: 33379, 33221)
Gulf Air runs international flights between Zanzibar and Europe (and other destinations in Arabia and the Indian Ocean) going via Abu Dhabi or Muscat. There are three flights per week. The Gulf Air office is on the seafront road (Mizingani Road) near the Big Tree.

Oman Air
This company has an office near the Big Tree, in the same building as Kenya Airways, and flights from Oman to Zanzibar are due to commence in 1997.

Regional air companies
Several small private air companies operate in Kenya and Tanzania, mostly serving tourist centres. Some have expanded their networks in the last few years to include Zanzibar, which makes access considerably easier for visitors.

Coastal Travels
This company is based in Dar es Salaam (tel: 051 31216, mobile: 0811 325673) and also has an office at Zanzibar airport (tel: 33112). They operate regular flights between Dar, Zanzibar, Mafia Island, Selous and Ruaha. Between Dar and Zanzibar there is one flight each day in each direction. Fares are: Zanzibar–Dar $44, Zanzibar–Mafia $99, Zanzibar–Selous $110.

Eagle Aviation
This is a Kenya-based company, with regular flights between Zanzibar and Mombasa for around $55 a seat. The service operates on the days when Kenya Airways doesn't. From Mombasa you can connect on Eagle services to Nairobi or several of Kenya's national parks. Eagle's main Zanzibar representative is Skyland Travel (tel: 32652, 31744), but some other agents also sell their flights.

Precision Air Flight Services
This charter company is based in Arusha, with a modern fleet and daily flights between Zanzibar and Dar or Kilimanjaro International Airport (with road connections to Arusha), plus many other destinations all over East Africa. In Zanzibar Town, Precision's agents are Air Zanzibar (listed under *Air charter companies* below), and Maha Tours (listed in the *Tour Companies* section, page 110). Some sample fares from Zanzibar to: Dar $55; Kilimanjaro International $146; Arusha $165.

Air charter companies
If time is short, you might consider flying from Zanzibar Town to Pemba Island or Mafia Island. Or you might decide to get to Zanzibar by air from Dar es Salaam, Mombasa or elsewhere on the mainland. It is also possible to fly direct from Zanzibar to national parks on mainland Tanzania such as Sadaani, Selous and Ruaha, or even direct to the northern parks such as Serengeti and Kilimanjaro.

If you are in a small group, you can charter your own plane. However, lone travellers can still fly by charter aircraft, as most companies also run regular 'coach services' where seats are sold on a single basis, or sell spare seats on a plane which somebody else has chartered. Planes sometimes fly one way empty and seats may be available then too.

Air Zanzibar (PO Box 1784, tel: 32512, 33615, 33767, fax: 33098, email: air@zanzibar.net)
This is one of the largest charter companies on the island, with various aircraft of different sizes available for private charter to any destination in eastern Africa, including Pemba, Dar, Nairobi, Mombasa, Mafia Island, Arusha and the national parks in Kenya or mainland Tanzania. Rates vary according to the aircraft and destination, so you should contact the company direct for details; but as an example, a five-seater plane between Zanzibar and Dar costs $240 to $280, a seven-seater is around $320 and a nine-seater around $350. Five-seaters to Pemba start at $380, Mombasa $750. All prices attract an extra 10% sales tax.

On charter flights, spare seats on the plane may be sold to the public. For example, Zanzibar to Dar is $44 a seat. Air Zanzibar runs a thrice-weekly scheduled service between Zanzibar and Dar, with one-way fares also $44. Air Zanzibar also offers flight, safari and accommodation packages to the Selous National Park direct from Zanzibar, charging $450 for one night and $610 for two nights.

The company advertises flights and spare seats on posters in hotels and tour companies around town, or you can call in at their main office on the airport road or their sales office on Kenyatta Road, near the old post office, to see what is available.

ZanAir (PO Box 2113, tel: 33768, 32993, tel/fax: 33670, mobile: 0811 321061)
Also one of the largest air charter companies in Zanzibar, with an office in the Malindi area, opposite Malindi Sports Club, near the Ciné Afrique. They deal in charter flights only, but spare seats are often sold to individuals when available. Rates vary according to the aircraft and destination, so you should contact the company direct for details; but as an example, a five-seater between Zanzibar and Dar is $230, Zanzibar–Mombasa $690, Zanzibar–Pemba $360. (A 10% sales tax is added to all these charter fares.)

Travel agents
United Travel Agency (PO Box 122, tel: 32258, 30874, fax: 32391)
This is one of the few specialist airline agents in Zanzibar, dealing mainly in international flights rather than local business. They represent all airlines (from Zanzibar and from Dar es Salaam) and are the only IATA approved agent in Zanzibar. Their office is on Gizenga Street behind the Fort.

Shipping companies
Several shipping companies operate passenger and vehicle ferries between Zanzibar, Pemba, Dar es Salaam and other points on the mainland. The services used by most tourists are operated by the following companies, which all have their offices in the new port area in Zanzibar Town. Schedules and prices are usually chalked up on a board outside each office. You can reserve a seat in advance, or buy a ticket on the day.

Africa Shipping Corporation (tel: 32312, 33031/2)
This company operates the *Flying Horse*, a fast catamaran which runs once daily in each direction between Zanzibar and Dar, taking about three hours. All seats cost $30 by day, $15 by night. If you take the night boat to Dar, it docks in Dar at midnight but you can sleep on board until customs open at around 06.00 – mattresses are provided. There are plans for *Flying Horse* to start services to Mombasa some time in the future. See also *Chapter Three*, page 45.

Azam Marine Ltd (tel: 31262, 33046)
This company operates the *Muungano* ferry-boat between Zanzibar and Dar, which goes daily, takes about four hours and costs $30 for all seats. They also operate the *Serengeti* ferry-boat between Zanzibar and Pemba, which goes three times a week in each direction and also costs $30. A similar boat, called the *Condor*, has the same service for the same price.

Mega Speed Liners (mobile: 0811 326413)
This new efficient company runs a fast ship called the *Talieh* twice daily between Zanzibar and Dar, charging $30 for the 105-minute journey. They also run the *Sepideh* which storms up and down between Dar es Salaam, Zanzibar and Mombasa, with plans to extend the service to Lamu. The ship goes between Dar es Salaam and Zanzibar once a day, with a service to Pemba five times weekly in each direction, plus a twice-weekly service to Mombasa and Tanga. For travellers crossing between Zanzibar and Kenya, this service is ideal: the Zanzibar-Mombasa fare is $45 one way. Between Zanzibar and Pemba or Dar is $30. Mega Speed have a ticket office at the port, and their main office above Kenya Airways, near the Big Tree. In Dar or Mombasa you can buy their tickets from most travel agents.

Sea Express Ltd (tel: 33013, 33002)
A fleet of large hydrofoils, all called *Sea Express*, runs five times daily in each direction between Zanzibar and Dar, taking about 70 minutes. First-class seating costs $35, second-class seating $30. Sea Express plan to start services to Mombasa sometime in the future.

Zanzibar Shipping Corporation (PO Box 80, tel: 31300/4)
This is the state-owned line, operating the *Mapinduzi* and the *Maendeleo* between Zanzibar, Pemba and Dar. These are primarily cargo ships with deck space, and the service is used by local people as it is cheap: about $3 for Zanzibar to Dar. Some travellers on a tight budget also use it as tickets can be paid for with TSh; however the service is irregular and unreliable. The company's office is in the Mambo Msiige Building in the Shangani part of Zanzibar Town, but you can also get information and tickets from an office at the Marine Studies Institute, opposite the Old Dispensary. A noticeboard outside the office shows details of the next departures and arrivals.

Adecon Marine
This company operates the *Canadian Spirit* – a large cargo ferry which runs between Mtwara and Dar once a week, via Mafia Island and Zanzibar. Deck space for passengers reportedly is cheap, and there is also more comfortable first- and second-class accommodation, but the timetable is difficult to pin down. It's only worth persevering with this if you want to reach Mafia or the far south of Tanzania without flying.

Most of the tour companies listed below in this chapter can also help you with boat tickets. This can often save time and hassle, and usually does not cost you any more money.

Travel by dhow

Non-Tanzanians are not allowed to travel by dhow in any direction between Dar and Zanzibar (see page 47), although a few travellers do find dhow captains willing to take them on board for the Zanzibar-to-Dar run. Travel by dhow is permitted for tourists, however, between Zanzibar and Pemba or Mombasa, or between Pemba and Tanga or Mombasa. Most of these boats are motorised, but you may find a few still travelling under sail.

Dhows between Zanzibar and Dar go most days, and between Zanzibar and Pemba or Mombasa once or twice weekly, but timings are irregular and prices are variable (although apparently not negotiable). Journeys between Zanzibar and Mombasa are supposed to take about 12 hours, but can take more than two days, and cost about $10 to $15, payable in TSh. It may appear to be a romantic way to travel, but dhow voyages are not for the faint-hearted. See page 47 for more details. If you still want to travel this way, the agent for dhows out of Zanzibar can usually be found at the Malindi Sports Club: a white house on Malawi Road, almost opposite the Police Station.

Details on dhows out of Pemba are given in *Chapter Seven*.

TOUR COMPANIES

The companies listed in this section mainly organise tours within Zanzibar. The most popular are boat excursions to Prison Island and trips around the plantations (generally called 'spice tours'). Most companies also arrange tours to the Jozani Forest Reserve, and visits to old palaces and other ruins in the Zanzibar Town area or elsewhere on the island. You can usually arrange transport to the beaches on the East Coast and other parts of Zanzibar with a tour company, and most can also make hotel and ship reservations, flight bookings, car hire arrangements, and so on.

Tour prices are usually quoted in US dollars (although they can be paid for in other currencies), and tend to vary considerably between the different companies, but some standard examples for groups of between four and nine people are: Prison Island Tour $15 per person; City Tour $20; Spice Tour $35; Jozani Forest Tour $30; East Coast Tour $45; Dolphin Tour $45.

Prices for groups of one, two or three people are higher, but for groups of ten and over they drop further. For example, a full-day tour for four people may cost $45, but will be $100 if you go on your own, and only $35 per person for ten or more. If you've got the time to shop around, you will almost certainly find cheaper deals than this, especially during quiet times: in the low season groups of ten can get spice tours for $10 each. Note, however, that price generally reflects the quality of service, and you should be aware of cut-price operations which may offer sub-standard trips.

All tour companies have to be licensed by the Government of Zanzibar and, if you have a reason to be dissatisfied, you can complain to the Ministry of Tourism who may take action against the company on your behalf, although in reality there's little control. It is therefore worth comparing a few tour companies before finally arranging your tour. Your best source of recommendations (good or bad) is always other tourists and travellers, so talk to some of them if you can before signing up for anything.

Also, beware of completely bogus tour outfits. We heard of a group of travellers who arranged things with a private operator, and were then attacked and robbed when their minibus was on a remote stretch of road. The whole thing appeared to be a scam set up between the driver and the robbers.

Most of the companies can arrange things on the spot (or with a day's notice), but you can also make prior arrangements by phoning, faxing or emailing in advance (see box below). Alternatively, you could try writing. Include the PO Box number in the address and allow between three and five weeks for a reply.

Tour companies (all based in Zanzibar Town) that have been recommended by readers in the past include the following (listed alphabetically):

Chemah Brothers Tours & Safaris (PO Box 1865, tel/fax: 33385, mobile: 0812 750158)
A long-established and well-respected company, arranging good quality spice tours, city tours, dolphin tours, island tours and beach tours, plus trips to Pemba. They also arrange self-catering accommodation and make reservations for beach bungalows. Other services include flight and boat bookings, car hire and the hosting and handling of cruise ships.

Dolphin Tours (PO Box 138, tel: 33386)
This company has an office in the Mkunazini area, near the UMCA Cathedral, and offers spice tours, boat trips and all the usual services.

Equator Tours (PO Box 2096, tel: 33799, fax: 33882)
With an office on Soko Muhogo Street, this company claims to offer 'eco-tours', although most seem to be the standard selection of trips to Jozani Forest, Ras Nungwi and Kizimkazi, or city and spice tours.

Fisherman Tours (PO Box 3537, tel/fax: 33060, fax: 33762, mobile: 0811 321441, 0812 750113, email: fisherman@costech.gn.apc.org)
This well-established and experienced company has efficient staff, and caters for overseas incentive and tour groups, as well as individuals, offering a total guided and escorted service. They organise wildlife safaris on mainland Tanzania, as well as the usual tours around Zanzibar, plus car hire, hotel bookings, ground transfers and so on. They also have credit card facilities. The office is on Vuga Road, near Air Tanzania.

Jasfa Tours (PO Box 4203, tel: 30468)
A well-established company, with an office near the Africa House Hotel. They can arrange car hire and diving excursions, plus a wide range of excursions such as spice tours and boat trips. They can also arrange guides (English-, French-, Spanish- or Arabic-speaking) for tours of the Stone Town or any of the ruins elsewhere on Zanzibar Island.

Maha Travel (tel: 30029, fax: 30016)
With offices on Vuga Road, this efficient company deals mainly in flights (they are agents for Precision Air), but also offers the standard range of tours around the island.

TELEPHONING ZANZIBAR

If you want to phone or fax anywhere in Zanzibar (Zanzibar Island and Pemba) from elsewhere in Tanzania, Kenya or Uganda the area code is 054. For calls from other countries, the international code for Tanzania is +255, then 54 for Zanzibar.

GUIDES AROUND ZANZIBAR STONE TOWN

Local youths in Zanzibar Town may offer to be your guide for the day, but guides are unnecessary as the Stone Town is not very large, and getting seriously lost is unlikely. (If you don't know where you are, keep walking – you'll come out on to Creek Road or one of the streets alongside the sea eventually.) In fact, for many visitors getting lost in the labyrinth of narrow streets and alleys is all part of the fun.

However, if your time is limited, or you want to find some specific sites of interest, you may want to hire a guide to take you from place to place. Rather than hiring the services of a *papaasi* (see the box on *Papaasi* in the *Hotels* section of this chapter), who will be more interested in souvenir shops and commissions, ask your hotel or a reputable tour company to put you in touch with someone. We have heard from readers who employed a local schoolboy, who was also very happy to practise his English, and this seems an excellent idea. About $3 (in TSh) for a day's work would be a suitable fee.

If you are seriously interested in the history of Zanzibar, a local artist and historian, John da Silva, is occasionally available for private guided tours around Stone Town. John knows the history of every public building and every house (and literally every balcony and door) in the town. His rates are $20 for a tour lasting two to three hours. Ask one of the reputable tour companies to put you in touch, or phone him direct on 32123.

Rainbow Tours & Travels (PO Box 2173, tel/fax: 33469, fax: 33701)
This enthusiastic company offers a wide range of services, including all-day or half-day spice tours, boat and island excursions, and tours around Zanzibar and Pemba islands. Rainbow also arrange tours for cruise-ship groups, and set up deep-sea game fishing trips and sailing excursions. Tours with a wildlife bias include trips to Jozani Forest to see monkeys and to Kizimkazi to see dolphins. They have an office on Gizenga Street and another on Soko Muhogo Street in the Vuga area.

Sama Tours (PO Box 2276, tel: 33543, fax: 33020, 33543,
email: step@www.intafrica.com)
This company has an office on Gizenga Street, behind the House of Wonders. As well as spice tours, boat trips and all the usual services, they arrange cultural tours, giving visitors an opportunity to meet local people. Guides speak English, French, German and Italian.

Sama also offer coconut tours, and a 'special' spice tour, organised by one of the owners, Salim Abdullah, who is very knowledgeable about the spices and fruits grown on Zanzibar. He knows their names in several languages (ideal for visitors who do not use English as a first language themselves). His tours include visits to ruined palaces among the plantations and a meal in a local village where different foods using all the spices can be sampled.

As well as being a knowledgeable naturalist, Salim is a bit of a small-screen star, having appeared on at least one British TV travel programme. Sama also have complete tailor-made tours, which include pick-ups from the port or airport (or from Dar), hotels, excursions, car hire etc. Prices depend on the length of the tour, the services required and the number in the group.

Sama's UK representative is Footloose Adventure Travel (tel: 01943 604030, fax: 604070).

Serene Tours (PO Box 326, tel/fax: 31816)
A new company, trying hard to please, with the usual range of tours (city, spice or Prison Island) and some good deals on car and moped hire. The office is on Kenyatta Street.

Suna Tours (PO Box 2213, tel: 33597)
This company represents several mid-range hotels on the East Coast and can assist with transport and tours to that side of the island. Suna also organise good-quality spice tours and trips to the islands. They have to be good: the company is run by the formidable Naila Majid Jiddawi, who also happens to be Director of Hotels and Tour Operations for the island's Chamber of Commerce, as well as being the unofficial 'first lady' of Zanzibar tourism. The office is in a small white building at the end of Forodhani Gardens, near the Arab Fort.

Sun N Fun Tours (PO Box 666, tel: 32132, 33018, 33065, fax: 30863)
In the same building as the Sea View Indian Restaurant, and with the same enthusiastic management, this company can set you up with anything. They run tours of Zanzibar Town and the island, provide transfer services to the airport or East Coast, and can help with general tourist information regarding Zanzibar and elsewhere in Africa. They can also assist with visas, car and bike hire, boat trips and flight tickets.

Zanea Tours (PO Box 620, tel: 30413)
An up-market company with very high-quality tours of the island, in good vehicles with knowledgeable local guides, aimed at more discerning visitors. They specialise in making hotel bookings and local tour arrangements in advance, especially for visitors who may have limited time.

ZanTours (PO Box 2560, tel/fax: 33116, mobile: 0811 335291)
This company confidently entered the tourist scene in 1997, with a smart office in the Malindi area, trained staff, a fleet of modern vehicles and an impressive range of tours, transfers, excursions and safaris. They are closely allied to ZanAir (listed under Charter air companies) and many tours utilise their fleet of planes.

Zanzibar Tourist Corporation (PO Box 216, tel: 32344)
ZTC is the state travel service, mainly handling transport, tours and reservations for groups from overseas. For individuals, ZTC offers the standard range of island tours and handles reservations for the ZTC bungalows on Chunguu Island and the East Coast. The main office is in Livingstone House, on the northeast side of town on the main road north towards Bububu. (The house itself was used by David Livingstone, the explorer, in 1866.) For general information, ZTC also has an office on Creek Road, where you can also buy postcards and maps.

As well as those tour companies listed above, there are many more to choose from in Zanzibar. In fact, the number is growing fast, although for every two that open another closes just as quickly. As with so many things, your best source of information is always other visitors; try to ask around for recommendations before booking anything. We have heard from readers who recommended:

Fazea Tours, just off Mkunazini Street near the Big Tree, PO Box 1224, tel/fax: 33326
Madeira Tours, opposite Baghani House Hotel, PO Box 251, tel/fax: 30406

Mazsons United Tours, Kenyatta St, near Mazsons Hotel, PO Box 1043, tel: 33694, fax: 33695
Mreh Tours, near the Chavda Hotel, PO Box 3769, tel: 33476, fax: 30344
Maya Tours, behind ZanAir, PO Box 3508, tel: 30986, fax: 33021
Stone Town Safaris, Mkunazini, near the Cathedral, PO Box 2209, tel: 30423, mobile: 0811 323491, fax: 33816
Zenith Tours, behind the Fort, PO Box 3643, tel/fax: 32320,33973.

Independent tour guides

It is possible to arrange a tour of the spice plantations, a boat trip to the islands or transport to the East Coast with an independent guide. Many double as taxi drivers. One driver, a Mr Mitu, has been doing these tours for many years and has been recommended by many visitors, although sometimes he subcontracts work to other drivers. These days he's so popular that instead of Mr Mitu in his taxi you might find yourself joining a large group touring the island in a fleet of minibuses. Either way, his tours leave from outside the Ciné Afrique every morning.

There are several taxi drivers who also organise their own spice tours., Most will undercut the tour companies (about $30 for the car seems average), although you may not get the same degree of information that you'd get with a specialist guide. We've also been told about a driver called Saleh Mreh, who organises 'eco' tours around the island, concentrating on environmental aspects.

You are almost certain to meet some of the local independent 'guides' (see box on the *Papaasi*, page 87) who tout for business outside hotels and restaurants, or along the streets of the Stone Town. For spice tours, *papaasi* prices are often cheaper than those offered by regular companies; but the tours are usually shorter and do not include a proper guide, which usually makes the whole thing pointless unless you are a fairly skilled botanist.

For boat trips to the island, it doesn't usually make much difference if you go with a *papaasi* or a regular company; although if you deal with the *papaasi* and things go wrong, it is very difficult to complain or get your money back.

For more details on local guides see the *Places to visit* section later in this chapter.

DIVING, SAILING AND FISHING COMPANIES

As an island archipelago in the Indian Ocean, Zanzibar has much to offer fishing and watersports enthusiasts. Even if you're only a casual angler or sailor, there's still plenty to attract. The activities take place on the coasts, the smaller islands or out at sea off-shore from Zanzibar and Pemba, but most companies organising fishing and watersports are based in Zanzibar Town, so are listed here.

Above: *Building a traditional dhow, Nungwi* (DE)

Below: *Old Dhow Harbour, Zanzibar Town* (CB)

THE NATURAL WORLD

Centre: *Kirk's red colobus monkey* (Colobus badius kirkii) (RG)

Clockwise from top left: *Coral trout* (Cephalopholis miniata); *lobster* (Panilurus ornatus); *juvenile green turtle* (Chelonia mydas); *Masked booby* (Sula dactylatra) *on Latham Island* (FM); *starfish* (Pentaceraster mammillatus) (MR)

MARINE HABITATS

Left: *Exposed coral at low tide* (MR)

Right: *Mangroves* (MR)

Left: *Rice fields on the west coast* (CO)

Above right: *Turmeric* (CO)

Below right: *Nutmeg and mace* (CO)

Diving companies

The reefs around the islands of Zanzibar are reported to offer some of the best diving in the Indian Ocean, and in the last few years several dive centres have opened in Zanzibar Town to take advantage of these conditions. Prices for open-water dives vary slightly between the companies, but are around $40 for one dive, between $50 and $60 for two dives, and $80 to $90 for three dives. The dive centres also offer various training courses, ranging from an escorted beginner's 'fun-dive' for around $35, through a one- or two-day 'resort course' for $80 to $100, to an advanced four- to six-day course (with lectures, pool sessions and open-water dives) leading to an internationally recognised PADI qualification for around $300.

Generally, the dive centres in Zanzibar Town include hire of equipment in their rates, although you should check this, as some places charge extra or make a reduction if you bring your own. Reductions are also often available for groups of four or more, so if you're on your own it might be worth teaming up with some other people before arranging anything. Most of the dive centres also offer night dives, underwater photography courses, special training sessions, tank filling, snorkel trips, and so on. As with so many things on Zanzibar, the best thing to do is shop around on the spot (or in advance by writing/faxing) between the various dive centres.

There are several other dive centres based at coast hotels (listed in *Chapter Six*) including the Tamarind Hotel, Matemwe Bungalows, Ras Nungwi and Uroa Bay. Prices are similar to those companies in Zanzibar Town, although generally dive prices do not include equipment (this is hired separately). For more details see the hotels listed in *Chapter Six*.

Dive companies in Zanzibar Town include the following:

Indian Ocean Divers (PO Box 2370, tel/fax: 33860, mobile: 0811 323096)
Part of a South African-run operation with other bases on the East Coast of Africa, this branch is on the seafront road (Mizingani Road), near the Big Tree. They offer a range of dives and specialist courses.

Zanzibar Dive Centre–One Ocean (PO Box 608, tel/fax: 0811 323091, mobile: 0811 328206)
Based under the Africa House Hotel, this is the only PADI five-star centre on the island, open every day, with two dive trips per day, modern gear and keen staff. The owner informs us that rates are not negotiable: 'We know we're good, so we don't need to cut prices.'

Cat-Diving Ltd (PO Box 3203, tel/fax: 31040, mobile: 0812 781376)
This experienced and high-quality company's operations are based around the German-built 24-metre catamaran *Inula*, which runs one-day sailing and snorkelling trips for $45 per person. One dive, including equipment, costs $25 extra.

Cat-Diving also offer all-inclusive live-aboard trips to the waters around Pemba, starting at $490 per person for three days to $980 per person for seven days, including all accommodation and three dives per day. Drift dives are common. Only divers with some experience can take part (there's no provision for training beginners). The boat has compressors, tanks and two large inflatables. Some equipment is available for rent, although most clients have their own. Windsurfing is also available from the catamaran.

When not at sea, *Inula* is usually moored at Forodhani Gardens, and more details are available from the Café Sea View nearby.

Sailing companies

For a short taster, **Zanzibar Dive Centre** (details above) offer a classical dhow cruise most evenings from 17.30, with a minimum of two people, costing $20 per person including drinks. **Cat Diving** also offer day trips (details above). **Mtoni Marine Centre** (see page 97), based at Mtoni, 4km north of Zanzibar Town, also has a dhow and offers various sailing trips to smaller islands, plus diving and fishing excursions.

A company called **Adventures Afloat** uses traditional wooden dhows (fitted with engines), and offers a wide range of trips. Full-day excursions in the bays around Fumba at the southern end of Zanzibar Island, where dolphins are usually seen, cost $60 per person, including land transfers, good quality snorkelling equipment, instruction if required, lunch and soft drinks. A sunset cruise costs $50 including dinner; and a moonlight cruise $60 including a seafood barbecue on Bawe Island. (All prices rise by about 15% at the Christmas and New Year peak season.) Private charter is also available, for as many days as you like. Prices vary according to the length of the charter and the route. Diving trips can also be arranged. You can make enquiries and bookings direct to Adventures Afloat (tel: 0811 321066), or through the Zanzibar Dive Centre (listed above) or Mbweni Ruins Hotel (see page 96).

Fishing companies

The waters around Zanzibar and Pemba Islands are reckoned by experts to offer some of the best fishing in the world, especially the Pemba Channel or around Mafia Island, south of Zanzibar. Big game fish include barracuda, kingfish, sailfish, wahoo, dorado and blue marlin. Some of the diving and sailing centres listed above also organise fishing trips on request. **Adventures Afloat** (listed above) operate a full day of game fishing in the Zanzibar Channel, with good quality rods and reels provided, for $400. A half-day trip is $300.

Specialist operators include **East African Fishing Club** (PO Box 3870, tel/fax: 33001) which has a specially designed sportfishing catamaran, fully equipped with high-quality tackle. Novice and experienced anglers are welcomed. For details of trips and prices East Africa Fishing Club can be contacted direct, or through their representative at the Arab Fort. The **Zanzibar Fishing Club** can be contacted through Mtoni Marine Centre, see page 97.

Around the island, other fishing operators include **Chinook Sport Fishing** at Nungwi, and Uroa Bay Fishing Club at the Uroa Bay Village Resort, reckoned to be one of the best outfits in Zanzibar.

SHOPPING

Since the early 1990s many shops have opened up in Zanzibar Town to cater for the growing tourist numbers. Die-hard deal-hunters will be hard pushed to visit them all. A selection is listed here.

Gift shops

One of the best places to start is **The Gallery**, on Gizenga Street, behind the Fort. This shop has many rooms and sells carvings, paintings, jewellery, materials, postcards, antiques and real pieces of art. You can also buy local pickles and honey and even banana-flavoured bubble bath. It's also a bookshop with a very good selection of guidebooks and coffee-table books on Zanzibar and other parts of Africa, animal and bird field guides, maps, histories and general novels. The shop is run by local photographer Javed Jafferji; his own books (signed) are also for sale here.

On the same street are several other souvenir and gift shops, all with similar lines, but without The Gallery's sheer range. Sellers offer carvings and paintings from pavement stalls nearby. Also recommended is the **Zanzibar Curio Shop** on Hurumzi Street, near the Clove Hotel, which has a good stock of antiques dating from Omani and British colonial times. Other places with antiques include the nameless shop behind the House of Wonders, opposite Sama Tours. There are several more antique shops on the street between St Joseph's Cathedral and Soko Muhogo crossroads.

There are several spice and craft shops in the **Arab Fort** in Zanzibar Town. Also in the fort are a pleasant shady café, an art and dance studio and a theatre with regular plays and music or dance shows, so you can easily combine sightseeing, shopping, watching, eating and drinking!

KHANGAS AND KIKOIS

A *khanga*, the traditional coloured wrap worn by local women, makes an ideal souvenir. You can use it as a beach mat on the coast, a sheet to cover bare mattresses in cheap hotels, and then hang it on your wall when you get home. A *khanga* normally comes as two matching squares, each about 1m². Local women cut them into two parts; one half is worn as a wrap-over skirt and the other is worn as a head scarf. (A knot is usually tied in one corner and used for keeping money in.) Prices for a *khanga*, from the market or local cloth shop, start at about $3.

On Zanzibar, and elsewhere on the coast, men traditionally wear a *kikoi*, a wrap-around 'kilt' of woven cotton, usually striped, and usually thicker than a *khanga*. Once again, a *kikoi* also has many practical travel uses before you take it home to use as a seat cover. Prices start at $8.

If you want to combine African and Western clothing, you could even have a local tailor make up a shirt or a pair of baggy shorts from a *kikoi*. For more ideas see the excellent little book *101 Uses for a Khanga*, by David Bygott, available in Zanzibar bookshops.

Local craftwork can also be found in the **Orphanage Shop**, near the fort. The orphanage is a large building with the main seafront road (Mizingani Road) in a tunnel passing right through the middle of it. The shop is on the side nearest the sea. Pieces made by local artists and by the children themselves are sold here to raise money. The shop also sells fabric (or you can bring your own) and the in-house tailors can make clothes to your own design, ideal if you need another beach-shirt or pair of casual trousers.

The tailor at **Mnazi Boutique**, near the Kiponda Hotel, can also copy any shirt, skirt or trousers you like, from material you buy in the shop or elsewhere in town. Prices start at $8, and go up to $25 for a complicated

---

THE SHORTEST WAR IN HISTORY

Sultan Hamad died on August 25 1896 while the British Consul, Arthur Hardinge, was on leave in England. The acting British Consul, Basil Cave, recommended that Hamoud (Hamad's cousin) be appointed sultan, but when Cave and Sir Lloyd Mathews reached the palace of Beit el Sahel in Zanzibar Town they found the doors barred.

Khaled bin Barghash (another cousin of Hamoud) had arrived before them with about 60 armed men, entered the palace by climbing through a broken window, and been quickly joined by more than 2,000 supporters.

Khaled proclaimed himself sultan, and raised the red flag of Zanzibar on the palace roof. But Basil Cave refused to recognise his claim: British ships in the harbour landed guards of marines, which were posted at the British Consulate (where the British women sought refuge), the Customs House, and elsewhere around the town. Many foreigners gathered on the roof of the English Club, where they had a clear view of the harbour and the palace.

On the morning of August 26 the three British ships were reinforced by the timely arrival of two others, and the following day, at dawn, the British fleet under Rear-Admiral Harry Holdsworth Rawson delivered an ultimatum: Khaled was to surrender, disarm, evacuate the palace and be at the Customs House by 9.00am, or the British ships would open fire. At 8.00am Khaled sent an envoy to Cave, asking for a chance to discuss peace, but his request was refused.

The palace clock struck three (9.00am British time) and at 9.02am the bombardment started. In half an hour Beit el Sahel and the adjoining palace of Beit el Hukm were badly damaged. The lighthouse outside the palace was in flames and the nearby House of Wonders was also hit a few times. Many of Khaled's supporters had fled, leaving 500 dead and wounded laying about the palace grounds.

At 9.40am Khaled surrendered. He lowered the flag, the firing ceased and the war was over. This dispute over the succession is listed in *The Guinness Book of Records* as the shortest war in history.

Khaled escaped through the narrow streets and fled to the German Consulate, where he was given asylum. As the steps of the consulate led on to the beach, Khaled was able to board the German warship *Seeadler* without risking arrest. Khaled was taken to Dar es Salaam where he lived in exile. He died in Mombasa in 1927, aged 53.

This event is covered in detail by the booklet *Zanzibar and the Shortest War in History*, listed in *Further Reading* on page 213.

dress. If you prefer traditional African clothing, consider a *khanga* or a *kikoi* (see box on page 117).

Tabasam Shop, near the Africa House Hotel, sells a selection of clothes and fabrics, plus carvings and paintings. Nearby, under the Africa House and next to the Dive Centre, is **Saifa Shop**, where Omi the tailor makes ethno-stylish clothes and bags, and sells hand-printed T-shirts, sandals and jewellery.

More elaborate clothing and jewellery can be bought at the **African Heritage**, part of the famous Kenyan chain, in a small 'mall' called Galleromer near the Tembo Hotel on Kenyatta Road. In the same building is **Kazuri Beads** and **Tinga Tinga Clothing** – other Kenyan off-shoots.

If you would like something simple and portable to remember Zanzibar by, some of the spices which make the islands famous can be bought from local shops and from the market. A wide selection, plus other local craft items aimed more specifically at tourists, is available from the **House of Spices** between the market and Kiponda Street.

THE DANGERS OF LEMON GRASS OIL

The exotic herbs and spices of Zanzibar can be dangerous. We heard from a traveller who sent us the following warning:

'In Zanzibar I bought some lemon grass oil, which smelt *wonderful*. I decided to spoil myself and applied a liberal coating to my face. Having rubbed it all in well it started to burn. It was worse than the very very hottest curry in your mouth. My skin went red and I thought blisters would appear, it hurt so much. Cold water and other plain oils helped after about 20 minutes, but any longer and I would have gone to hospital. Only later did I find a tiny slip of paper in the bottom of the packet which warned of skin and eye irritation. I strongly urge all other spice enthusiasts not to exceed the recommended dose!'

Art galleries

Shops with paintings for sale include **Zanzibar Roots**, next to Eagle Bureau de Change, on the corner of New Mkunazini and Kajificheni Streets, and **Suvaka** next to Sama Tours on Gizenga Street, behind the House of Wonders. Both display paintings and batiks by various local artists. Other places for paintings and batiks include **Paul's Gallery** above St Monica's Hostel near the Anglican Cathedral (where you can also buy hand-painted T-shirts), and the **Tower Workshop** at the Old Fort.

Tinga Tinga is a distinctive contemporary East African painting style which originated in Zanzibar. Examples of this brightly coloured, highly stylised art are sold in most of the gift shops mentioned above. There are also some dedicated Tinga Tinga shops; the most notable is Saidi's **Tinga Tinga Workshop** near St Joseph's Cathedral.

LOCAL SERVICES

Tourist information

The Zanzibar Tourist Corporation (ZTC) is the state travel service. It has offices in Livingstone House, on the northeast side of town, on the main road towards Bububu, where you can make reservations for the ZTC bungalows on the East Coast. You can also make general tourist enquiries, but there's little in the way of information here. You'll get more joy at the ZTC office on Creek Road, where the staff are a bit more helpful. You can also buy postcards and maps.

For general information, some tour companies are happy to help, even if you don't end up buying a tour from them. Try Sun N Fun Tours, listed on page 113.

Also worth visiting is the information desk at the Arab Fort, which has details of local musical, cultural and sporting events and some tour company leaflets to give away. For less formalised (but equally useful) information, check the noticeboard at the open-air café-restaurant inside the Fort, or the noticeboard near the bar at the Africa House Hotel (see page 94).

Banks and money-changing

Many of Zanzibar's currency regulations that restricted visitors in the past have been lifted in the last few years. At the time of writing (1997), currency declaration forms are not used, and it is no longer necessary to change a certain amount of money for each day of your visit. Basically, you only have to change as much as you need. (For more information see *Money* in *Chapter Three*.)

For changing money, you can go to a bank or a change bureau. Both offer tourists 'free market rates', which means the rates are not artificially fixed (and therefore usually good for tourists), but change bureaux tend to have a faster service and slightly better rates. Banks and bureaux accept most foreign currencies, but staff are most familiar with US dollars, and these get relatively higher rates than other hard currencies. There's usually some difference in the exchange rates offered between the various banks and bureaux, and for cash or travellers cheques: you may want to shop around if you've got the time and inclination.

Banks changing money are the People's Bank of Zanzibar, near the Fort, or the Greenland Bank on the Malindi end of Creek Road. Do not change money at the Commercial Bank of Zanzibar; this is mainly for business transactions, and the rates are bad. Change bureaux include the Shangani Bureau de Change (Kenyatta Road), Eagle Bureau de Change (Mkunazini) and Malindi Bureau de Change near the Port Gates. Most large hotels will also change money (although some deal only with their own guests). One of the best is the bureau at the Hotel International (Ukatani area), which welcomes everyone and usually offers good rates. There are also change bureaux at the port and airport.

HENRY MORTON STANLEY

The man known to the world as Henry Morton Stanley was born John Rowland on January 29 1841 at Denbigh in Wales. He spent nine years in a workhouse and two years as a farmhand, before joining a ship from Liverpool to New Orleans, which he reached in 1858. In New Orleans he was adopted by his employer, a cotton merchant, from whom he took his new name, Henry Stanley. 'Morton' was added later.

By 1869 Stanley was a correspondent for *The New York Herald*. The manager of the newspaper, James Gordon Bennett, despatched him to Africa with orders to cover the inauguration of the Suez Canal, and then find Livingstone if he were alive, or bring back his bones if he were dead.

Stanley arrived in Zanzibar on January 6 1871. He borrowed a top hat from the American Consul, John Francis Webb, and went to visit Sultan Barghash who gave him letters of recommendation to show his agents in the interior. Stanley set off from Zanzibar in March that year, just two days before the start of the rainy season. His provisions included American cloth, beads of glass, coral and china for trading, plus two silver goblets and a bottle of champagne for the day he met Livingstone.

Stanley finally met Livingstone at Ujiji on November 10 1871 (see box, page 122), and returned to Zanzibar on May 7 1872, before travelling to London.

Stanley gave up journalism to return to Africa as an explorer. He reached Zanzibar again in September 1874, and left for the mainland in November the same year. On this expedition he rounded the southern shore of Lake Victoria, went through Buganda (now Uganda), and followed the Congo River to the Atlantic Ocean, which he reached on August 12 1877, thus crossing Africa in 999 days.

From 1879 to 1884, Stanley returned to the Congo for King Leopold II of Belgium. He established and governed the Congo Free State, and the town of Stanleyville (now Kisangani) was named after him.

After another expedition from 1887 to 1889, Stanley returned to Britain a celebrity. He was married in Westminster Abbey in 1890, elected to Parliament as a Liberal Unionist for North Lambeth in 1895, and knighted in 1899. He died in London on May 10 1904.

It is worth trying not to change more than you need into TSh, as it can sometimes be difficult changing this back into hard currency. The bank often just refuses to do it (or will only accept money that you have already exchanged at the People's Bank of Zanzibar, not money changed at banks on the Tanzanian mainland), and private change bureaux may offer poor rates or not have foreign currency available.

When calculating the amount of money you need to change into TSh, remember that many items, such as hotels, car hire and air tickets, are payable in hard currency only (usually US dollars). Many other items, such as bike hire, boat trips and souvenirs, can also be paid for with US dollars and, if you know the various exchange rates, you can sometimes get a better bargain.

Drawing cash on a credit card is either impossible or very expensive; see the notes on credit and debit cards on page 53. One major exception to this

DAVID LIVINGSTONE

David Livingstone was born on March 19 1813 in the village of Blantyre, near Glasgow, in Scotland. In 1841 he went to South Africa as a missionary doctor. There he married Mary Moffat, a missionary's daughter. On his early expeditions in southern Africa he crossed the Kalahari Desert and, in November 1855, became the first European to see *Mosi oa Tunya* ('the smoke that thunders') which he renamed the Victoria Falls. Livingstone made his fourth major expedition from 1858 to 1864 in the area around the Lower Zambezi and Lake Nyasa (present-day Lake Malawi). He was accompanied by Dr John Kirk, another Scot, who joined the expedition as medical officer and naturalist. After the expedition, in April 1864, Livingstone spent a week in Zanzibar before travelling back to Britain.

Livingstone returned to Zanzibar in January 1866. He had been asked by the Royal Geographical Society to explore the country between Lake Nyasa and Lake Tanganyika and solve the dispute over the location of the source of the Nile. He left for the mainland on March 19 1866, and travelled around the southern end of Lake Nyasa.

After several years of exploring the region, during which time little news of his travels had reached the outside world, Livingstone met with the Welsh-born American journalist Henry Stanley at Ujiji on Lake Tanganyika on November 10 1871. According to Stanley's own description of the meeting, Stanley took off his hat, held out his hand, and said: 'Doctor Livingstone, I presume?'. When Livingstone answered 'Yes', Stanley continued with 'I thank God that I have been permitted to see you', to which Livingstone gravely replied 'I feel thankful that I am here to welcome you'.

Livingstone was suffering from terrible foot ulcers, fever and dysentery, and had only a few days' supply of cotton with which to buy food. But two weeks later his strength had returned sufficiently to set out on a small expedition with Stanley. They explored the northern shores of Lake Tanganyika, establishing that the River Ruzizi flowed into (not out of) the lake. Livingstone and Stanley left Ujiji on December 27 1871 and reached Kazeh, half way to the coast, in February the following year. Livingstone was in good health, so Stanley continued on alone and arrived in Zanzibar in May 1872.

Livingstone stayed at Kazeh until August 1872, then set out on a short expedition around the southern shores of Lake Tanganyika. He was still looking for the source of the Nile when he became ill again with dysentery. He died at the village of Chitambo, a few miles south of Lake Bangweulu, in present day Zambia on May 2 1873. Two of his loyal companions, called Susi and Chumah, removed his heart and buried it under a tree at the spot where he died. They dried his body in the sun for two weeks, then carried it to Zanzibar, wrapped in bark and cloth, where it was identified by a broken bone in the left arm, once crushed in the jaws of a lion. Livingstone's body rested at the British Consulate before being taken to London for burial. Stanley and Kirk were among the pall bearers at his funeral in Westminster Abbey on April 18 1874.

rule is Mtoni Marine Centre (listed on page 97). As the official assistance agent for Visa International, they seem to be able to give cash on a card with the minimum of fuss and expense.

Post

Zanzibar Town's main post office (GPO) is a large building in the new part of town on the road towards the stadium. It is open from 08.00 to 16.30 every day, except Sunday when it closes at 12.30. If you are receiving letters via the Poste Restante service, they will be sent here. For everything else you can use the old post office on Kenyatta Road, in the Shangani area. The old post office closes at 12.30 on Saturday and is closed all day Sunday.

Letters to destinations inside Tanzania cost about $0.20, while postcards to countries outside Africa are about $0.75 (slightly more for letters). The service is reliable, with letters taking about a week to ten days to reach their destinations. Some mail does get lost and there have been rare instances of post office staff steaming stamps off letters and selling them again. To avoid this, you can take your letters to the post office and have them postmarked in front of you. Most hotels offer this service and are reliable.

If you need to send anything fast and securely, DHL (the international courier service) has an office in the Malindi area, near the Port Gates. The service is run by Air Zanzibar (listed on page 108).

Telephone

You can telephone or send faxes from the international telephone counter at the old post office, which stays open until 20.00 Mondays to Saturdays, and until noon on Sundays. A phone call within Zanzibar is less than $1 for three minutes (minimum), and about $2 to mainland Tanzania. A call or fax to Europe costs about $25 (payable in TSh) for three minutes (minimum). The system is fairly efficient: you give your money and the number required to the operator at the desk who then dials the number for you. If you don't get through, you get your money back. A telegram costs about $1 per word, with a $25 minimum charge.

Phone cards were introduced in 1997. These can be bought at the telephone office at the old post office and used in the phones there. A 150-unit card gives you a 50-second international call for $7. A 1,000-unit card gives you seven minutes for $30.

Alternatively, for phone calls and faxes, try Zanzibar Global Communications (tel: 32664), a privately run bureau on Mkunazini Street (near the Flamingo Guest House). Alternatively, for telephone, fax, email, photo-copying or secretarial work go to Next Step Services (step@www.intafrica.com), on Gizenga Street behind the Clove Hotel.

Zanzibar has no area codes; within Zanzibar (Zanzibar Island and Pemba Island) you just dial the four- or five-digit number. If you need to phone a number in Zanzibar from elsewhere in Tanzania (or Kenya or Uganda) the area code is 054. Mobile phones have six-digit numbers and have a code of either 0811 or 0812. The international code for Tanzania is +255.

Hospitals, medical centres and pharmacies

The main public hospital for all of Zanzibar Island is at Mnazi Moja, on the south side of the Stone Town. (During the island's revolutionary heyday it was called the Lenin Hospital, but this title has now been quietly dropped.) Like many hospitals in developing countries, the staff are dedicated but the wards are badly under-funded and under-supplied, and not in good condition. More worrying is the pile of rubbish (including drip-feeds and needles) simply dumped on the beach behind the hospital.

Most tourists go to one of the private medical centres where staff speak English and the service is usually better. Of course, this has to be paid for, and costs around $50 per consultation, but all fees should be covered by your travel insurance. The medical centres also have pharmacies selling medicines and other supplies.

Most expatriates recommend the Zanzibar Medical and Diagnostic Centre (PO Box 1043, tel: 33113), just off Vuga Road, near the Majestic Cinema. This fully equipped centre is run to European standards and the staff speak several European languages. For emergencies, the after-hours number is 33062.

If your insurance covers only major medical problems, and you want to keep costs down for something minor, you could go to one of Zanzibar's other medical centres. One of the best seems to be the Fahaud Health Centre near St Joseph's Cathedral, where consultations cost $1 and a malaria blood test is $0.50. Should your test prove positive, they also sell Fansidar at $0.50 per tablet. Others clinics include: Afya Medical Hospital (tel: 31228) near the Zanzibar Hotel, and Mkunazini Hospital (tel: 30076) near the market.

In the case of real emergency, the nearest major hospital, fully staffed and equipped, is the Aga Khan Hospital in Mombasa. You may even need to fly there (by charter plane if necessary) if things are really serious, but this should be covered by your insurance.

If you need to buy medicines, Zanzibar Town has several pharmacies stocking drugs, mostly imported from Europe and India, and other items such as toiletries and tampons. Stocks are not always reliable, so if you know you're likely to need a specific drug during your visit, it's best to bring a sufficient supply with you. There is a pharmacy near the Musoma Bookshop, another on Creek Road near the market, and another in the Malindi area, behind Ciné Afrique. 'Over-the-counter' medicines, toiletries and tampons are also available at the 'container stores' (listed on page 105) on Creek Road.

Police

In case of emergency the main police station is in the Malindi area, on the north side of the Stone Town. Robberies can be reported here (travel insurance companies usually require you to prove you have notified the local police), but you should not expect any real action to be taken as the police are not particularly well-motivated.

Zanzibar also has a patrol of Tourist Police, although many people question their effectiveness. They are mostly seen driving around town in fancy new patrol cars, while touts continue to hassle tourists unimpeded.

Embassies and consuls

Countries with diplomatic representation on Zanzibar include China, Egypt and Oman. Likely to be of more use to tourists in case of emergency, the British Consular Correspondent is Mr Carl Salisbury at ZanAir (listed under Air Charter companies on page 108). The equivalent for visitors from the USA is the American Warden, Mr Emerson Skeens, at Emerson's House hotel (listed on page 91). The German Honorary Consul is Mr Meffat, with an office near the post office in the Stone Town. These people have limited powers and are unable to assist with technical matters such as visas or with simple problems such as illness or theft of belongings, although they will try to help in more serious cases such as *wrongful* arrest or imprisonment. Most countries have embassies or high commissions in Dar es Salaam, or in Nairobi.

If you do lose your passport in Zanzibar, you can get an Emergency Travel Document from the Ministry of the Interior. This will allow you to leave Zanzibar and either go directly back to your own country, or reach Dar where most countries have representation and you should be able to get a replacement.

Newspapers and books

Newspapers from Kenya and mainland Tanzania, some international magazines, and a reasonable range of books, are available from the Masumo Bookshop, off Creek Road, near the market, or from Tee-Dee's, near the junction of Kenyatta Road and Shangani Road, in the Shangani area. Most large hotels have gift shops which also sell local newspapers, international magazines and books.

One of the best bookshops in Zanzibar is The Gallery, on Gizenga Street behind the Fort. Although primarily a souvenir shop, they have a very good selection of guidebooks and coffee-table books on Zanzibar and other parts of Africa, animal and bird field guides, maps, histories and general novels.

Maps

A straightforward tourist map, *Zanzibar Town & Zanzibar Island,* is available from the Zanzibar Tourist Corporation offices, and from some bookshops and hotels in the town. It costs around $2. An excellent hand-drawn map of *Zanzibar Stone Town & Zanzibar Island* has been produced by local artist Giovanni, and is widely available. He has also produced *Zanzibar at Sea*, covering dive sites around the island, with particular detail on the Mnemba Atoll. These are part of a wider series of maps, including the national parks of mainland Tanzania.

Good-quality maps of Zanzibar and Pemba Islands, produced by the British Directorate of Overseas Surveys at scales of 1:50,000 and 1:10,000, are available from the Map Office in the Commission of Lands and Planning, part of the Ministry of Environment, near the People's Bank of Zanzibar and the fort. Maps cost about $2.

Film
Slide and print film for cameras is available in several hotel giftshops. The best place to buy film is Majestic Quick Foto, behind the Majestic Cinema, near the Flamingo Guest House. The shop is air-conditioned and films are recent. Slide film costs about $10, print film is cheaper.

Cinemas
The main cinema on Zanzibar is the Ciné Afrique on Malawi Road, in the

---

THE EAST AFRICAN SLAVE TRADE

From the earliest times, slaves were one of the many commodities exported from Africa to Arabia, Persia, India and beyond. In the 18th century the demand increased considerably, and Arab trading caravans from Zanzibar penetrated mainland Africa in the search for slaves. Various contemporary accounts describe all aspects of the trade, from the initial capture of the slaves to their sale in the infamous market of Zanzibar Town.

In the interior, the Arab traders would often take advantage of local rivalries and encourage powerful African tribes to capture their enemies and sell them into slavery. In this way, men, women and children were exchanged for beads, corn or lengths of cloth.

When the Arab traders had gathered enough slaves (maybe up to a thousand), they returned to the coast. Although the Koran forbade cruelty to slaves, this was ignored on the long journey to Zanzibar: the slaves were tied together in long lines, with heavy wooden yokes at the neck, or iron chains at the ankles, which remained in place day and night until they reached the coast. The trade in slaves was closely linked to the trade in ivory: the Arab traders also bought tusks from the Africans and some of the captured slaves may have had to carry these on their heads as they marched towards the coast. In addition, women often carried a child on their backs. If they became too weak to carry both child and ivory, the child would be killed or abandoned to make the ivory load easier to carry. Any slaves too weak to march were also killed and left behind for the vultures and hyenas. The passage of a slave caravan was marked by a long line of decaying corpses.

After many weeks or months of marching, the slave caravans reached the coast at ports such as Kilwa and Bagamoyo. Here, the slaves were loaded on to dhows, seldom more than 30m to 35m long, and carried to Zanzibar. Each dhow carried between 200 and 600 slaves, all crammed below decks on specially constructed bamboo shelves with about three feet of headroom. There was not enough room to sit, or kneel or squat, just a crippling combination of the three. Sometimes slaves were closely packed in open boats, their bodies exposed day and night to the sea and the rain. They were thirsty, hungry and seasick and many died of exhaustion. Meals consisted of a daily handful of rice and a cup of stagnant water.

Malindi area, near the Port Gates. There is also the Majestic Cinema on Vuga Road and the Empire Cinema near the market.

Television

Tanzanian television is available in Zanzibar, and the islands also have their own service, called ZTV. The news in English is broadcast at 20.30 on Saturdays. The ZTV headquarters is on Creek Road, near the Peace Memorial Museum. (These are the oldest TV studios in East Africa.)

Swahili lessons

If you would like to learn a few words (or even more than a few words) of the local language, the Taasisi Kiswahili Institute on Vuga Road (next to the Air Tanzania office) charges $80 for a week's course of four hours per day. Single lessons and longer courses, which include lodgings in the house of a teacher or local family, are also available.

Sanitation was non-existent and disease spread rapidly. When any illness was discovered infected slaves were simply thrown overboard.

By the time the slaves reached Zanzibar, they were suffering from starvation and the cramped conditions. It was sometimes a week after landing before they could straighten their legs. The slave traders paid customs duty on all slaves who landed, so any considered too weak to live were thrown overboard as the ship approached the port. Even so, many more slaves died in the Customs House or on the streets between the port and the market.

Before being put on sale, the slaves that did survive were cleaned so that they would fetch a better price. Men and boys had their skins oiled and were given a strip of material to put around their waist. Women and girls were draped in cloth, and sometimes even adorned with necklaces, earrings and bracelets. Generous layers of henna and kohl were smeared on to their foreheads and eyebrows.

The slaves were put on sale in the market in the late afternoon. They were arranged in lines, with the youngest and smallest at the front and the tallest at the rear, and paraded through the market by their owner, who would call out the selling prices. The owner would assure potential buyers that the slaves had no defects in speech or hearing, and that there was no disease present. Buyers would examine the arms, mouth, teeth and eyes of the slaves, and the slaves were often made to walk or run, to prove they were capable of work. Once their suitability had been established, they were sold to the highest bidder.

After being sold to a new owner, slaves were either put to work in the houses and plantations of Zanzibar or else transported again, on a much longer sea voyage, to Oman or elsewhere in the Indian Ocean. However, the slaves were relatively well treated when they arrived at their new homes. They were fed, housed and clothed, and given small plots of land, with time off to tend them. Young mothers were rarely separated from their children, and good slaves were often freed after a few years. Many took paid jobs, such as gardeners and farmers, for their previous masters: some even became leaders of slave caravans or masters of slave ships.

Source: The Lunatic Express, Charles Miller, Macmillan, New York, 1971

PLACES TO VISIT IN ZANZIBAR TOWN

In the old Stone Town of Zanzibar you can spend many idle hours and days just wandering through the fascinating labyrinth of narrow streets and alleyways. One writer has compared the town to a tropical forest with tall houses instead of trees rising up towards the sky, and overhanging balconies instead of foliage to block out the sun. Most visitors agree that the Stone Town is certainly an exotic and fascinating place.

The Stone Town was originally built on a peninsula which has probably been inhabited since the first people arrived on Zanzibar (although the creek that separated its eastern edge from the rest of the island has now been reclaimed). Ras Shangani, at the western tip of the peninsula, is thought to have been the site of a fishing village for many centuries, and at least one of Zanzibar's early Swahili rulers, the Mwinyi Mkuu, had a palace here. In the 16th century, Portuguese navigators built a church and trading station on the peninsula as it had a good harbour and was easy to defend. When the Omani Arabs began to settle on the island in the 18th century, they built a fort on the site of the church, and today's Stone Town grew up around the fort.

Most of the houses that can be seen today were built in the 19th century when Zanzibar was one of the most important trading centres in the Indian Ocean region. The coralline rock of Zanzibar Island was easy to quarry and made a good construction material, so that many of the houses were built in grand style with three or four storeys. Until this time most of the houses on Zanzibar had been much smaller, built with mangrove poles and palm thatch, so the fine white buildings of the Stone Town were even more exceptional.

Today, nearly all of these old houses are still inhabited, although many are in a very bad state of repair. The coralline rock was a good building material but it is also easily eroded. Crumbling masonry, along with dilapidated woodwork, is an all too familiar sight in the Stone Town.

However, since the end of the 1980s, several buildings in the Stone Town have been renovated. The Zanzibar government, with assistance from the United Nations Centre for Human Settlements (the Habitat Fund) and the Aga Khan Foundation, plans to preserve many more, eventually restoring the whole Stone Town to something like its original magnificence. The Stone Town Conservation and Development Authority has been established to co-ordinate this work.

During the 19th century many of the people living in the Stone Town were wealthy Arabs and Indians. Consequently, the houses were built in two main styles: the Arab style, with plain outer walls and a large front door, leading to an inner courtyard; and the Indian style, with a more open facade and large balconies decorated with ornate railings and balustrades, designed to catch sea breezes and dispel the humid atmosphere.

Many of the buildings have doors with elaborately carved frames and

panels, decorated with brass studs and heavy locks. The size of the door, and the intricacies of its decoration, was a sign of the family's wealth and status. The use of studs is thought to have originated in Persia or India, where they were used to prevent doors being battered down by war-elephants, although in Zanzibar they are purely for decorative purposes.

As you walk through the town, between the houses, you will come across mosques, churches and other public buildings, almost hidden in the maze. The Stone Town also has a few streets of shops, or bazaars. Some of the shops are very small, no more than a kiosk, with a few dusty food tins or a couple of jars of sweets on the shelf; others are larger, catering for locals and visitors, with a wider range of foods, books, fabrics, furniture or electrical goods. There are also antique and curio shops, and an increasing number of places selling locally produced arts and crafts, aimed specially at the growing tourist market.

When walking around the narrow streets, you should remember that Zanzibar Town is very much a real community, where real people live and work. It is not a museum piece created for tourists. You should show respect for local sensibilities (see the *Clothing* section) and should not enter any private house or courtyard unless expressly invited to do so. Mosques are not usually open to non-Muslim visitors. Taking photos of buildings is generally acceptable, but you should never take photos of people without their permission.

The market

The market is about halfway along Creek Road and a good place to visit even if you don't want to buy anything. The long market-hall is surrounded by traders selling from stalls, or with their wares simply spread out on the ground. It's a very vibrant place where everything, from fish and bread to sewing machines and second-hand car spares, is bought and sold. People bring their produce here from all over the island, and other people come to buy things they can't get in their own villages.

Towards the end of the 19th century, the town's marketplace was inside the old fort. Today's market-hall was built in 1904. Some very early photographs of the market displayed in the museum show that very little has changed since then.

On some evenings, a public auction is held in the street behind the market where furniture, household goods, old bikes, and all sorts of other junk is sold. It is very entertaining to watch, but make sure you don't bid for anything by mistake. Keep your hands still!

The Old Dhow Harbour

The old harbour is at the northern end of the Stone Town, beyond the Malindi Guesthouse. This is a busy place, with wooden dhows from Tanzania, Kenya and other parts of the coast unloading their goods onto the quayside. Between December and March it is also possible to see large ocean-going dhows from the Arabian Gulf.

This is also where the fishing boats come in, and there are several fish stalls in the street outside the harbour. Like ports all over the world, this area has a rough edge to it. Wandering around alone, or with an expensive camera over your shoulder, may be inviting trouble. The old harbour should also be avoided at night.

North of the Old Dhow Harbour, and beyond the Bwawani Plaza Hotel, is a shallow bay. The Zanzibar government plans to develop this area, as far as Mtoni, into a modern marina.

Livingstone House
On the northeast side of the town, this old building is now the main office of the Zanzibar Tourist Corporation (ZTC). It was built around 1860 for Sultan Majid (sultan from 1856 to 1870). At this time Zanzibar was used as a starting point by many of the European missionaries and pioneers who explored eastern and central Africa during the second half of the 19th century. David Livingstone, probably the most famous explorer of them all, stayed in this house before sailing to the mainland to begin his last expedition in 1866 (see box on page 122). Other explorers, such as Burton, Speke, Cameron and Stanley, also stayed here while preparing for their own expeditions. The house was later used by members of the island's Indian community, and in 1947 it was bought by the Colonial government for use as a scientific laboratory for research in clove diseases. After independence and the revolution it became the Zanzibar headquarters of the Tanzania Friendship Tourist Bureau, the forerunner of today's ZTC.

The Old Dispensary
Opposite the new port buildings, on Mizingani Road, this is a grand four-storey building with a set of particularly decorative balconies. It is also called the Ithnasheri Dispensary, and lettering at the top of the front wall reads 'Khoja Haji Nasser Nur Mohammed Charitable Dispensary'. The dispensary was originally built in the 1890s as a private house for a prominent Ismaili Indian merchant called Tharia Topan, who was a customs advisor to the sultans, and probably one of the wealthiest individuals on Zanzibar at the time. In 1899 he gave up the house to be used as a dispensary, also funding the medicine and other services. Topan also provided money (with the Aga Khan and Sultan Ali) for a non-denominational school which opened in Zanzibar in 1891. The dispensary fell into disrepair during the 1970s and 1980s, but was renovated in 1995 with funding from the Aga Khan Charitable Trust.

The Big Tree
Just west of the Old Dispensary, about 100m along Mizingani Road, is a large tree originally planted by Sultan Khalifa in 1911. Known simply as the Big Tree (or in Swahili as *Mtini* – the Place of the Tree), it has been a

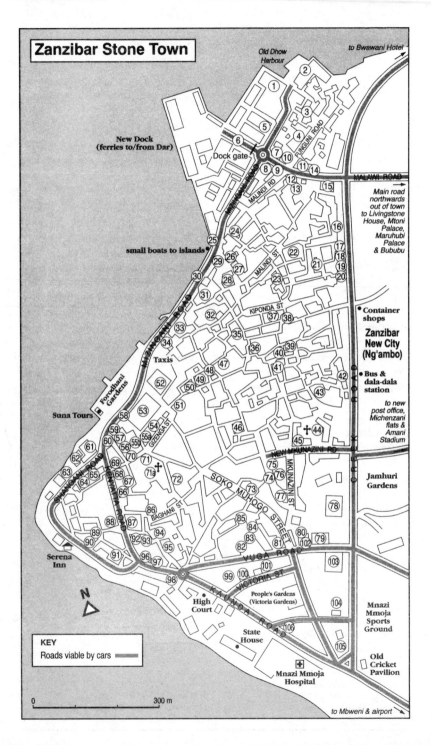

Zanzibar Stone Town

Old Dhow Harbour

to Bwawani Hotel

New Dock (ferries to/from Dar)

Dock gate

FUNGUNI ROAD

MALAWI ROAD

Main road northwards out of town to Livingstone House, Mtoni Palace, Maruhubi Palace & Bububu

small boats to islands

MALINDI RD

MALINDI ST

KIPONDA ST

Container shops

Zanzibar New City (Ng'ambo)

Bus & dala-dala station

to new post office, Michenzani flats & Amani Stadium

Taxis

Forodhani Gardens

Suna Tours

GIZENGA ST

NEW MKUNAZINI RD

MKUNAZINI ST

Jamhuri Gardens

MKANGANI ROAD

TARRADA ROAD

SOKO MUHOGO STREET

BAGHANI ST

SHANGANI ROAD

Serena Inn

VUGA ROAD

VICTORIA ST

People's Gardens (Victoria Gardens)

High Court

KAUNDA ROAD

State House

Mnazi Mmoja Sports Ground

Old Cricket Pavilion

Mnazi Mmoja Hospital

N

KEY
Roads viable by cars ▬▬▬

0   300 m

to Mbweni & airport

ZANZIBAR STONE TOWN MAP: KEY

1 Clove Distillery
2 Pagoda Chinese Restaurant
3 Malindi Guesthouse
4 Warere Guesthouse
5 Fish Market
6 Shipping company offices (most in this area)
7 Ciné Afrique
8 Malindi Restaurant
9 DHL office
10 Malindi Guesthouse Annex
11 Malindi Sports Club (dhow tickets)
12 Passing Show Restaurant
13 ZanAir
14 Petrol station
15 Malindi Police Station
16 Al Jabry Restaurant
17 People's Bank of Zanzibar
18 Zanzibar Tourist Corporation
19 Petrol station
20 Taxi rank
21 Karwan Serai Hotel
22 Narrow Street Hotel
23 Pyramid Guest House
24 Old Dispensary
25 Pychi's
26 Gulf Air
27 Ijumaa Mosque
28 Kenya Airways, Oman Air, Mega Speed Liners
29 Big Tree, The
30 Sea View Indian Restaurant
31 Old Custom House
32 Kiponda Hotel
33 Palace Museum
34 1001 Nights
35 Aga Khan Mosque
36 Spice Inn
37 Ithnasheri Mosque
38 Narrow Street Hotel Annex II
39 House of Spice
40 Hotel International
41 Emerson's House
42 Market
43 Masumo Bookshop
44 Anglican Cathedral/UMCA
45 St Monica's Hostel
46 Hamamni Baths
47 Emerson's and Green Hotel
48 Bottoms Up Bar
49 Clove Hotel
50 Zanzibar Curio Shop
51 Sama Tours
52 House of Wonders
53 Arab Fort
54 Gallery, The
55a People's Bank of Zanzibar (main building)
55b People's Bank of Zanzibar (foreign exchange)
56 Coco de Mer Hotel
57 Karibu Inn
58 Orphanage
59 Le Bistrot
60 National Bank of Commerce
61 Old British Consulate
62 Tembo Hotel
63 Starehe Club
64 Fisherman Restaurant
65 Le Pecheur Bar
66 Air Zanzibar
67 Blue Ocean Hotel
68 Post office
69 Luna Mare Restaurant
70 Luis Yoghurt Shop
71 Fahaud Medical Centre
71a St Joseph's Catholic Cathedral
72 Chit Chit Restaurant
73 Equator Tours
74 Green Garden Restaurant
75 Zanzibar Roots Gallery
76 Jambo Guesthouse
77 Flamingo Hotel
78 Haile Selassie School
79 Kiswahili Institute
80 Air Tanzania
81 Fisherman Tours, Maha Tours
82 Florida Guesthouse
83 Culture Music Club
84 Haven Hotel
85 Manch Lodge
86 Chavda Hotel
87 Sunrise Restaurant and Pub
88 Mazson's Hotel
89 Tippu Tip's House
90 Jasfa Tours
91 Africa House Hotel
92 Dhow Palace Hotel
93 Baghani House Hotel
94 Zanzibar Hotel
95 Afya Medical Centre
96 Camlur's Restaurant
97 Maharaja Restaurant
98 Chemah Brothers Tours
99 Two Tables Restaurant
100 Bar Baraza
101 Victoria Guesthouse
102 Majestic Cinema
103 Ben Bella School
104 Peace Memorial Museum Annex
105 Peace Memorial Museum
106 Zanzibar Milestone

ISLAM

Most of the people in Zanzibar are Muslims, followers of the Islamic faith. Islam was founded by the Prophet Mohammed, who was born around AD570 in Arabia. He received messages from God during solitary vigils on Mount Hira, outside his home town of Mecca. When driven out of Mecca by his enemies, he migrated to Medina. Here, at the age of about 53, he started to convert the world to Islam. Mohammed died in AD632.

By the early 8th century Arab Muslims had conquered all of northern Africa, and by AD1100 Islam had spread along the East Africa coast from Arabia and the Horn of Africa down to Sofala, in present-day Mozambique.

The five main tenets of Islam are prayer (five times a day), testimony of the faith, fasting (the period of *Ramadan*), alms giving, and the pilgrimage to Mecca (the *Haj*).

The Muslim calendar dates from the *Hejera*, the flight of Mohammed from Mecca to Medina, which corresponds to July 16 AD622 in the Christian calendar. The Muslim year consists of twelve lunar months of 29 or 30 days each, making 354 days. Eleven times in every cycle of 30 years a day is added to the year. This means Muslim festivals fall 11 or 12 days earlier every year, according to the Western calendar.

major landmark for many years. It can be seen on numerous old photos and etchings of Zanzibar Town viewed from the sea, and it is still clearly visible on the seafront from ships approaching the port. Today, traditional dhow-builders use the tree as a shady 'roof' for their open-air workshop.

Mosques

Zanzibar Town has many mosques. The oldest is Malindi Mosque, a small inconspicuous building near the port, with a minaret which is thought to be several hundred years old. Three of the larger mosques are also in the northern part of the Stone Town: the Ijumaa Mosque (Sunni); the Ithnasheri Mosque (Shia); and the Aga Khan Mosque (Ismaili). These were all built in the 19th century.

Compared to the large mosques of other Islamic cities, often decorated with domes and tall minarets, the mosques of Zanzibar are relatively plain and unpretentious. However, in 1994 the Ijumaa Mosque (near the Big Tree) was completely renovated in a modern Arabesque style, and the other large mosques may follow this trend. (Ijumaa simply means Friday, the Muslim holy day, and is the term given to any large mosque.)

Non-Muslims are not normally allowed to enter any mosque in Zanzibar Town, although, if you have a genuine interest, a good local guide might be able to speak to the mosque's elders on your behalf and arrange an invitation. Men will find this easier than women. There are usually no restrictions on non-Muslims (men or women) visiting the area around a mosque, although photos of local people praying or simply congregating should not be taken without permission.

The Old Customs House

On Mizingani Road (the main seafront), overlooking the sea, this large building has a plain façade and is fairly featureless, apart from its portico of green metal pillars and a beautiful set of carved wooden doors. These have been decorated in the Arab style with fish, lotus and anchor chain motifs. Hamoud, grandson of Sultan Said, was proclaimed sultan here in 1896.

In 1995, the Customs House was renovated with funds provided by Unesco, the United Nations cultural organisation, and is due to be opened as a conservation training school. (The equally large building next door to the Customs House was formerly Le Grand Hotel and then became a private house before being abandoned. In 1995 it was also renovated and is due to be converted into a hotel once again.)

The Palace Museum

This is a large white building with castellated battlements situated on Mizingani Road, where it runs very close to the sea. Originally called the Sultan's Palace, it was built in the late 1890s for members of the sultan's family. From 1911, it was used as the Sultan of Zanzibar's official residence. It was renamed the People's Palace after the 1964 Revolution, when Sultan Jamshid was overthrown, and was used as government offices until the early 1990s.

In 1994 the palace was turned into a museum dedicated to the history of the sultans of Zanzibar. Remarkably, much of their furniture and other possessions survived the revolutionary years and it can now be seen by the public for the first time. The museum is well organised and informative: the ground floor is dedicated to the early years of the sultanate (1828 to 1870), while the upper floors contain exhibits from the later, more affluent period of 1870 to 1896. These exhibits include thrones, banqueting tables and ceremonial furniture, and also more personal items such as beds and the sultan's personal water-closet. There is also a room devoted to Princess Salme, the daughter of Sultan Said who eloped to Hamburg with a German merchant in 1866. (See *Salme's Story*, page 142.) In the palace garden are the graves of sultans Said, Barghash, Majid, Khaled, Khalifa and Abdullah.

The museum opens at 09.00 every day and closes at 18.00 Tuesdays to Saturdays, at 15.00 Sundays, Mondays and holidays. An excellent little leaflet is available containing a clear, concise historical background with plans and descriptions of all the palace rooms.

The House of Wonders

This is a very large, square-shaped building, with several storeys, surrounded by tiers of pillars and balconies, and topped by a large clocktower. It was built in 1883 as a ceremonial palace for Sultan Barghash (sultan from 1870 to 1888), on the site of an older palace used by Queen Fatima, the Mwinyi Mkuu (ruler of Zanzibar) in the 17th century.

The building was designed by a marine engineer, and the construction makes great use of steel pillars and girders. The interior was decorated with a marble floor and panelled walls, and it was the first building on Zanzibar to have electric lighting, and also one of the first buildings in East Africa to have an electric lift. Not surprisingly, when it was built, local people called it Beit el Ajaib, meaning the House of Wonders. It is still one of the largest buildings on Zanzibar today.

In 1896 the House of Wonders was slightly damaged by naval bombardment during an attempted palace coup which started when Sultan Hamad suddenly died and his cousin Khaled tried to seize the throne. (See *The Shortest War in History*, page 118.)

From 1911 the House of Wonders was used as offices by the British colonial government and after the 1964 coup it was used by the ASP, the ruling political party of Zanzibar. In 1977 it became the headquarters of the CCM (Chapa Cha Mapinduzi, the Party of the Revolution) then the sole political party of Tanzania.

The building was virtually abandoned by government and party in the early 1990s, but the inside remains closed to visitors. However, it is possible to walk around the outside and look at the huge carved doors, and the two old bronze cannons which have Portuguese inscriptions. It is thought that these cannons were made in Portugal some time in the early 16th century, but they were probably brought to Zanzibar by the Omanis, after taking them from Persian forces who had originally captured the guns from the Portuguese in 1622.

The House of Wonders is due to open as the National Museum in 1998.

The Arab Fort

The Arab Fort (also called simply the Old Fort, or *Ngome kongwe*) is next to the House of Wonders. It is a large building, with high, dark brown walls topped by castellated battlements. It was built between 1698 and 1701 by the Busaidi group of Omani Arabs, who had gained control of Zanzibar in 1698, following almost two centuries of Portuguese occupation. The fort was used to defend themselves against the Portuguese and against a rival Omani group, the Mazrui, who occupied Mombasa at that time.

The fort was constructed by the Busaidi Omani Arabs on the site of a church which had been built between 1598 and 1612 by the Portuguese. In the main courtyard of the fort, remnants of the old church can still be seen built into the inside wall. In the 19th century the fort was used as a prison, and criminals were executed or punished here, at a place just outside the east wall. (The Swahili word *gereza*, meaning prison, is thought to be derived from the Portuguese word *ireja*, meaning church.)

In the early 1900s, the fort was also used as a depot for the railway line which ran from Zanzibar Town to Bububu, then in 1949 it was rebuilt and the main courtyard used as a ladies' tennis club.

Today, the fort is open to visitors. It is possible to reach the top of the battlements and go on to the towers on the western side of the fort.

In 1994 a section of the fort was turned into an open-air theatre. The development was imaginative yet sympathetic to the overall design and 'feel' of the original building, with seating in the style of an amphitheatre and the fort's outer walls and House of Wonders forming a backdrop. The theatre is used for contemporary and traditional music, drama and dance, with regular performances during the tourist season.

The fort is home to an art gallery, where local painters create and exhibit their work, and is the current location of 'Zanzibar Dance!', a performing arts studio which arranges various classes, workshops and performances and is a vibrant focal point for music and dance on Zanzibar. (For more details see the section on *Music and dance* in *Chapter Four*.)

The fort also houses a tourist information desk, with details on performances in the amphitheatre and other events around town, plus a selection of books for sale and a range of tour company leaflets to browse through.

Also in the fort are several spice and craft shops and a pleasant café, serving drinks and snacks under the welcome shade of a large tree. There are even some very clean public toilets. Even if historical ruins don't interest you, it is well worth stopping by at the fort. With all these attractions and facilities, it's easy to spend quite a few hours here!

Forodhani Gardens

The Forodhani Gardens (also called Jamituri Gardens on some maps) are between the Arab Fort and the sea, overlooked by the House of Wonders. (*Forodhani* actually means 'Customs' – the original Customs House was near here.) The gardens were first laid out in 1936 to commemorate the Silver Jubilee of Sultan Khalifa (sultan from 1911 to 1960) and were called Jubilee Gardens until the 1964 Revolution. This is a popular place for local people in the evenings and there are some stalls serving drinks and snacks. In the centre of the gardens is a podium where the band of the sultan's army used to play for the public. Nearer the sea is a white concrete arabesque arch which was built in 1956 for the visit of Princess Margaret (sister of Queen Elizabeth II of Britain), although this was never officially used, as the princess arrived at the dhow harbour instead. She did visit the gardens, however, and planted the large tree with creepers that can still be seen today.

The Orphanage

Next to the fort, the road runs through a tunnel under a large building that is the island's orphanage. Built in the late 19th century, the building was used as a club for English residents until 1896, and then as an Indian school until 1950. There is a small craft shop on the ground floor opposite the gardens.

The Upimaji Building

Between the orphanage and the People's Bank of Zanzibar, this building is now the Commission for Lands and Environment. In the 1860s it was the offices and home of Heinrich Reute, the German merchant who eloped with Princess Salme. (See *Salme's Story*, page 142.)

The Old British Consulate

This fine old house was used as the British Consulate from 1841 to 1874, after which the consulate was moved to the Mambo Msiige Building (see below). The first consul was Lieutenant-Colonel Atkins Hamerton, posted here to represent the interests of Britain after Sultan Said had moved his capital from Oman to Zanzibar.

Later consuls here played host to several of the well-known British explorers, including Speke, Burton, Grant and Stanley (see box on page 121), before they set out for their expeditions on the East African mainland. In 1874, the body of David Livingstone was brought here before being taken back to Britain for burial at Westminster Abbey.

From 1874 to 1974 the building was used as offices by the trading company Smith Mackenzie, but it was taken over by the government in the late 1970s. It is still used as government offices today, and visitors are not allowed to enter, but there is not much to see on the inside; most of the building's interest lies in its grand exterior.

THE PALACES AT MIZINGANI

The Palace Museum (formerly the People's Palace, and before that the Sultan's Palace) was constructed on part of the site of an even older palace called Beit el Sahel (the House of the Coast), which was originally built for Sultan Said between 1827 and 1834. Contemporary accounts describe Beit el Sahel as a two-storey whitewashed palace, with a roof of green and red tiles. Sultan Said spent three days of each week at Beit el Sahel, and the rest of the time at his country palace at Mtoni, about 5km north of Zanzibar Town. He often walked from the town to Mtoni even though his stables were full of Arabian horses.

The Beit el Sahel Palace was separated from the beach by a high wall, with a grove of pomegranates behind. Every morning, the best horses were brought out from the stables and fastened to the seaward side of the wall with long ropes, to roam about and wade in the soft sand at low tide.

Another palace, called Beit el Hukm (the House of Government), was built later behind Beit el Sahel. Then, in 1883, Beit el Ajaib (the House of Wonders) was also built. These three adjoining palaces were connected by a series of covered ways and passages. A lighthouse in front of the palaces was nicknamed the 'Sultan's Christmas tree' by British Navy officers, due to its many rows of lamps.

Beit el Sahel, Beit el Hukm and the lighthouse were all destroyed in the bombardment of 1896 (see *The Shortest War in History*, page 118). The palace that exists today (now the museum) was constructed partly on the site of Beit el Sahel. On the site of Beit el Hukm a private house was built, which is now the offices of the Stone Town Conservation and Development Authority, easily seen between the Palace Museum and the House of Wonders, set back from the road. The building has a well-maintained garden with palm trees and shrubs. Outside the main entrance is a pair of cannons, made in Boston, Massachusetts, in 1868.

The Mambo Msiige Building

This grand house, overlooking the open 'square' at the far western end of Shangani Road, was originally built around 1850 for a wealthy Arab, incorporating a variety of architectural styles. Its name means 'look, but do not imitate'. The building was sold to the British Foreign Office in 1875 and used as the British Consulate until 1913. From 1918 to 1924 it was used as the European hospital, after which it was used as government offices. Today, the Zanzibar Shipping Corporation is based here.

The Extelcoms Building

The grand Serena Inn was originally Zanzibar's External Telecommunications Building. For more details see box, page 98.

Tippu Tip's House

Tippu Tip (also spelt Tippoo Tib and Toppu Tob) was a slave-trader, whose real name was Hamed bin Mohammed el Marjebi. He was born in the 1840s and began to participate in the slave trade at the age of 18. His nickname is thought to come from a local word meaning 'to blink', as he apparently had a nervous twitch affecting his eyes, or because his eyes resembled those of a type of bird called Tippu Tib locally because it had characteristic blinking eyes.

During the mid-19th century, Tippu Tip travelled for many years across the East African mainland, trading in slaves and ivory. He also helped some of the European explorers such as Livingstone and Stanley with their supplies and route-planning.

Contemporary records describe him as tall, bearded, fit and strong, with dark skin, an intelligent face and the air of a well-bred Arab. He reportedly visited his concubines twice a day, and is said to have argued with missionaries that Abraham and Jacob (men of God, who appeared in the Bible and the Koran) had both been slave-owners themselves. Tippu Tip became very wealthy and by 1895, after many years of trading on the mainland, he owned seven plantations on Zanzibar and 10,000 slaves. He died in 1905.

The house where Tippu Tip lived is near the Africa House Hotel, behind the offices of Jasfa Tours. Until the 1960s it was a private residence, but after the revolution it was turned into a block of flats and is now occupied by several families. The house has not been maintained since its transformation, and one writer has called it 'the most magnificent squat in all of Africa'. It is not open to visitors. However, the huge carved front door (a sign of Tippu Tip's great wealth) leading into the courtyard can still be seen.

St Joseph's Catholic Cathedral

This large cathedral, with prominent twin spires, is off Kenyatta Road in the Baghani part of town. Although its spires are a major landmark from a distance, the cathedral can be surprisingly hard to find in the narrow streets. It was built between 1893 and 1897 by French missionaries and local converts, who had originally founded a mission here in 1860. The plans were drawn by the same French architect who designed the cathedral in Marseilles, France. The tiles and the stained-glass windows were imported from France, and the murals on the inside walls, painted just after the cathedral was completed, also show a clear French influence. (Some of the murals have been recently – and none too carefully – restored.)

The cathedral is in regular use by the town's Catholic community, a mixture of Zanzibaris, Tanzanians from the mainland, Goans and Europeans. There are several masses each Sunday, and one or two on weekdays too. Outside mass times, the main cathedral doors may be locked, and entrance is via the back door reached through the courtyard of the adjoining convent.

The Hamamni Baths

In the centre of the Stone Town, east of St Joseph's Cathedral and northwest of New Mkunazini Road, are the Hamamni Baths. The area is called Hamamni, which means simply 'the place of the baths' from the Arabic *Hamam* (bath-house).

This was the first public bath-house in Zanzibar, commissioned by Sultan Barghash and built by an architect called Haji Gulam Hussein. It is one of the most elaborate on Zanzibar, and is constructed in the Persian style. (Such baths are found in many Arab and Islamic countries, and are commonly known by Europeans as 'Turkish Baths'.) Today the baths are no longer functioning, but it is still possible to go in and look around. Inside, the bath-house is surprisingly large, with several sections including the steam room, the cool room and the cool water pool.

The caretaker lives opposite; he will unlock the door, make a small entrance charge, give you a guided tour and sell you an informative leaflet about the baths' history and function.

The Anglican Cathedral

The Cathedral Church of Christ, also called the Cathedral of the Universities Mission in Central Africa (UMCA), is near the junction of New Mkunazini Road and Creek Road on the eastern side of the Stone Town. It stands on the site of the slave market, used in the 18th and 19th centuries when Zanzibar was a large slaving centre.

A group of UMCA missionaries had originally come to East Africa in 1861, following the call of the explorer David Livingstone to oppose the slave trade and spread Christianity across Africa. In 1864 they settled in Zanzibar, after a number of earlier sites proved unsuccessful. When the slave market was closed by Sultan Barghash in 1873 the missionaries bought the site and almost immediately started building the cathedral. Some adjoining land was donated to the mission by a wealthy Indian merchant called Jairam Senji.

When the first service was held in the cathedral, on Christmas Day 1877, the roof was not finished. It was finally completed in 1880. Tradition has it that the cathedral's altar stands on the site of a tree to which the slaves were tied and then whipped to show their strength and hardiness.

Today, nothing of the old slave market remains, although the cellar of the nearby St Monica's Hostel is reputed to be the remains of a pit where slaves were kept before being sold in the market. The man who was the force and inspiration behind the building of the cathedral was Bishop Edward Steere, who was Bishop of Zanzibar from 1874 to 1882. (He was also the first compiler of an English-Swahili dictionary, using the Roman alphabet; until then Swahili had been written using Arabic script.) He trained local people as masons and used coral stone and cement for building materials. Sultan Barghash is reputed to have asked Bishop Steere not to build the cathedral tower higher than the House of Wonders. When the Bishop agreed, the Sultan presented the cathedral with its clock. The tower was finished in 1883.

The memory of David Livingstone lives on in the cathedral: a window is dedicated to his memory, and the church's crucifix is made from the tree that marks the place where his heart was buried at the village of Chitambo, in present-day Zambia.

The mosaic decorations on the altar were given to the cathedral by Miss Caroline Thackeray (see the section on *Mbweni Ruins,* page 148 for more details), who was a teacher at the mission here from 1877 to 1902.

Behind the altar is the bishop's throne and twelve other seats for the canons. They are decorated with copper panels and show the names of several biblical figures, written in Swahili. The window behind the altar has been decorated with pictures of African saints, from Egypt, Carthage and Ethiopia.

Around the church are many plaques, dedicated to the memory of missionaries who died here, and to the sailors and airmen who were killed in action during the East Africa Campaign of World War I.

Today, services are held every Sunday (in Swahili). An English service is held on the first Sunday of the month. The cathedral is also open to visitors. A small entrance charge is made outside service times.

A leaflet called *Guide to Christ Church Cathedral,* with good notes on historical background and the cathedral's features, is also sometimes available.

The People's Gardens

The People's Gardens are on Kaunda Road, at the southern end of the Stone Town, near the main hospital. They were originally laid out by Sultan Barghash for the use of his harem. Many of the trees and bushes in the garden, including eucalyptus, coffee, tea and cocoa, were added by Sir John Kirk, the British Consul on Zanzibar from 1873 to 1887. The gardens were given to the people of Zanzibar by Sultan Hamoud on the occasion of

SALME'S STORY

Salme was a daughter of Sultan Said. She was born at the Mtoni Palace in August 1844. Her mother was a *surie* (concubine with the status of wife) from Circassia, in southern Russia. Salme later wrote *Memoirs of an Arabian Princess*, from which we learn many interesting details about life at court and the events of the time.

In her book she decribes her early childhood at the Mtoni Palace, where she lived until she was seven years old. Here she learnt sewing, embroidery and lace-making from her mother. She and her brothers and sisters had a private teacher and lessons were conducted in an open gallery containing just a single large mat and a *Koran* (Islamic holy book) on a stand. The royal children were taught the Arabic alphabet, reading and a little arithmetic. The boys were also taught to write, using home-made ink, and the well-bleached shoulder blade of a camel for a slate. But Salme was rebellious and taught herself to write in secret.

Twice a day, early in the morning and in the evening, all children above five years had riding lessons. When they had made sufficient progress, the boys received Arabian horses, while the girls received white donkeys from Muscat. When the princesses rode their donkeys to the clove plantations, slaves ran by the side of each animal with a large parasol to protect the riders from the sun. The children also learnt to swim in the sea at an early age.

Salme was given her own African slaves as personal attendants. At bedtime, one slave would massage her, while another fanned gently, until the princess fell asleep, still fully dressed. Slaves fanned the princess all night. In the morning, her slaves massaged her gently until she awoke. Her bath was filled with fresh spring water. Slaves laid out the day's clothes, on which jasmine and orange blossoms had been strewn overnight, and which were scented with amber and musk before wearing. Windows and doors were left open throughout the year, even in colder, wetter weather when a charcoal fire was burning. The fresh air helped to disperse the strong scents. Slaves washed the linen daily. It dried in little more than half an hour, was smoothed flat (not ironed) and put away.

As a child, Salme was allowed to mix freely with boys of her own age. After she was nine years old, the only men allowed to see her were her father, close male relatives, and her slaves. She wore trousers, a shirt reaching to her ankles, and a handkerchief for the head. The skirt and trousers were always of a different pattern. On her walks, she wore a *schele*, a large shawl of black silk. When she appeared before a stranger, the law required her to be veiled; part of the face, the neck and chin, and above all, the ankles, had to be completely covered.

In October 1859 Salme became involved in family intrigue between her older brothers, Barghash and Majid. She helped Barghash escape to the Marseilles

Queen Victoria's Jubilee in 1899 and they were renamed Victoria Gardens. The building in the centre of the gardens was called Victoria Hall. It was built over the baths of the harem and used as the Chamber of the Legislative Council.

The large house opposite the gardens was built in 1903 as the official British Residency. After the 1964 Revolution, the Victoria Gardens were renamed the People's Gardens and the old British Residency became the State House – official residence of the president. Today, the gardens are open to the public and are still being tended in a half-hearted manner.

clove plantation, after his attempt to overthrow Majid failed. (See *The Escape to Marseilles*, page 154.) Majid never punished Salme for her part in the plot but by siding with Barghash she lost the friendship of many of her other brothers and sisters. When she renewed her friendship with Majid, she isolated herself from her fellow conspirators.

By 1866 Salme was living in Zanzibar Town. Although 22 years old, she was still unmarried. Rejected by her family, she began socialising regularly with many of the foreigners on the island. She became friendly with a young German merchant from Hamburg, Heinrich Reute, who was living in a house next to hers. They began a covert friendship, speaking to each other from their balconies across the narrow street, and meeting secretly in the countryside beyond the town.

In July 1866 Salme discovered she was pregnant and was forced to leave Zanzibar in a hurry, as an illegitimate pregnancy would have brought disgrace to her family and the whole Busaidi dynasty. She escaped on a British warship, and for several months after her departure a wave of anti-European feeling spread through Zanzibar Town. Another British warship was sent to suppress any possible reprisals against Europeans.

Salme reached Aden, where she stayed with some European friends. She renounced Islam and was baptised into the Anglican Church, with the name Emily. In Zanzibar, Heinrich wound up his affairs then joined Salme in Aden. They were married immediately and travelled to Heinrich's home in Hamburg.

In the following three years Salme and Heinrich had two daughters and a son. Tragically, in August 1871, Heinrich fell whilst jumping from a tram, and was run over; he died three days later. No longer welcome in Zanzibar, Salme remained in Germany, making one short visit to London in 1875, and two brief returns to Zanzibar in August 1885 and May 1888, but her attempts at reconciliation were unsuccessful. She lived in exile in Syria until 1914 and died in Germany in 1924. Among the possessions found after her death was a bag of sand from the beach at Zanzibar.

CR

The Palace Museum in Zanzibar Town has a room devoted to Salme's life and writings. In 1994 the Sayyida Salme Institute (SASI) was established to raise awareness about the life and writings of this remarkable woman, and to promote training and research relevant to Zanzibar. The director of SASI, Saidi el Gheithy, can be contacted through the Africa Centre in London (38 King St, WC2E 8JT, tel: 0171 240 0199).

The building next door to the State House was the embassy of the Soviet Union. It is now the offices of the Zanzibar Investment Promotions Agency (ZIPA), a government agency set up to attract foreign business capital to Zanzibar.

The Zanzibar Milestone

Near the People's Gardens is this octagonal pillar, built with marble taken from the palace at Chukwani, showing the distances from Zanzibar Town to other settlements on the island. For complete accuracy, the distances were measured from this exact point.

The distance to London is also shown: 8,064 miles. This is the distance by sea. (By 1870, ships between Zanzibar and London travelled via the Suez Canal. Before this all voyages were much longer, via the Cape of Good Hope.)

The Peace Memorial Museum

The museum is at the southern end of the Stone Town, near the junction of Creek Road and Kaunda Road in the area called Mnazi Moja. It is also known by its local title: Beit el Amani (House of Peace). It was designed by the British architect J H Sinclair, who also designed the High Court, the British Residency and several other public buildings around Zanzibar Town.

If you can, it is a good idea to visit the museum twice during your visit: the first time to get an introduction to the history, and to get a 'feel' for the town and islands; and the second time to get a deeper understanding after you have actually visited the various buildings and sites of interest.

The museum is informative although some exhibits are becoming quite decrepit. The main building has sections on archaeology, early trade, slavery, palaces, mosques, sultans, explorers, missionaries, colonial administrators, traditional crafts and household items, stamps, coins, fishing and clove cultivation. Highlights include Dr Livingstone's medical chest, a section of track from the short-lived Zanzibar Railroad, and some old bicycle lamps customised to run on coconut oil. And be sure not to miss the old lighthouse

---

ZANZIBAR DOORS

When a house was built in Zanzibar, the door was traditionally the first part to be erected. The greater the wealth and social position of the owner of the house, the larger and more elaborately carved his front door. The symbolic designs and quotations from the Koran were intended to exert a benign influence. Patterns include waves of the sea climbing up the door-post, representing the livelihood of the Arab merchant to whom the house belonged, frankincense, and date-palms symbolising wealth and plenty.

Some designs are thought to date from before the Koran: the stylised lotuses could be associated with Egyptian fertility symbols, and the fish could possibly represent the Syrian protecting-goddess Atargatis, or the ancient fish-god of the Egyptians.

Many doors are studded with brass spikes and bosses. This may be a modification of the Indian practice of studding doors of medieval castles with sharp spikes of iron to prevent their being battered in by war elephants. In AD915, an Arab traveller recorded that Zanzibar island abounded in elephants, and around 1295 Marco Polo wrote that Zanzibar had 'elephants in plenty'. But the elephants must have been extinct long before the Arabs built houses in Stone Town, and the studs and bosses seen today are purely for decoratation.

The oldest carved door in Zanzibar, which dates from 1694, is now the front door of the Peace Memorial Museum in Zanzibar Town.

IN ZANZIBAR MUSEUM

1 We ask you O our Lord the glorious, so give us from your great generocity, clearance in our all abouts
2 And save us from bottlenecks and guide us for your generocity, O the one with access generocity and riches
3 And for the great effort and glory that lengthened and proceeded its construction
4 So we ask you O the Merciful to pass to those who did wrong among us that repentance
5 And give us from your grace by your wealth in a gracious way, and blessing on us
6 So in your gracious and protection which come before every and we have promised good dids
7 And means of living in plenty in comfort and give us security and faith and give us good garment
8 For your limitless knowledge acceed your blessing and give us prosperity in agriculture with perpatual livestock
9 And grow to us abundance of grass so as to be fed by the livestock
10 I have with me five people who cool hot stream water which burns skin instantly
11 The Apostle (Muhammad) and Ally and their two sons (Hassan and Hussein) and Fatima
12 So the Almighty God suffice them from every evil for he is all hearing, all knowing

Today is the 16th of the Holy Month of Shaaban
year 1276 A.H. (1856 A.D.)

---

lamp upstairs!

The museum annexe has a small library and the natural history sections, with some tatty stuffed exhibits, snakes in jars, photos of mutant fish, and the bones of a dodo. In the garden, a herd of giant tortoises do their best to keep the grass short.

The museum is open from 09.00 to 18.00 every day except Sunday. There is a small entrance charge, and visitors are often asked to make an extra donation by the somewhat over-enthusiastic curator.

Opposite the museum, on the other side of Creek Road, is Mnazi Moja Sports Field. (*Mnazi Moja* means 'one coconut tree'.) This area used to be a swamp at the end of the creek that separated the Stone Town peninsula from the rest of the island. The land was reclaimed and converted to a sports field during the colonial period, hence the English-style cricket pavilion in the corner. In the 1920s part of the sportsground was set aside for exclusive use by members of the English Club; it contained tennis courts, a croquet lawn and the only golf-course on the island. Today, Mnazi Moja is used mainly for football matches and, although the creek itself has been reclaimed, the sports field is still prone to flooding in the rainy season.

The road leading southeastwards out of the town (now called Nyerere Road) was originally built as a causeway across the swamp by Bishop

Steere of the Universities Mission in Central Africa. Today the road is a pleasant avenue lined with giant casuarina trees.

The Zanzibar Archives

For real aficionados, the Zanzibar Archives (*Nyaraka za Taifa* in Swahili) contain some fascinating material. These include many books and manuscripts in Arabic dating from the 1600s, when the Omani sultans took control of Zanzibar, Consular and Protectorate Records from the British Colonial times, papers and documents relating to the various European expeditions that started from Zanzibar in the second half of the 19th century, plus a lot of contemporary material such as stamps, newspapers, maps and photographs. If there is something of special interest, the staff on duty can help you search through the collections. If you just want to browse there is an exhibition room, where some selected items of interest are on display.

The Archives are open from 07.30 to 15.30 Mondays to Fridays and until 12.00 on Saturdays. Entrance is free. They are situated outside the

---

WILLIAM LLOYD MATHEWS

William Lloyd Mathews was a Welshman born in Madeira in 1850. He entered the British Navy in 1864, and from 1870 he served in the slave patrolling boats of *HMS London*. In August 1877 Mathews was seconded from the navy and appointed to command and organise a European-style army for Sultan Barghash, who wanted to enforce his sovereignty over the interior. Until then, the sultan's army had been composed of Arabs and Persians only, but the new army contained 500 Africans, with a uniform of red caps, short black jackets and white trousers. The Arab officers wore dark blue frock coats and trousers, with gold or silver lace, possibly modelled on uniforms of the British Royal Navy. The British government donated 500 rifles, and by the beginning of the 1880s Mathews had about 1,300 men under his command.

One of the new army's first tasks was to stop the slave smuggling between Pemba and Pangani on the mainland and they were soon successful, capturing several slave smugglers and hindering the illicit trade. Mathews was released from the navy and became Brigadier-General Mathews, Commander-in-Chief of Zanzibar's army.

A leading slave trader at this time was called Hindi bin Hattam. His dhow was captured by a British Navy ship, captained by one Captain C J Brownrigg, between Zanzibar and Pemba. Brownrigg found about 100 slaves on board Hindi bin Hattam's dhow but before any action could taken Hindi's men killed Brownrigg, and most of the British crew, and sailed away. In another ship General Mathews pursued Hindi bin Hattam to Wete in Pemba, and took him prisoner after a battle. Hindi died later of gunshot wounds. Brownrigg was buried on Grave Island.

In 1891, when a constitutional government was established in Zanzibar, General Sir Lloyd Mathews was appointed as His Highness's First Minister, and he was awarded a knighthood on March 3 1894. On October 11 1901 Sir Lloyd Mathews died in Zanzibar, of malaria, at the age of 51. He was buried with full naval and military honours in the English cemetery outside Zanzibar Town.

main town, about 2km along Nyerere Road from the Mnazi Moja Hospital, in an area called Kilimani. To get there take a dala-dala on Route U and asked to be dropped at Nyaraka za Taifa, or at the prison. The dala-dala will stop at the bottom of Kinuamiguu Hill (the only hill on this road); turn left (north) off Nyerere Road, then take the first road on the right.

More information is available from the Head of the National Archives, PO Box 116, Zanzibar, tel: 30342.

PLACES TO VISIT NEAR ZANZIBAR TOWN

The following places of interest can be reached easily, or without too much difficulty, from Zanzibar Town. They make good day-trips by hired scooter, hired bike, or a combination of foot and public transport. (For details on travelling beyond the town see *Travel around Zanzibar Island* on page 161.) If you prefer not to travel independently, visits to any of the places mentioned here can also be arranged with a tour company.

Some of the palaces and bath-houses mentioned in this section are included in the 'spice tours' arranged by tour companies and independent guides. If you are planning to join one of these tours, check where it goes to avoid unnecessary duplication.

South of Zanzibar Town
Mbweni

The area of Mbweni is on the coast, about 3km directly south of Zanzibar Town. It was originally a plantation bought by the Universities Mission in Central Africa (UMCA) in 1871. Bishop Tozer (Bishop of Zanzibar from 1863 to 1873) planned to build a mission station here. His successor Bishop Steere (Bishop of Zanzibar from 1874 to 1882) oversaw the building of a church and other mission buildings, and also used the area as a colony for freed slaves.

To reach Mbweni, take the main road out of town going towards the airport. Go uphill through the area called Kinuamiguu ('lift your legs'). After a few kilometres, at a signpost to Mbweni and Chukwani, fork right, then turn right again after 500m on to a smaller road. Continue down this road towards the sea to reach Mbweni. Dala-dalas on Route U run between the town and the airport and go past the main Mbweni and Chukwani junction.

St John's Anglican Church

At the heart of Mbweni (on the right side of the small road leading towards the sea) is this English-style church, complete with tower and surrounding cemetery. It was opened in 1882 by UMCA missionaries and converts, and consecrated in 1904. Descendants of freed slaves continued to live in the area. Today, the sexton at the church is Peter Sudi, a descendant of John Swedi, one of the first five freed slave boys taken in by the mission.

The church has a marble altar inlaid with mother-of-pearl (colourful shell pieces) and a wooden chair made for Bishop Tozer by sailors from the ship *HMS London,* famous for its slave-dhow captures. Miss Caroline Thackeray (see the section on *Mbweni Ruins,* following) is buried in the cemetery here. The nearby hotel, Inn by the Sea, was originally the old clergy house.

There are Anglican church services at 09.00 every Sunday.

Sir John Kirk's House

Along the road which passes northwards in front of St John's Church is the house of Sir John Kirk, who was British Consul General in Zanzibar from 1873 to 1887. Kirk first came to Africa as medical officer and naturalist to Livingstone's Zambezi expedition in the 1850s. As Consul General he was very active in the suppression of the slave trade, often regarded as the 'power behind the throne' during the rule of Sultan Barghash, his close friend. The house was built as a gift from the sultan and was used by Kirk and his family as a country retreat.

Kirk was an experienced botanist and established a large experimental garden here, which later provided the core species of all the boating gardens of Zanzibar and mainland Tanzania. He imported many new plant species to the islands, and worked on improved varieties of useful and edible crops. Kirk also collected trees and flowers from the mainland of Africa which formed the basis of the then standard work *Flora of Tropical Africa.*

In 1887 Kirk left Zanzibar, and sold his house to Miss Caroline Thackeray, the headmistress of the School for Girls at Mbweni (see the section on *Mbweni Ruins,* below). While she lived here, Miss Thackeray opened the grounds of the house for a yearly garden party. She retired in 1902, but continued to live in Kirk's house until her death, aged 83, in 1926.

The house was then sold by the church to a wealthy Arab, who used it until the early 1960s. The house is now privately owned and not open to the public.

Mbweni Ruins

If you continue past St John's Church towards the sea, the dirt road leads past the gates of the Inn by the Sea Hotel to the Mbweni Ruins Hotel, set in the grounds of Mbweni Ruins. These ruins are the remains of St Mary's School for Girls, built between 1871 and 1874 by the missionaries based at Mbweni under the leadership of Bishop Steere. The land, then known as Mbweni Point Shamba, had originally been bought by Bishop Tozer in 1871, when there was an old Arab house on the property which was incorporated into the school entrance.

The school was a large square building, based around a central courtyard. The head teacher from 1877 until 1902 was Caroline Mary Defflis Thackeray (a cousin of the famous English novelist William Makepeace Thackeray). In 1926 she died at Kirk's house (see above) and was buried at St John's Church nearby.

The school educated orphaned girls who had been freed from captured slave-dhows, and daughters of freed slaves who lived at the mission, each with their own house and small garden. Most of the girls were trained as teachers, and were taught reading, writing, arithmetic, geography and sewing. In 1877 Caroline Thackeray had an Industrial Wing built (at her own cost) where vocational training in basketry, stitching, laundry and cooking was given to the girls who were less academically inclined.

St Mary's had its own chapel which is still in good condition today, though without a roof. In 1906 the school became a convent and in 1920 the buildings were sold by the church to a consortium of the Bank of India. They slowly became ruins and were never used or lived in until the present time.

The owner of the Mbweni Ruins Hotel, Flo Liebst, has written an informative book called *Zanzibar, History of the Ruins at Mbweni*, which also touches on the general history of Zanzibar and the UMCA missionaries of East Africa.

Chukwani Palace

The Chukwani Palace is near the small village of Chukwani, to the south of Zanzibar Town, about 5km beyond Mbweni. It was built by Sultan Barghash in 1872 and used mainly as a place to recuperate after illness as the air here was supposed to be particularly healthy. The palace was built as a smaller version of the House of Wonders, without the tower. During the reign of Sultan Ali bin Hamoud (sultan from 1902 to 1911) the palace was used by government officers. Today, most of the palace has been demolished, leaving only the bath-house. The front door of the palace is on display in the Peace Memorial Museum. The new buildings around the ruins are used by the army, so visitors are not allowed to enter, but you can get a good view from the air if you fly out of Zanzibar as the palace lies only a few kilometres to the southwest of the airport.

Fumba

Fumba is a small village at the end of the peninsula, about 15km south of Zanzibar Town. It can be reached by bus or hired vehicle. A local villager called Issa Kibwana conducts small tours of the nearby fruit and spice plantations.

North of Zanzibar Town
Maruhubi Palace

The Maruhubi Palace is on the coast, about 4km north of Zanzibar Town. It was built in 1882 for Sultan Barghash (sultan from 1870 to 1888) and at one time he reputedly kept 100 women here; one official wife and 99 concubines. (The sultan himself lived at the palace in Zanzibar Town.) The palace's name comes from the original owner of the estate who sold the land to Sultan Barghash.

The palace was built with coral stone and wood, and was reported to have been one of the most ornate on the island. Large walls were built around the palace grounds, thought to have been inspired by the park walls seen by Sultan Barghash on his visit to England in 1875. Unfortunately, the palace was destroyed by a fire in 1899. All that remains today are the great pillars which supported the upper storey, and the Persian-style bathhouse. The separate bathrooms for the women, and the large bath for the Sultan's own use, can still be seen. The original water tanks, now overgrown with lilies, also remain in the grounds of the palace. To the north of the pillars, at the back of the beach, is a small set of arches and steps; this was part of the palace's reception area. (The Peace Memorial Museum in Zanzibar Town contains a photo of the palace taken at the end of the 19th century when it was still in use.)

To reach the palace, take the main road north out of Zanzibar Town towards Bububu. Pass Livingstone House on your right and, after a few kilometres, the Maruhubi Palace is signposted on your left. Dala-dalas on Route B run between the town and Bububu village, past the palace entrance gate.

Mtoni Palace

Just north of Maruhubi is the ruined Mtoni Palace, which was built for Sultan Said (sultan from 1804 to 1856) on the site of an older house believed to have belonged to Saleh bin Haramil, the Arab trader who imported the first cloves to Zanzibar (see *Chapter Two* for more details). Mtoni, which means 'place by the river', is the oldest palace on Zanzibar.

One of Sultan Said's daughters, whose name was Salme, later married a German trader who lived and worked in Zanzibar in the 1860s. She eloped with him to Germany and later wrote a book about her life on Zanzibar (see box, page 142). In her book, Salme describes Mtoni Palace in the 1850s: it had a large courtyard where gazelles, peacocks, ostriches and flamingos wandered around, a large bath-house at one end and the sultan's quarters at the other, where he lived with his principal wife, an Omani princess whose name was Azze.

Salme records that over 1,000 people were attached to the sultan's court in the palace. She describes how the sultan would pace up and down on a large round tower overlooking the sea, where he could see his fleet anchored off the shore. If visitors came by boat, he would greet them on the steps of his palace as there was no landing pier. Salme and the other princesses were carried out to their boats on chairs.

In her book, Salme also describes her own return visit to Zanzibar in 1885. The palace at Mtoni had been abandoned and was already in ruins. Today, only the main walls and parts of the roof remain. The palace was turned into a warehouse during World War I, and evidence of the alterations can still be seen.

To reach the palace, turn left off the main road on to a dirt track, about 2km north of Maruhubi. There is a small signpost.

Beit el Ras Palace

Further north along the coast, this palace was built for Sultan Said as an 'overflow' house for his children and their servants (see box, page 152). Building started in 1847 but was not completed by the time of Said's death in 1856. Sultan Majid (Said's successor) did not continue the project and much of the stone from the palace was used during the construction of the Zanzibar Railroad (see below). The remaining ruins were abandoned and finally demolished in 1947 to make room for a school and teacher training centre. Today, only the giant porch of the original palace remains, with high arches and steps leading up one side.

The palace is in the grounds of the training centre, now called the Nkrumah Teacher Training College (*Chuo Cha Ualimu Nkrumah*), and is reached by turning off the main road a few kilometres beyond Mtoni. Beit el Ras means 'the palace on the headland' and from the porch you get good views over this part of the coast and out towards the group of small islands off Zanzibar Town.

Kibweni Palace

North of Beit el Ras, this 'palace' was built in Arabic style by the British authorities in 1915. In the village of Kibweni, its official title was Beit el Kassrusaada (Palace of Happiness), although this name seems to have been forgotten. Sultan Khalifa II (sultan from 1911 to 1960) used the palace as a country residence. After the revolution it was taken over by the government and is still used as an official residence. It is not open to the public.

Chuini Palace

About 10km north of Zanzibar Town, on the coast near the village of Chuini, lie the ruins of Chuini Palace. (*Chuini* means 'place of the leopard'.) It was built for Sultan Barghash, added to by Sultan Ali bin Said, and destroyed by fire in 1914. The ruins are on private land and cannot be visited.

The Zanzibar Railroad

In the early 1900s a light railway (36-inch gauge) was built and operated by an American company. Construction begun in 1904 and ended in 1905 and the line ran from a point outside the Arab Fort in Zanzibar Town, along the seafront and up the coast to the village of Bububu. The service was used mainly by local people but a special firstclass coach was joined to the train so that passengers from the steamers that put in to Zanzibar could get a brief glimpse of the island. The line was closed in 1928, but railway buffs can still see the remains of bridges and embankments from today's main road. A piece of the original track and some old photos of the line can be seen in the Peace Memorial Museum.

In his book *Sketches in Mafeking and East Africa* (1907), Lord Robert Baden-Powell quotes from a description of the Zanzibar train by an American writer called Miss Kirkland. 'Have you ever been to Bu Bu Bu?

THE WIVES AND CHILDREN OF SULTAN SAID

During his lifetime, Sultan Said (Sultan of Oman and Zanzibar from 1804 to 1856) had three legitimate wives or *harino* (singular *horme*). (Under Islamic law, he was allowed up to four *harino* at a time.)

In 1827, he married Azze binte (daughter of) Seif bin Ahmed, a grandchild of Sultan Ahmed, and thus a cousin of Said's. Like any *horme*, Azze was considered to have equal status with her husband. Strongwilled, she ruled the household with an iron hand and no act of state was carried out without her advice and approval.

In 1847 Said married his second wife, Binte Irich Mirza, nicknamed Schesade, a beautiful and extravagant princess, and grand-daughter of the Shah of Persia. She came to Zanzibar in 1849 and Said built the baths at Kidichi for her in 1850, using stonemasons and plasterers from Persia. Schesade had no children so Said divorced her and sent her back to Persia. In the 1850s Schesade was a prominent member of the Persian army, fighting against her former husband.

Said's third wife was Binte Seif bin Ali, of which little is known.

Said also possessed a great many concubines. Once they had given birth, they were known as *sarari* (singular *surie*), immediately freed and given equal status with the legal wives.

Said was credited with 120 children (99 daughters and 21 sons). When he died in 1856, he left a single widow, Azze binte Seif, and 75 *sarari*. Of his 120 children, only 36 were still alive: 18 sons and 18 daughters. Two of his sons, Thuwaini and Turki, became sultans of Oman. (The present Sultan of Oman, His Excellency Sultan Qaboos bin Said, is a direct descendant of Sultan Turki.) Four more sons, Majid, Barghash, Khalifa and Ali, became sultans of Zanzibar.

If not, do not call yourself a travelled person,' she wrote. 'Bu Bu Bu is a settlement in a shady grove on the island of Zanzibar, and is the terminus of a new and important railroad – six and a half miles long.'

It has been suggested that the name Bububu comes from the sound made by the train's whistle, but maps dating from before the building of the railway show the village already had this title. It is more likely that the name was inspired by the sound of the freshwater springs which bubble to the surface just outside the village. (Most of Zanzibar Town's water supply comes from here.)

For a detailed history of the railroad, see *Zanzibar and the Bububu Railway* listed in *Further Reading* on page 213.

Kidichi Persian Baths

The Persian Baths at Kidichi lie to the northeast of Zanzibar Town, about 4km inland from the main coast road, in the island's main clove and coconut plantation area. The baths were built in 1850 for Sultan Said. He owned land in this part of the island, and he and his wife, Binte Irich Mirza (also called Schesade, more often written Sherazade), would come here for hunting or for overseeing the work being done on their plantations. The bath-house was constructed so that they could refresh themselves after the journey from town, or after hunting. Schesade was a granddaughter of the Shah of Persia, so the baths were built in the Persian style, with decorative stucco work. An underground furnace kept the water warm. A small resthouse was also built nearby, but none of this remains.

Today, you can enter the bath-house, and see the bathing pool and toilets. Unfortunately, the bath-house has not been well maintained, and there is mould growing on much of the stucco. A colony of bats seems to have taken residence here as well.

To reach Kidichi, continue up the main road northwards from Zanzibar Town, to reach the village of Bububu. Turn right here on to a dirt road that leads through coconut palms and clove plantations, and past a few collections of huts and small houses. Follow the road eastwards for about 4km until the bath-house, a low white building, is seen on the right, just a few metres off the dirt road.

Kizimbani Persian Baths

The Kizimbani Baths are near Kidichi. These baths were also built in the Persian style for Sultan Said, at about the same time as the baths at Kidichi which they resemble, though there is no inside decoration.

To reach them from Kidichi, continue eastwards along the dirt road to a crossroads, where you go straight on, passing through plantations to reach the Kizimbani Experimental Station headquarters. The baths are on the right of the track.

The experimental station is the island's centre for agricultural research. The surrounding plantations originally belonged to Saleh bin Haramil, the Arab trader who imported the first cloves to Zanzibar, but they were confiscated by Sultan Said on the grounds that Saleh was a slave smuggler (see *Chapter Two* for more details).

Mangapwani Coral Cavern

Mangapwani (meaning 'Arab shore') lies on the coast, about 20km north of Zanzibar Town. The Coral Cavern is a large natural cave in the coral with a narrow entrance and a pool of fresh water at its lowest point. Water was probably collected from here by early inhabitants of this part of the island but at some time in the past vegetation grew across the entrance and the cavern was 'lost'. Later, the area became the property of a wealthy Arab landowner called Hamed Salim el Hathy who had many slaves working on his plantations. During this time, the cavern was re-discovered by a young boy searching for a lost goat. Local people were able to use the water again, and Hamed Salim arranged for his slaves to collect the water regularly for his own use. It has been suggested that the cavern may have been used as a hiding place for slaves after the trade was officially abolished in 1873.

To reach the cavern from Zanzibar Town, take the main road through Bububu to reach Chuini, then fork left towards Bumbwini. After 7km, in Mangapwani village, fork left again and head westwards towards the coast.

(Buses on Route 2 link Zanzibar Town and Mangapwani village, but services are not frequent. You're better coming by hired bike or car, or on a tour.) About 1km from the junction, a narrow dirt road leads off to the left. Follow this to reach the cavern. A flight of stone steps leads through the entrance down into the cavern itself.

Mangapwani Slave Cave

The Mangapwani Slave Cave is a few kilometres further up the coast from the Coral Cavern. In fact, it is not a cave at all, but a square-shaped cell that has been cut out of the coral, built as a chamber for storing slaves. Its construction is attributed to one Mohammed bin Nassor Al-Alwi, an important slave trader. Boats from the mainland would unload their human cargo on the nearby beach, and the slaves would be kept here before being taken to Zanzibar Town, elsewhere on the East African coast, or to Oman. It is thought that some time after 1873, when Sultan Barghash signed the Anglo-Zanzibari treaty which officially abolished the slave trade, the cave was used as a place to hide slaves, as an illicit trade continued for many

THE ESCAPE TO MARSEILLES

In October 1859 Barghash was plotting to overthrow his brother, Majid, who was Sultan of Zanzibar. Barghash was living in a house in Zanzibar Town, close to the palace of Beit el Sahel, with his sister, Meje, and 11-year-old brother, Abdil Aziz. Two more sisters, Salme and Khole, were living in a house immediately behind his, separated by a narrow street. Two of his nieces, the princesses Shembua and Farschu, also lived nearby. The three houses formed a centre for the conspiracy.

Majid, aware that his brother was plotting against him, arranged to have the three houses watched and ordered Barghash's house to be blockaded. Several hundred soldiers were posted outside the front of the house with strict orders to shoot any suspicious person and cut off all communications. But Barghash had plenty of provisions, and his fellow conspirators smuggled water to him through the back of the house. Meanwhile, at the fortified plantation of Marseilles, in the centre of the island, the conspirators stored arms, ammunition and food supplies in preparation for a siege. (The plantation had been named Marseilles by another brother, Khaled, who had a predilection for all things French.)

At midnight on October 8 1859 Salme and Khole went to Barghash's house with a large escort including Shembua and Farschu. Bluffing their way past the soldiers on duty (Arab women did not normally speak to strange men), they were allowed to pay the prisoner a short visit. They brought women's robes and veils so that Barghash could leave the house unnoticed, but the plan started to go wrong when he refused to wear them. At last Barghash agreed to be wrapped in a voluminous black robe, which left only his eyes free. The tallest women walked alongside him to make his height less conspicuous. To their great relief, the guard on the door made way respectfully for the royal party.

Salme and Khole had arranged a rendezvous with some of Barghash's other supporters outside the town. If the royal party did not arrive at the given time, the escort would disperse, but they were now late and Barghash grew increasingly agitated.

years. Today, the cave itself remains, although the wooden roof under which the slaves were hidden has now gone.

To reach the Slave Cave from the Coral Cavern, retrace the narrow track to the road and turn left. Continue for 1km to reach a large house overlooking the sea. (The house once belonged to a wealthy Arab family, but it is now used by the army and is closed to visitors. Nearby, a narrow path leads down to a small beach. A new hotel is under construction in this area.) Just before you reach the house a small dirt track branches off to the right. Follow this for 1km to reach the Slave Caves. With care, you can reach the steps that lead down on to the cavern floor.

Fuji Beach

After an energetic day's sightseeing in the area north of Zanzibar Town, Fuji Beach, near Bububu village, is a good place to go for a rest before heading back to town. A small dirt road leads down to the beach from near the police station in the centre of Bububu village. This is the nearest place to the town where swimming is advisable and it makes a good place for a

---

The party walked through the inhabited part of the town at a normal pace, but once on the outskirts, they put out their lanterns, took to their heels and ran. The fields were muddy but the royal party scrambled over the hedges and ditches in their embroidered slippers. They only slowed as they reached the appointed meeting place hidden amongst the trees.

The escort had waited. Barghash threw off his disguise, said farewell, and disappeared into the darkness. The exhausted sisters returned home to face the consequences.

Majid soon heard news of Barghash's escape, and knew that he had reached Marseilles with many followers. Majid mustered 5,000 soldiers and appealed to the British Consul, Sir Chistopher Rigby, for help in quelling the revolt. Rigby provided Majid with nine soldiers and a gun from the British warship *HMS Assaye*.

Majid marched to Marseilles and started to bombard the house, but Barghash's supporters emerged from their fortifications, and fought off Majid's troops until sunset. Several hundred lives were lost. Majid retreated for the night but, as he and his army slept, Barghash and his supporters slipped back into town. On the morning of October 16, Majid readvanced on Marseilles and smashed open the gates, only to find it abandoned.

By this time, Barghash had returned to his house and remained concealed, refusing even to go to the window. Rigby arranged for *HMS Assaye* to be anchored just offshore. A detachment of marines landed and marched to the front of Barghash's house. On October 17 Rigby called on Barghash to surrender. When there was no answer, the marines started to fire their guns at the front of the house. Khole, calling from her house across the street, persuaded her brother to surrender. Cries of *Aman! Aman!* (Peace) were heard and the firing stopped. Rigby rapped on the door with his walking stick and demanded immediate surrender. Minutes later the door opened and Barghash emerged. Rigby arrested him and put him on board the *Assaye*. He was taken to India, where he lived in exile for two years. Abdil Aziz insisted on accompanying his older brother and stayed in India after Barghash's return in 1861.

day trip if you fancy just relaxing for a while.

Local legend has it that the beach's name was due to one Mr Honda, a Japanese engineer who came to Zanzibar to build roads, but fell in love with a local girl and decided to stay. He built a 'taverna' called Fuji Beach Bar, at the time the best on the island, and the name stuck. Even though Mr Honda is no longer around, his legacy remains. The bar still sells beers and snacks, and the staff will look after your gear while you are swimming. (There have been reports of robberies here, so this is worth arranging.) If you want to stay for more than a day, nearby is the Bububu Guesthouse (see page 98).

Islands near Zanzibar Town

A few kilometres from Zanzibar Town are several small islands, some of which are good destinations for a relaxing day's outing. Boat trips to the islands can be arranged with a tour company, or with one of the independent 'guides' (*papaasi*). Costs range from $20 to $60 for the boat, or from $6 to $20 per person, depending on who you deal with, the number of hours you want, and on the quality of the boat. Other factors might be lunch or snorkelling gear included in the price. You can hire a boat for yourself, or reduce costs by getting your own small group together. If you're alone, it's usually easy to link up with other travellers for a boat ride. The papaasi will organise things, or tell you just to come to the beach by the Big Tree on Mizingani Road (the seafront), from where boats go across to the islands every morning.

Changuu Island

This island is also called Prison Island, and was originally owned by a wealthy Arab who used it as a detention centre for disobedient slaves. After the abolition of slavery, in 1873, the island was bought by General Lloyd Mathews, commander of the Sultan's army, who built a house here (see box on page 146). In 1893 a prison was built on the island, but it was used instead as a quarantine station for the whole East African region. In the 1920s passengers arriving from India had to spend between one and two weeks on Changuu before proceeding to Zanzibar Town. On some old maps, Changuu is called Kibandiko Island, but this name now seems to be forgotten.

Today, the island is owned by the government and non-Tanzanian visitors must pay a $2 entry fee (TSh are not acceptable). You can still see the quarantine station, and the house built by General Mathews which is now used as a restaurant. A path leads right round the island (about an hour's easy stroll), also passing some old pits where coral has been dug out to make building stone.

The island's other highlight is the large number of giant tortoises which can be seen on the lawn outside the Mathews' house and all over the island. How and why the tortoises were brought to the island is unclear, but they are believed to have been brought from the Seychelles in the 18th century. They delight in fresh mango peel, and also seem to spend a large amount of time mating, a long and noisy process but apparently successful, as the island's tortoise population is said to be growing.

Changuu Island has a small beach, and you can go snorkelling on the nearby reef. Masks and flippers can be hired from the ticket office. The island also has a small restaurant and ZTC guesthouse (see the list of hotels on page 99). A tour company intends to lease the restaurant, and co-operate with ZTC to improve the service and quality, whilst also taking responsibility for maintaining the island itself. Unrestricted visitor numbers have resulted in damage to some parts of the island. Litter disposal facilities (or lack of them) is another problem. The tour company plans to 'clean the place up a bit', and their efforts should be applauded. There are also long-term plans to lease the guesthouse and improve the quality here as well.

Chapwani Island
This is also called Grave Island as a small section of it has been used as a Christian cemetery since 1879. Most of the graves belong to British sailors who were killed fighting against Arab slave ships (including Captain Brownrigg, page 146); others date from World War I (1914–1918) when the British ship *Pegasus* was bombarded and sunk by the German ship *Konigsberg* in Zanzibar Town harbour. There is a small beach on the island, and a small hotel (see page 99).

Snake Island
This is the popular name for the very small island between Changuu and Chapwani islands. Boats do not usually land here as there is no beach.

Bawe Island
To the south of Changuu Island, this uninhabited island is rarely visited, although the snorkelling is reported to be of good quality. In the 1870s telegraph cables were brought ashore here, linking Zanzibar with the Seychelles, Aden and South Africa. Another line was run from Bawe Island to the External Telecommunications building in the Shangani area of Zanzibar Town. The old 'Extelcoms' building has now been converted into the Serena Inn, and another hotel is being built on Bawe Island itself. It is not known if they will use the original phone line...

Chumbe Island
The coral reef surrounding Chumbe Island was officially gazetted as a Marine National Park (the first in Tanzania) in 1994. The island itself has been declared a Forest Reserve, and the island and reef together are known as Chumbe Island Nature Reserve or Chumbe Island Coral Park (CHICOP). The coral is such good condition because until recently the island was inside a military area and public access was not allowed.

CHICOP's own information publicity states: 'Chumbe Island is a rare example of a still pristine coral island eco-system in an otherwise heavily overfished and overexploited area. It includes a reef sanctuary and a forest and bird sanctuary of exceptional biodiversity.' This has been verified by various global conservation and scientific bodies, including IUCN, WWF and UNESCO. A specialist from the Australian Institute of Marine Sciences called Chumbe 'one of the most spectacular coral gardens to be found anywhere in the world'.

Over 350 species of fish have been identified in the reef and surrounding area. Other marine wildlife usually seen includes turtles, dolphins and the rare giant coconut crab. On the island, 60 species of bird have been recorded, including breeding pairs of the rare roseate tern. Another rare animal, Aders' duiker, used to occur on Chumbe but was wiped out by hunters in the 1950s. There are plans to reintroduce this duiker, as populations are coming under increased pressure elsewhere on Zanzibar.

Tourism is being developed on Chumbe in a sensitive and appropriate manner. Money paid by tourists visiting the island or snorkelling on the reef is channelled back into educational and conservation projects. Forest and intertidal nature trails have been established, and permanent moorings have been built to allow visitors in boats to reach the coral without needing to drop anchor. Local fishermen have been employed as marine park rangers.

Buildings of historical and cultural interest on Chumbe include a lighthouse built by the British in 1904 (still clearly visible from ships approaching Zanzibar from Dar), now converted to an observation tower, and an ancient mosque built in an Indian style unique to Tanzania. An education centre – aimed primarily at local schoolchildren and fishermen – has been constructed in a cottage originally built for the lighthouse-keepers.

Day trips to the island are available (these cost $50 including all transfers, snorkelling equipment, guides and lunch), but visitors are encouraged to overnight in the reserve. Accommodation is available. For more details see page 99.

Only authorised tour companies are allowed to bring visitors to Chumbe, as the diversity, quality and management of the island's marine and terrestrial wildlife is of a much higher standard than on many of the other islands around Zanzibar Town.

The team of people who campaigned to establish Chumbe as a conservation area should be congratulated and supported as much as possible. It is hoped that the Zanzibar government also recognise the island's potential as a tourist attraction and flag-ship environmental project.

For more information contact Chumbe Island Coral Park (CHICOP), PO Box 3203, Zanzibar, tel/fax: 31040, radio 156.725/ch74. Alternatively, you can make enquiries at any reputable tour company, or at Mbweni Ruins Hotel (see page 96) where boat trips to the island depart.

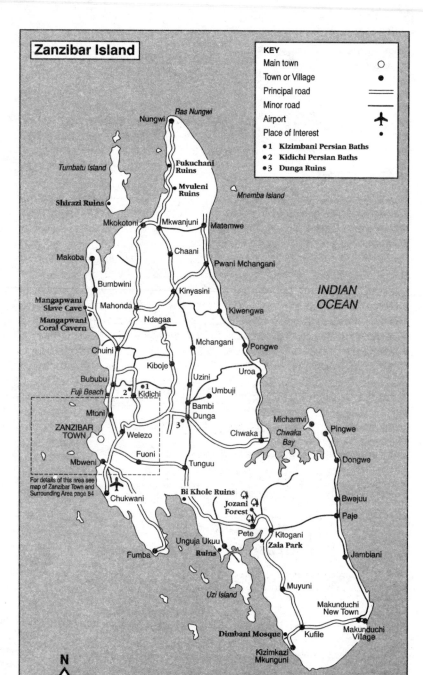

Zanzibar Island

KEY

Main town	○
Town or Village	●
Principal road	═══
Minor road	───
Airport	✈
Place of Interest	●

- ● 1 **Kizimbani Persian Baths**
- ● 2 **Kidichi Persian Baths**
- ● 3 **Dunga Ruins**

Ras Nungwi

Nungwi

Tumbatu Island

Fukuchani Ruins

Mvuleni Ruins

Mnemba Island

Shirazi Ruins

Mkokotoni   Mkwanjuni   Matemwe

Chaani

Makoba   Pwani Mchangani

Bumbwini   Kinyasini

Mangapwani Slave Cave   Mahonda   Kiwengwa

Mangapwani Coral Cavern   Ndagaa

INDIAN OCEAN

Chuini   Mchangani   Pongwe

Kiboje   Uroa

Bububu   Uzini

Fuji Beach   2 Kidichi ● 1   Umbuji

Mtoni   Bambi   Dunga

ZANZIBAR TOWN   3

Welezo   Chwaka   *Chwaka Bay*   Michamvi   Pingwe

Fuoni

Mbweni   Tunguu   Dongwe

For details of this area see map of Zanzibar Town and Surrounding Area page 84

Chukwani   **Bi Khole Ruins**   Bwejuu

Jozani Forest   Paje

Pete   Kitogani

Unguja Ukuu   **Zala Park**

Fumba   **Ruins**   Jambiani

Muyuni

Uzi Island   Makunduchi New Town

Dimbani Mosque   Kufile   Makunduchi Village

Kizimkazi Mkunguni

N
△

0   10 km

Chapter Six

Zanzibar Island

After enjoying the unique sights and atmosphere of Zanzibar Town, you can start to explore the rest of Zanzibar Island (or Unguja, to give it its correct local name). The island is an ideal place to enjoy travel simply for its own sake; to wander slowly among plantations and farmland, and pass through small towns or fishing villages. Once you move away from the somewhat 'touristy' parts of the island you will find a very different, and more authentic, world where local people continue with their everyday lives in a manner which has changed little over hundreds of years. It is refreshing to see this other side of Zanzibar, but you should not be fooled into regarding the island as some kind of rural paradise created only for tourists to admire. For local people this island is home, where the work in the fields or on the sea is hard, and where great poverty is not at all unknown. If you remember this, taking the time to see more of the island and its people, and getting beyond the picture-postcard image, your visit to Zanzibar will be greatly enriched.

TRAVEL AROUND ZANZIBAR ISLAND

You can travel around Zanzibar Island in several different ways: by hire-car, motorbike, scooter, bicycle, tourist minibus, dala-dala, bus, taxi, organised tour, walking, hitchhiking, or a combination of all of these. Outside Zanzibar Town the main roads are tarred, although some are in very bad condition, which can make travel by car or bus slow and uncomfortable. The main routes are gradually being resurfaced, which makes travel quicker and easier for tourists and locals. All other roads on the island are dirt or graded gravel which varies in quality. Along with that in the rest of East and southern Africa, traffic drives on the left in Zanzibar.

Car hire
Car hire is best arranged through one of the tour companies listed in *Chapter Five*. Some have their own vehicles, while others will make arrangements with another company on your behalf. Rates vary between the companies, but are generally between $40 and $60 per day for a small car (eg: Suzuki 'jeep') and around $100 per day for a larger car (eg: Landcruiser). However, quality is much more variable than price, and standards on Zanzibar are not always high; you should carefully check your car for defects and even

go for a short test drive before agreeing to hire.

The price usually includes unlimited distance, but you pay for the petrol yourself: it costs about $0.80 per litre. Insurance is also included in the price, although some tour companies seem a little vague about this, so it is worth checking your exact legal position should you be unfortunate enough to have an accident involving another car or person. Get this in writing.

A deposit and proof of identity are usually asked for. An international driving licence is also required. If you prefer not to drive yourself, most companies provide a driver at little extra charge.

Motorbike and scooter hire

It is possible to hire motorbikes (almost all are Honda DT 125s or similar) or scooters (Vespas and Lambrettas) from many of the tour companies listed in the *Zanzibar Town* chapter. Prices vary, but are generally around $15 to $25 per day for a scooter, $30 per day for a motorbike. For a cheaper deal, try **Nasor Aly Mussa's Scooter Service**, a small garage just off New Mkunazini Road, in Zanzibar Town, near the Anglican Cathedral. As with cars, you should take your scooter for a test drive to make sure everything works before agreeing to hire.

Some tourists to Zanzibar hire scooters, imagining them to be similar to Greek-island-style mopeds. However, scooters have larger engines and are harder to handle than mopeds, and there have been a number of accidents and injuries. You should not hire a scooter if you have never ridden one before; the dirt tracks and potholed roads of Zanzibar are not ideal places to start learning.

Bicycle hire

For getting around Zanzibar Town, or going further afield around the island, fit and adventurous visitors will find bicycles ideal. Most bikes are heavy steel Chinese-built roadsters, so you shouldn't plan on covering too many miles (it's too hot to cycle fast anyway). You can also hire mountain bikes, but most of these are pretty basic all-steel models, and only slightly lighter than the Chinese roadsters. They do have gears though, which makes them easier to ride.

Bikes can be hired through several of the tour companies listed in the *Zanzibar Town* chapter. Daily rates start at $5 for the Chinese roadsters, and $10 for mountain bikes. Take your bike for a short test ride before hiring to make sure everything works. Unless you plan extensive off-road forays, make sure your tyres are pumped up fairly hard, especially on the mountain bikes where semi-flat fat tyres can make for hard going. Your bike should come with a puncture outfit and pump, but if it doesn't these can be bought from the bicycle *fundi* (mechanic) in the market in Zanzibar Town.

Roads can be rough, but are generally flat, and traffic is very light once you're away from Zanzibar Town. If you get tired, you can put your bike on top of a bus or dala-dala and come home the easy way.

Tourist minibuses

Several tour companies and some 'independent guides' (see *Guides and the Papaasi*, page 87) arrange minibuses for tourists from Zanzibar Town to the popular beaches on the southern part of the East Coast, and also to Nungwi.

Transport arranged by tour companies is smooth and reliable, and costs around $20 per person, or around $50 for the vehicle (with driver). In the high season, Sun N Fun Tours (listed on page 113) run a daily 'no-hassle minibus service' to the East Coast for $4 per person each way, or $5 to Nungwi.

Transport arranged by *papaasi* is cheap, but has a slightly rougher edge, and costs between $3 and $6 each way. Coming back to Zanzibar Town from the East Coast is nearly always more expensive than going the other way. (You're trapped – and they know it!) On top of this cost, sudden mid-trip price-rises can also occur, so make sure you agree on the fare before travelling. There's a certain degree of co-operation between the *papaasi* outfits, and usually at least one vehicle a day running in each direction, so you can stay on the beach for as long as you like.

To arrange transport by tourist minibus, or for more details, you can contact a tour company or ask your hotel to put you in touch with an independent guide (more often the *papaasi* will have found you first anyway). As other beaches become popular, tourist minibuses will probably start running here too.

Public bus and dala-dala

It is possible to reach many parts of Zanzibar Island by public bus; although few visitors use them, especially on routes covered by tourist minibuses. The buses are converted lorries with seats and sides made from wood. All buses leave from the market area, or from Darajani Bus Station, both on Creek Road in Zanzibar Town. Fares are very cheap: for example, it costs about only $1 to travel half the length of the island between Zanzibar Town and Bwejuu. Note, however, that prices can rise suddenly if there is a fuel shortage.

On most routes, especially the longer ones, there is only one bus each day. They usually leave Zanzibar Town around midday to take people back to their villages after visiting the market. They reach their destinations in the evening, and 'sleep' there before returning to Zanzibar very early in the morning (between 02.00 and 04.00) in time for the start of that day's market. Some of the longer journeys can be very slow. For example, Zanzibar Town to Nungwi takes three to five hours, Zanzibar Town to Makunduchi between four and eight hours.

The bus route numbers and destinations are:

Route No 1   to Nungwi on the northern tip of the island, via Mahonda, Kinyasini and Chaani, or via Mkokotoni
Route No 2   to Bumbwini and Makoba on the west coast, north of Zanzibar town, via Mangapwani
Route No 3   to Kidichi and Kizimbani, an area of plantations, to the northeast of Zanzibar Town, via Welezo

Route No 4	to Mchangani, in the centre of the island, northeast of Zanzibar Town, via Dunga, Bambi, and Uzini (some buses also go to Umbuji)
Route No 5	to Ndagaa, in the centre of the island, northeast of Zanzibar Town, via Kiboje
Route No 6	to Chwaka, about halfway down the east coast (some buses continue to Uroa)
Route No 7	to Fumba, at the end of a peninsula, south of Zanzibar Town, via Kombeni
Route No 8	to Unguja Ukuu, about halfway down the southwest coast, opposite Uzi Island
Route No 9	to Paje, on the east coast, and sometimes to Bwejuu and Jambiani
Route No 10	to Makunduchi, at the southern end of the east coast, via Tunguu, Pete and Munyuni
Route No 11	to Fuoni, about 7km east of Zanzibar Town.

Buses do not always go to their final destination. For example bus No 1 (the route for Nungwi) may go only as far as Mkokotoni. Therefore, always check that the bus *is* going to the destination you think it should be.

Some of the bus routes listed above are also covered by *dala-dalas* (small pick-up vans), which fill the gaps in the bus service 'timetables'. Dala-dalas are usually slightly more expensive than the buses, but also tend to be quicker.

Hitchhiking

Hitching around Zanzibar Island is possible, but there are few private cars on the island and traffic is very light, so you will need a lot of patience. However, a combination of public transport, walking and hitching is sometimes the only way to travel, unless you hire a bike or car. In the northern part of the island, there are occasional vehicles on main roads between Zanzibar Town and Nungwi (via Kinyasini), and between Zanzibar Town and the junction near Dunga, where the roads to Bambi New Town and Chwaka divide. In the southern parts of the island, the main road between Zanzibar Town and Kitogani (where the road to the beaches on the southern part of the East Coast branches off) is slightly busier, so you may be able to hitch a lift here, or get picked up by one of the tourist minibuses that travel up and down this route.

Travellers report that hitching around Zanzibar and Pemba islands is relatively safe, when compared to many other parts of Africa, although of course this can never be guaranteed. It seems that there are no particular dangers for women hitching alone, any more than for lone men or couples, as long as the usual sensible precautions are taken. Some local drivers expect payment for giving a lift – normally the same as the equivalent bus or dala-dala fare – so check this before accepting a ride.

HOTELS AND GUESTHOUSES

Around Zanzibar Island, nearly all the hotels and guesthouses are built on or very near the coast. This is where you find idyllic tropical beaches with palm trees, clean white sand, and the warm blue waters of the Indian Ocean.

Some travellers come here for a couple of days, just to relax after seeing the sights of Zanzibar Town, and linger for a couple of weeks instead. Visitors on tighter time restrictions always wish they could stay for longer...

On the coast there are several different kinds of place to stay, ranging from large hotels and 'club-resorts' with many facilities, through small but comfortable lodges and bungalows, to local-style guesthouses which are basic but adequate. Some places deal almost exclusively with package tourists who fly in from Europe (particularly Italy) and spend most or all of their time on Zanzibar within the confines of their hotel. These hotels may not even be able to take guests who simply 'walk in' and want a room. At the middle and lower end of the range there are many places which normally deal with 'walk-in' guests, although reservations at busy times are recommended. For budget backpackers there's a huge choice, and even if you could reserve a room (if they had a phone, and it was working) it would be a very unusual thing to do.

As the number of tourists visiting Zanzibar continues to grow, the number of hotels on the coast increases also. The following list describes a wide selection, but cannot hope to be complete. You should expect to find more new places by the time you arrive. Most of the hotels and guesthouses have restaurants, where the food and prices reflect the quality of the hotel itself. If you have a stove and want to cater for yourself, you can buy fish and a few vegetables in the villages, but supplies are often quite limited so it is better to bring some items from Zanzibar Town.

Throughout this chapter, all prices quoted for hotels are high season rates. You can normally get discounts of 25% to 50% in the low season, and there may be additional premiums at the Christmas and New Year peaks. At any time of year, rates may be negotiable if you're in a small group, or plan to stay several nights. All places include breakfast, unless otherwise stated . Other meals are available – at all but the smartest places lunches and dinners usually have to be ordered several hours in advance.

Note Not all the hotels on Zanzibar Island are positioned near specific tourist sights or places of interest. Similarly, not all the places to visit have a place to stay nearby. Consequently, they are listed separately. For details see the *Places to Visit* section later in this chapter.

Places to stay on the East Coast – northern part
The northern part of the East Coast, between Nungwi (at the northern tip of Zanzibar Island) and Chwaka Bay, was until recently seldom visited by tourists. Public transport was limited and accommodation was virtually non-existent. However, since the early 1990s several hotels have been built along this stretch of the coast, and many more are planned for the future.

Nungwi
This large village at the far northern end of Zanzibar Island is traditionally the centre of Zanzibar's dhow-building industry, and until five years ago

was rarely reached by tourists. When we came here in 1992 to write the first edition of this book there was quite simply nowhere to stay. In the second edition we listed a couple of fledgling guesthouses. Now you can choose between at least ten places, ranging from basic to total luxury.

Nungwi is a popular place for diving and fishing, and a number of operators have set up bases here. The main beach (just west of the village) is favoured by some visitors as the reef does not extend immediately from the shore so the water is deep enough for swimming, whatever the state of the tide. As the beach faces west it is also good for watching the sun go down. (On the east coast, of course, you only get sunrises.) However, there are fewer palm trees here than on the East Coast, and so less shade. It's a matter of taste.

Despite the influx of tourists, Nungwi is a traditional, conservative place. It was one of the last coastal settlements of any size on Zanzibar to have a hotel, or any tourist facilities. As recently as the mid-1990s proposals for large developments in the area were fiercely opposed by local people (although see box on page 168 for more news on developments at Nungwi). Today, local people are not unfriendly, but they are proud and independent. You rather get the impression tourists are here on sufferance. If you're trying to make friendly contact, a little bit of respect and politeness goes a long way.

Nungwi can be reached by bus, tourist minibus or hired vehicle. From Zanzibar Town the main road to Nungwi goes via Mahonda, Kinyasini and Chaani New Town. The road directly north from Mahonda to Mkokotoni is in poor condition – although it does go through better scenery.

For somewhere to stay, the first place reached as you come to the beach from Nungwi village is **Baraka Guesthouse**, owned and managed by the friendly Mr Baraka himself, where simple en-suite bungalows with verandas cost around $30 a double. There are also some triples and a few older bungalows which cost $10 per person. Next door, and slightly closer to the beach, is the **Paradise Guesthouse** with a similar range of rooms and prices. Nearby are some local shops selling postcards, drinks, biscuits, and other odds and ends. Also nearby is the base of Chinook Sport Fishing, a smart outfit running trips to the Pemba Channel. Indian Ocean Divers (see page 115) also have a base here.

A short distance along the beach is **Amaan Bungalows**, probably the largest and most organised of the budget places, where double en-suite bungalows are $25 to $30, and simple rooms $10. There's a well-stocked bar and food is available. At the attached East Africa Diving & Watersports Centre, single dives cost $30, multiple dives $25, and five-day instruction courses $300. Fishing boats can be hired for $25 per hour including equipment, and sailboards from $5 per hour. You can contact Amaan Bungalows direct (PO Box 2750, tel: 0811 327747, fax: 0811 30556) and use the phone to make calls to the mainland or any other part of the world.

In Amaan's back yard are two more straightforward locally run places:

Kigoma Beach Guesthouse and **Safina Bungalows**, both charging $8 per person in simple rooms, or $10 in a small hut with veranda.

Back from the beach are two more cheap places, which are worth trying if the others are full or if you just want a different atmosphere: **Ikibal Guesthouse** and **Ruma Guesthouse**.

On the east side of Nungwi are some other places to stay. Just past the lighthouse are **Mnarani Beach Cottages**, one of the few places on Zanzibar where you can see sunrise *and* sunset, with friendly staff, relaxed management and just six comfortable bungalows, pleasantly built in local style, costing $70 for doubles. Half board and full board are both available. For reservations, contact their Zanzibar Town office: tel: 33440, mobile: 0811 334062.

A few kilometres further down the coast is the **Ras Nungwi Beach Hotel**, one of the smartest establishments on this part of the island, with 35 chalets, 19 lodge rooms, two bars, restaurant, shop, fully equipped dive and deep-sea fishing centres, and facilities for other sports like wind-surfing and snorkelling. Although there are other similar resort set-ups on Zanzibar, Ras Nungwi has resisted the urge to be giant and offers guests a relatively intimate experience. Additionally, efforts are made to attract visitors from several overseas countries, to avoid the domination of any one nationality. High-season rates for chalets are $80 per person, for lodge rooms $65 per person, full board (three meals each day). Low-season rates are about 20% less. Transfers from Zanzibar town or airport are $20 per person, less for groups of more than five. For diving the hotel charges $25 per dive, or $300 for a PADI Open Water 1 five-day course. Specialist courses, air fills and equipment hire are also available. Although diving is a big thing here (the lodge makes full use of its position at the tip of the island and boats can reach a range of dive sites), and watersports are popular, many guests come to Ras Nungwi simply to laze on the beach! Only non-motorised watersports are allowed near the beach (no waterskiing) so lazers are not disturbed. You can make enquiries or reservations through agents overseas or in Zanzibar Town, or direct to Ras Nungwi's Zanzibar Town office (tel: 33767, fax: 33098, email: rasnungwi@zanzibar.net).

Surprisingly close to Ras Nungwi are **Saleh's Beach Bungalows** which cost $25 per person per night.

A few kilometres south of Nungwi, on the west coast beach, is **Kendwa Rocks**. Originally established as a low-key campsite in the mid 1990s, over the years some rustic *bandas* (shacks) and bungalows have been built, although the *very* mellow atmosphere remains intact. Camping is $4 (or $5 to borrow a tent), bandas are $6 per person, and bungalows are $20 a double. All prices include breakfast. Other meals, snacks and drinks are sold. Boat rides to Tumbatu Island are arranged, and you can hire kayaks and snorkel gear. You can get here by boat from Nungwi (there's one free run per day) or you can walk for 30 minutes along the beach. If you've got a car, it's about 5km from Nungwi, first on the main road, then on rough tracks. Next door, a new place connected to Amaan Bungalows should be completed by 1998.

Interesting things to see near Nungwi include the Mnarani Natural Turtle Aquarium, and the ruins at Fukuchani and Mvuleni. More details are in the *Places to visit* section later in this chapter.

The skilled traditional dhow builders are fascinating to watch, but some do not like having their photos taken so ask before you use your camera. (Some dhow-builders are happy to be photographed but ask for payment.) The lighthouse at Ras Nungwi is still in operation, and not open to visitors. The marines guarding it do not allow photos.

Matemwe

Matemwe is a small village, about 15km south of Nungwi. At the northern end of the village are **Matemwe Bungalows**, a small and simple but comfortable hotel, with whitewashed walls and thatched roofs, on a low coral cliff overlooking the sea. The hotel has been here for about ten years, and was well known around the world for its 'eco-tourism' philosophy long before this became a trendy, and all too easily applied, buzzword.

This is a low-key development, where the management are taking great steps to reduce their impact on the local people and surroundings. New grass has been planted to prevent soil erosion, and visitors are encouraged not to damage the nearby reef, nor buy coral and shells from villagers. The hotel buys as much fresh produce locally as possible, and has provided finance to support local artists and a women's co-operative which makes money from selling local handicrafts. The hotel also runs a small sea-turtle nest protection project. Local people are paid a fee to report finding a turtle nest, and a bonus for every hatchling which makes it to the sea.

Full-board accommodation in an en-suite double bungalow is $70 per person per day. Non-en-suite bungalows are $55. The hotel is proud to advertise that there is no telephone and no electricity. The rooms and restaurant are lit by lamps. Speedboat trips are not offered, but you can go sailing in a traditional outrigger. You can even go fishing, and the chef will prepare your catch for dinner.

THE FUTURE FOR NUNGWI?

Despite the local inhabitants' original resistance to large-scale development at Nungwi, the December 1996 issue of *Tantravel*, a magazine published by the Tanzania Tourist Board, proudly reported that a multi-million-dollar joint venture between the Zanzibar government and a British development company planned to convert 50 square kilometres of the Nungwi area into a complex of luxury hotels, resorts and a pleasure-boat marina.

According to the magazine, the $500-million project will be in two phases. The first is the construction of a 200-room five-star hotel, complete with golf course. The second is the construction of community buildings (police station, medical clinic, hospital) and the setting up of an ambulance service.

Phase one is due for completion in the year 2000. The report doesn't say when phase two will be finished. Or started.

Based at the hotel is Dive Adventures Zanzibar, with standard dives and courses run in the same sensitive and responsible manner. A single dive is $35, double dive $35, four-day open water course $350, all including equipment. Dive sites include the nearby Mnemba Atoll. The resident fully-qualified dive instructor is also a marine biologist and offers a unique reef ecology course. Night dives and other special courses are also available. If you have your own gear, rates are lower. The hotel has also developed a short walking trail along the reef-edge.

For more details, or to make a reservation, contact Matemwe Bungalows direct (PO Box 3275, tel: 33789, fax: 31342), or visit their office at Kibweni, north of Zanzibar Town. Credit cards are accepted if payment is made in Zanzibar Town, not at the hotel. Alternatively, any tour company in Zanzibar Town will make a reservation for you.

Transfers can be arranged by the hotel or a tour company. If you are driving, you can approach Matemwe direct from Mkwanjuni (east of Mkokotoni), or via Kinyasini and Pwani Mchangani, then go up the small coastal track to Matemwe. The bungalows are difficult to reach by public transport – the nearest regular bus goes to Pwani Mchangani village, although dala-dalas go to Matemwe village (at the end of the road from Mkwanjuni) most days, from where the bungalows are a 4km walk through the palms.

North of Matemwe, a new hotel is being developed at Muyuni Beach, and several more are rumoured to be planned. South from here, towards Pwani Mchangani, yet more new hotels are planned, or under construction. It can only be hoped that they are developed with the same sensitivity as Matemwe Bungalows.

Mnemba Island

Mnemba Island lies about 3km off the coast, to the northeast of Matemwe. It is a small island, about 1km around, surrounded by a large circular coral reef. The island and reef together are known as Mnemba Atoll. On the island is **Mnemba Club**, a very exclusive group of cottages made mainly from local materials, offering what the owners call 'barefoot luxury'. Rates start at $350 per person per day, which includes everything except transfers from Zanzibar airport and champagne. A large game-fishing boat, complete with crew and tackle, is available for hire. The club is frequented by the rich and famous: some people, wanting complete exclusivity, hire the whole island. The club is run by a South African company called the Conservation Corporation. Advance reservations are essential, through any reliable travel agent in Zanzibar Town or specialist agents overseas.

Pwani Mchangani

About 6km south of Matemwe village is the larger settlement of Pwani Mchangani, which (along with Chwaka) is one of the island's main fish markets. About 2km north of here, or 4km south of Matemwe village, is **Mambo Guesthouse**, a small quiet locally-owned place set back from the beach, where doubles cost $30. In Pwani Mchangani village itself, there are two more places: **Tufikiniwe Guesthouse** and **Riziki Haiwanwa Guesthouse**. They are owned and run by a local women's co-operative group and are both reported to offer simple good-value accommodation. Also in the village is the **Dolphin Restaurant**, set up mainly to cater for guests from the large hotels further along the coast.

A new road along the coast links Pwani Mchangani and Kiwengwa. Less than 2km south of Pwani Mchangani village is **Mapenzi Beach Village**, a large resort (with some of the largest palm-thatch *makuti* roofs anywhere in Africa) catering almost exclusively for Italian fly-in package tourists. If you want a taste of luxury, a travel agent in Zanzibar or overseas will make a booking for you. Full board in en-suite bungalows, each with fan or air-conditioning, safety deposit box, telephone and hairdryer, costs $120 per person. Facilities include swimming pool, jacuzzi, two boutiques, a disco and nightly entertainment. Next along is the similar **Coral Reef Village**.

Just south of Coral Reef, at the northern end of Kiwengwa Beach, is the **Shooting Star Bar, Restaurant and Cottages.** This is a small friendly place run by English-Tanzanian couple Shelley and Eli. The food is good; many guests come to eat here, overlooking the beach, as a change from the nearby large hotels, but an increasing number come from Zanzibar Town on day trips by hire car or motorbike. Fresh fish, chicken, beef and vegetarian dishes are served, plus curries, crab and squid; three-course meals range from $9 to $17, lobster starts at $20. There are six cottages for rent, ideal for couples or families, at $50 per person full board, with cheaper rates for children; simple double bandas at $10 bed and breakfast; and luxury double en-suite bungalows for $140 full board. For more information contact PO Box 3076, tel: 33386.

Kiwengwa

Kiwengwa is a small coastal village. There are several hotels nearby. North of the village these include **Karibu Beach Resort** (part of the VentaClub chain) and **Kiwengwa Club Village** (Francorosso), both catering for Italian package tourists. Rates at the former are from $80 per person, at the latter $120, full board. Both places also have fully geared-up dive centres.

South of the village is the markedly different **Reef View**, a low-key, quiet place run by a friendly English-Zanzibari couple, still under development when we passed through but due to be ready for guests by late 1997. Simple bandas are $10 per person, bungalows $30. There will be a bar and restaurant, with simple meals available. Fishing boats can be hired.

Next along is **Pongwe Beach Hotel**, where bungalows on the beach are $50 to $70 a double.

Uroa

The small village of Uroa can be reached from Kiwengwa, along the coast track, or from Dunga via Bambi, but most easily (if you're coming from

Zanzibar Town) via Chwaka.

The large **Uroa Bay Village Resort** is regarded as one of the best on the island, charging around $150 per person per day in a double room for full-board accommodation. Facilities include swimming pool, watersports, sailing and fishing and a highly regarded fishing club. (Town office, tel: 33552, fax: 33504.) Nearby is the smaller **Sun & Sand Beach Bungalows**, with double rooms for $40 (en-suite $70). For enquiries and reservations contact their office (tel: 32449) in Zanzibar Town near the People's Bank of Zanzibar. Next door is the similar **White Villa**, another mid-range place recommended by some visitors.

At the southern end of Uroa is the **Tamarind Beach Hotel**, a pleasant group of villas with en-suite rooms and balconies overlooking the palm-lined seashore. Bed and breakfast rates are $77 single, $103 double, $150 triple, with discounts for children. Full board is an extra $35 per person. Bahani Divers are based at the Tamarind: one dive is $35, three dives $90, open water course $350. A full-day double dive trip to Mnemba is $75. Equipment can be hired. For reservations contact the Tamarind's Zanzibar Town office (PO Box 2206, tel/fax: 33041/2, mobile: 0811 323566) or their European office in Germany (tel: (06221) 642223, fax: 642225).

Chwaka

Chwaka is a large fishing village halfway down the East Coast. In the 19th century, Chwaka was a slave port, and during colonial times its ocean breezes made it a popular holiday resort for wealthy Zanzibaris and British colonial officials. Today, Chwaka has one of the island's largest fish markets, and a lively atmosphere in the mornings when the fishing boats land. There are a couple of hotels, but few tourists come here, so Chwaka is a place worth considering if you want to be amongst Zanzibaris rather than other foreigners. Chwaka can be reached by public bus, or by hired car or bike.

For accommodation in Chwaka your options are the large and frequently empty **Chwaka Bay Beach Hotel** (also called the Zanswede Hotel) at the north end of the village, costing from $45 for a double bungalow, and the small and basic **East End Guest and Restaurant** [sic] where singles are $10 and doubles $20.

If you come to Chwaka by bus, then want to continue travelling down the East Coast without going all the way back to Zanzibar Town, you can get a ride on a boat across Chwaka Bay to Michamvi or Pingwe on the peninsula north of Bwejuu. Local people travel this way, but only the occasional adventurous tourist is seen here. Boats from Michamvi come across to Chwaka fish market most mornings, then go back about noon, but there are no set schedules: you need to ask around on the beach. A ride will cost about $1. Alternatively, you can hire a boat for about $25 and go across when it suits you. The trip takes about two hours depending on wind and the availability of petrol for the motor. From Michamvi or Pingwe you can then walk along the beach or through the palms to Bwejuu in three to five hours.

Place to stay on the East Coast – southern part

The southern part of the East Coast, from Michamvi (on the peninsula east of Chwaka Bay) down towards Makunduchi, is probably the most popular area for visitors. There is a wide choice of accommodation here for all budgets and transport links to and from Zanzibar Town are good.

On this stretch of coast are the famous beaches of Bwejuu, Paje and Jambiani. Backpackers and independent travellers have been coming here for many years, and several low-to-mid-budget hotels have been built during this time. These areas can be reached by public bus, tourist minibus, car, scooter or bike, via the villages of Tunguu, Pete and Kitogani.

North of Bwejuu are several other hotels, which are more up-market. South of Jambiani there are no hotels at present (1997) but it can only be a matter of time before some appear. If you want to go north beyond Bwejuu or south past Jambiani, there's no public transport, so you'll need to have your own wheels or enjoy a good walk.

If you come to the Bwejuu-Paje-Jambiani area by tourist minibus, the drivers get commission from some of the hotels and will try to take you to these, unless you specifically say you want to go to one of the other places.

Paje

Paje is a small fishing village, where the road from Zanzibar Town meets the coast and the tracks to Bwejuu and Jambiani divide. There are several places to choose from here. The **Ufukwe Guesthouse** and the **Amani Guesthouse** have been recommended; both are simple, good-value places with double rooms for $8 per person, including breakfast.

Other places include **Paje Ndame Village,** where the food is good, and the very pleasant **Paradise Beach Bungalows**. These have a few more facilities and charge $10 per person. Also recommended is the larger and slightly more expensive **Paje by Night Hotel**, charging $15 per person. At least one large hotel is under construction in the village, and more may be planned.

If you don't want to eat at your hotel, a small **café** has been opened by the junction where the road to Zanzibar Town leaves the coast.

Also in the village is an old mausoleum, a low rectangular edifice with a castellated wall and inset with old plates and dishes. This design is thought to have originated in Persia, and may indicate that this part of the island was settled by Shirazi immigrants before the western side of the island near present-day Zanzibar Town.

Bwejuu

Bwejuu village is north of Paje. There is a **ZTC bungalow** here, with three rooms, which is clean but plain and dreary. Officially, it costs $20 to rent the whole bungalow (reservations should be made at the ZTC office in Zanzibar Town) but it might be possible to make an arrangement with the caretaker if you only want one room.

Other places to stay in Bwejuu village include the popular and constantly expanding **Dere Guesthouse** (tel: 31047, 31017), with rooms in the main house, set around a courtyard, for $8 per person, or $10 for en-suite. Rooms in the new wing all cost $10 per person. Rates for groups or long-stays are negotiable. The Dere has a small restaurant doing cheap, good-value food, with meals around $3 to $6.

Nearby is **Burghani Villa**, a small place with four double rooms for $10 per person. Meals can be cooked to order, by arrangement with the caretaker.

Almost next door is the **Palm Beach Inn**, a smarter place with a pleasant garden and quiet atmosphere. Nicely decorated en-suite double or triple rooms cost $15 per person. En-suite beach bungalows are $20 per person. Prices include breakfast. The Palm Beach has an airy restaurant with a good selection of local meals, including lobster, for between $4 and $8 (advance orders are appreciated), and a beach bar. For reservations, contact Suna Tours in Zanzibar Town (tel: 33385).

Another budget option is the **Seven Seas Guesthouse**, with rooms at $10 per person.

All the hotels do food but, if you want to eat elsewhere, Bwejuu village itself has a few local-style eating houses; several travellers have recommended **Jamal's Restaurant**, near the Palm Beach Inn. There's also a couple of small shops with a very limited stock, and you can buy fish and sometimes vegetables from sellers on the beach.

You can explore the offshore reef with snorkelling gear, hired from the Dere Guesthouse or Palm Beach Inn (around $3 per day for mask, snorkel and flippers), although this means walking out at low tide. You can also hire bikes ($4) or scooters ($40) from local villagers (arranged through the hotel) and ride a few kilometres north up the beach to the 'lagoon' at Dongwe, an inlet in the reef where its outer edge can be more easily reached.

North of Bwejuu
North of Bwejuu village, towards Dongwe, budget places include the **Kilimani Guesthouse** and the **Evergreen Resthouse**, both with rooms for $10 per person. There's also the **Twisted Palm**, two open-plan houses with five rooms each, pleasant and peaceful, and good value at $25 per person for half board or $10 per person bed only. Several travellers have recommended this place for its tranquil atmosphere and good food.

Further north (about 3km from Bwejuu village) is the small but smart, and frequently recommended, **Sunrise Hotel** (PO Box 3967, fax: 30344) set in lush gardens, with a great view of the sea from your bar-stool, where en-suite double bungalows cost $60 to $70. Meals in the restaurant (which has a Belgian chef) start at $6.

Beyond the Sunrise, all the way up the coast, through the villages of Dongwe, Pingwe and Michamvi, several more up-market hotels and club-resorts are being built, which are all likely to be in the $100 to $200 per person per night bracket, and mostly designed to cater for fly-in package tourists rather than one-off passing visitors. These include the **Blue Marlin**, the **Sultan Village** and the **Karafuu**. At least two others are planned. If these places open to passing trade when they are completed, more details will be available from tour companies in Zanzibar Town.

From Bwejuu, if you want to keep heading north up the coast, you can avoid back-tracking around Chwaka Bay by taking a boat from Michamvi across to Chwaka. See the section on Chwaka earlier in this chapter for details, or ask around at the hotels in Bwejuu for more information.

Jambiani

Jambiani is south of Paje. The village's name comes from *jambiya*, meaning an Arab-style dagger. Local legend holds that some early settlers found a dagger here: proof that even earlier visitors had been before them.

This is a very long settlement, spread for several kilometres down the coast, with a wide choice of low-budget places to stay. In between those mentioned below, other new budget-bungalow-type places are constantly popping up. The village also has a school (which invites visitors to donate money to improve facilities), several basic food stores, a local craft shop (which also sells delicious natural honey) and a bakery.

At the northern end of the village, reached first as you come in from Paje, are the **Horizontal Inn** and the **Manufaa Guesthouse**, both small family-run places, with clean rooms for $6 per person. Lunch and dinner are also available, for around $3, but you must order several hours in advance.

Next in line is the **ZTC bungalow**, offering the standard ZTC service for the standard ZTC price of $20 for five people. Ten years ago this was the only place to stay in Jambiani. Little has changed, apart from a coat of paint in 1990 and the installation of electricity in 1994, but if you're spending most of your time on the beach this is a fair deal. Nearby is the no-frills **Molly Beach Restaurant**, serving lunches, dinners and drinks.

In the same area is **Oasis Beach Inn**, with simple rooms at $8 per person. Nearby, but in a different league, is the **Sau Inn**, with comfortable en-suite rooms and cottages set in pleasant gardens, with a good restaurant overlooking the beach. Singles are $40, doubles $50, triples $60. Half-board and full-board rates are also available. Special rooms ('well furnished with high comfort') cost an extra $10 per person. You can make reservations direct to the hotel (PO Box 1656, tel: 32215) or through any travel agent in Zanzibar Town.

Further along the village 'main street', past the health centre and the school, is the popular **East Coast Visitors Inn**, which is clean and pleasant with rooms in the 'guesthouse' at $8 per person, en-suite doubles for $10 per person and a double en-suite cottage for $15 per person. Meals in the restaurant start at around $3. Next along is the **Jambiani Beach Hotel**, small and peaceful, with comfortable en-suite rooms facing the beach, good value at $10 per person. The hotel's restaurant serves local dishes for between $4 and $7, and has a quiet bar.

Beyond that, past the village shop (which also sells stamps) is the **Shehe Guesthouse**, a very friendly place, and popular too, although some travellers report that it's not as good as it used to be. Rooms, set round a sandy courtyard, cost $6 to $10 per person. Some travellers report that this price includes transport to/from Zanzibar Town, but this has to be negotiated separately. The guesthouse also has a small shop selling biscuits, soft drinks and a few items of tinned food, and a cafeteria serving cheap fixed-menu lunch and dinner (from $3) which must be ordered several hours in advance.

Beyond the Shehe, at the quieter southern end of the village, is the **Gomani Guesthouse** (tel: 31476), a clean and friendly place perched on low cliffs, with simple rooms for $6 per night, and more comfortable bungalows at $10 per person.

About two hours' walk outside Jambiani is a large underground cavern called Kumbi, which contains a natural spring. According to local legend, it was lived in at one time. Today it is a traditional shrine: local people go there to pray and make offerings. Around the village, you can also see several old tombs decorated with plates and dishes, similar to the one at Paje.

South of Jambiani

At the end of Jambiani village, the beach fizzles out and low coral cliffs, covered in vegetation, come right down to the sea. The dirt road heads inland and cuts through the scrub for 10km to Makunduchi. There are no hotels along this stretch of road, and no public transport. If you want to keep heading south to Makunduchi, you may be lucky and find a lift on one of the occasional vehicles passing this way. Otherwise, if you decide to walk, it takes about three to four hours.

Place to stay on the South Coast
Makunduchi

There are two parts to this settlement at the southern end of Zanzibar Island. On the coast is the small village of 'old' Makunduchi, which has some local huts and houses, a few holiday cottages, and a small beach. Very few visitors come here, and it is much quieter than Bwejuu or Jambiani (not that they are particularly noisy). Dolphins can often be seen from the shore. About 2km inland is Makunduchi New Town. Despite its grand title, this settlement is only a large village, with the additional features of a bank, post and telephone office, police station and small shop. The town also has a few blocks of flats, built as part of an East German aid scheme, similar to the ones in the new part of Zanzibar Town but even more inappropriate as Makunduchi has a poor electricity supply which means the residents have to cook indoors on charcoal stoves.

For a place to stay, you have to go to 'old' Makunduchi village, which is a better setting as it's on the beach. There are two **ZTC bungalows** here, but both seem to be seem to be permanently closed, although if you wanted to stay here you could make enquiries at the ZTC office in Zanzibar Town

---

THE MWAKA KOGWA FESTIVAL AT MAKUNDUCHI

If you happen to be visiting Zanzibar during the last week of July, try to reach Makunduchi. Every year there's a large festival here called the *Mwaka Kogwa* when local people come from all over the island for singing, dancing and drumming. The festival is also called *Mwaka Nairuz* and it originates from Persia, marking the start of the New Year in the Shirazi calendar. (For more details on the Shirazis in Zanzibar see *Chapter Two*.)

The festival involves several rituals, including a mock fight where men from different parts of the village beat each other with banana stems. It is believed that this fight gives each combatant a chance to vent his feelings, and in this way the disagreements and arguments of the past year are exorcised so that the new year can be started peacefully. (Although this is a mock fight, it can still get pretty serious. Fortunately the men are only fighting with banana stems – they used to do it with real clubs and cudgels.)

While the men are beating each other, the women have a far more pleasant way of celebrating: dressed in their finest clothes, they parade around the village singing. The songs contain comments about love, families and village life.

The next stage of the festival is the ritual burning of a traditional hut, which has been built especially for the purpose. A local healer goes inside before the fire is lit and runs out again when the hut is burning strongly. It is thought that the burning of the hut symbolises the passing of the old year and also ensures that during the coming year should any house in the village catch fire its inhabitants will escape unharmed.

After the fighting and the hut-burning, a large feast is held with all the villagers bringing food and eating together. People from other parts of Zanzibar are welcomed, as a local tradition holds that any villager without a guest must be unhappy.

After the eating, the dancing starts. The dances are traditional *Ngomas* and *Taarabs* (see the section on *Music and dance* in *Chapter Four*), but these days may include some amplified disco sounds as well. The locals dance into the night and die-hard party-goers move on to the beach to continue singing and dancing until dawn.

During the festival time, several of the tour companies listed in *Chapter Five* run day-trips to Makunduchi.

(see page 113). Your best option is a small locally run place called **Kigaeni Reef Lodge**, which has double and triple rooms for $8 per person. The lodge also has a small garden where you can camp. Simple meals are available in the restaurant to order. Fishing and snorkelling trips can be arranged through the lodge, as can tours from Zanzibar Town, which include transport to and from the lodge, full board accommodation, a visit to Jozani Forest and a boat trip to see the dolphins. It costs from $30 per person (depending on group size). If you don't want the tour, Kigaeni Reef Lodge arranges free transport from Zanzibar Town for groups of four or more. This can be arranged at the lodge's office in Zanzibar Town (PO Box 1741, tel: 31289), or at Sama Tours (page 112) or Suna Tours (page 113).

South of Kigaeni Reef Lodge, a new hotel seems to be under construction. About 1km further along the beach is a lighthouse.

Makunduchi can be reached by public bus, or by rented car, scooter or bike, but there are no tourist minibuses working regularly on this route, although you could hire one specially through a tour company or independent guide in Zanzibar Town, apart from the free transport arranged by Kigaeni Reef Lodge. You can also reach Makunduchi from Jambiani; see *South of Jambiani*, page 175.

Kizimkazi

To the west of Makunduchi, Kizimkazi is actually two villages: Kizimkazi Mkunguni and Kizimkazi Dimbani. The Mwinyi Mkuu (the traditional king of Zanzibar) once had a residence at Kizimkazi Mkunguni. Today the village has a few huts and houses, a school, a mosque, and a dispensary. The **Kizimkazi Beach Villa**, a fairly basic bungalow overlooking the beach, charges $8 per person. Meals (all in the $2 to $5 range) can be prepared to order.

Dolphins are seen in this area, and Kizimkazi has become a launch point for boats running 'dolphin tours' organised by companies in Zanzibar Town. If you don't take an all-in tour from town, or want to spend the night at Kizimkazi, you can usually hire a boat or arrange to join a group here. But read the box on *Dolphins* (page 182) carefully.

Kizimkazi Dimbani is about 2km north along the coast from Kizimkazi Mkunguni (3km by road), just off the road towards Kufile. There's no place to stay here, but the ancient Shirazi mosque (more details in the *Places to visit* section below) is worth looking at.

If you don't come to Kizimkazi by tourist minibus, or as part of a tour, you can get here by public bus: some buses running between Zanzibar Town and Makunduchi divert down to Kizimkazi Mkunguni. Otherwise you'll have to get off the bus at Kufile junction and walk to Kizimkazi Dimbani (4km) or Kizimkazi Mkunguni (6km). Your other alternative is to come by hired car, scooter or bike.

PLACES TO VISIT

Zanzibar Island divides roughly into two areas, north and south of a line drawn between Zanzibar Town and Chwaka Bay. All the places of interest described in this section can be reached by hire-car, scooter or bike, or by using a combination of public bus, tourist minibus, walking and hitchhiking. More details about how to get around are given towards the start of this chapter.

Places to visit on Zanzibar Island – northern area
Nungwi

Nungwi is a large fishing village at the northern end of Zanzibar Island, and the centre of Zanzibar's traditional **dhow-building** industry. Various hardwood trees, particularly good for boat-building, grow in this area. The teams of boat-builders work on the beach outside the village, under the shade of the palm trees. With great skill, and using only the simplest of tools, they turn planks of wood into strong ocean-going vessels. Another important material is rope made from coconut husks (coir). Little in the way of iron or steel is used.

It is a fascinating place to see the dhows at their various stages of construction. However, you should show respect for the builders, who are generally indifferent towards visitors, and keep out of the way. Most do not like having their photos taken (so ask before you use your camera), although a few have realised their photogenicity has value and ask for payment.

Nungwi's other industry is seaweed. Local women tend this newly introduced crop on the flat beach area just beyond the low tide mark. The seaweed is harvested, then dried in the sun and sent to Zanzibar Town for export. (For more details, see the box on *Seaweed farming*, page 80.)

Another attraction for visitors to Nungwi is **Mnarani Natural Turtle Aquarium**, at the north end of the west beach, very near the lighthouse which marks the actual headland of Ras Nungwi (in Swahili *ras* means head) and the northernmost tip of Zanzibar Island. With encouragement from various conservation bodies, the local people have created what is essentially a very large rock pool, where the water level goes up and down with the tide, which is home to a large 'family' of turtles. There are a few adults and several young which are released into the sea when they reach a certain size. Turtles are an endangered species, and are captured elsewhere on Zanzibar for food, while their shells are made into souvenirs (see the box on page 72 for more details). Tourists are charged $1 to enter the aquarium. It's interesting to see the turtles at close quarters, and money raised goes to various local community schemes. It may sound a bit zoo-like, but only if animals have a tangible value are local people likely to protect them.

The lighthouse at Ras Nungwi is still in operation, and not open to visitors. The marines guarding it do not allow photos. (*Mnara* means tower or lighthouse, and Mnarani is 'place of the lighthouse'.)

Places to stay in Nungwi are listed on pages 165 to 168.

Fukuchani Ruins

These remains of a large house, dating from the 16th century, lie to the south of Nungwi. The ruin is known locally as the Portuguese House but it is considered by archaeologists to be of Swahili origin, although some Portuguese settlers may have built houses on Zanzibar during this period. It is built of coral bricks, with arched doorways and rectangular niches in the walls of the main room, and surrounded by a stone wall in which small holes have been inserted for the purposes of defence. Buildings of a similar style have been found at other sites along the East African coast.

The ruins are in good condition, compared to many others on Zanzibar of a similar age, and quite impressive. Behind the ruin, a path leads to a small beach. Across the channel you can see Tumbatu Island, with the

Old Dispensary, Stone Town, restored by the Aga Khan Foundation (CO)

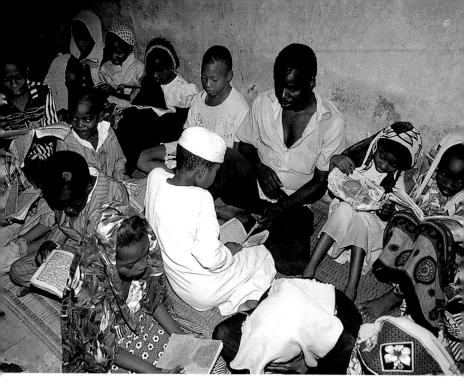

Above: *Koranic school, Stone Town* (CO)

Below left: *Wood carver, Old Arab Fort* (CO)

Below right: *Artist, Stone Town* (CO)

Above: *Rural house with baskets of charcoal* (CO)

Below left: *Grinding maize on a 'portable' grinding wheel, Kizimkazi* (PB)

Below right: *Preparing traditional food* (CO)

Above: *Mahambi Palace, built in 1882 for Sultan Barghash's harem* (CO)

Below: *House of Wonders and Old Arab Fort, Stone Town* (CO)

lighthouse at its northern tip clearly visible. At the southern end of the island are the remains of a large town, dating from around the 12th century (see below).

Fukuchani lies just to the west of the main road, about 8km north of Mkwanjuni and 12km south of Nungwi.

TUMBATU ISLAND

Tumbatu is one of the largest of Zanzibar's offshore islands, measuring about 8km long by 2km to 3km across. The people of the island, the Watumbatu, speak their own dialect of Swahili. They have a reputation for pride and aloofness, and are reputed not to welcome visitors on their island. The Watumbatu men are traditionally known as the best sailors on Zanzibar, or even on the whole East African coast.

On the southern end of Tumbatu Island are a group of Shirazi ruins, thought to date from the 12th century. An Arab geographer, writing in the 13th century, recorded that the Muslim people of Zanzibar Island were attacked (by whom is not clear) and retreated to Tumbatu Island where the people were also Muslims. The ruins were probably abandoned in the early 16th century, but the Watumbatu still claim to be descended from Shirazi immigrants.

Mveleni Ruins

This is another set of ruins, near Fukuchani, also sometimes described as Portuguese but also more likely to be of Swahili origin. The house was once larger than the one at Fukuchani, with thicker walls, but the ruins are in poor condition and overgrown with vegetation. The remains of the house well can still be seen in a natural cavern outside the main wall.

Mveleni Ruins lie just to the south of Fukuchani, on the other side of the road (east). From the roadside, next to a few huts and a small shop, a path leads through banana and palm plantations to reach the ruins.

Mkokotoni

Mkokotoni is a busy fishing village, with a market, a few shops, and a police station, on the main road between Zanzibar Town and Nungwi. In 1984, Chinese coins were discovered on the beach north of the village indicating that trade between China, India, Arabia and Zanzibar existed long before the arrival of the Europeans. Today, this village is an interesting place to wander around, if only because very few tourists ever stop here. There is no official accommodation. The island of Tumbatu can be seen from Mkokotoni (see above).

Dunga Ruins

Dunga Ruins are very near the modern village of Dunga, on the main road between Zanzibar Town and Chwaka. They are the remains of the palace built for King Mohammed, the Mwinyi Mkuu (Swahili ruler) of Zanzibar, some time between 1846 and 1856. They may have been built on the site of an earlier house. Before that, the residence of the Mwinyi Mkuu had been at Kizimkazi or Unguja Ukuu.

A Swahili royal line is believed to have already existed on Zanzibar when the first Shirazi immigrants arrived here from Persia in the 10th century AD. Leading figures among the Shirazis are thought to have married into the family of the Swahili ruler, as the Mwinyi Mkuu (literally the 'Great Chief') later claimed to be descended from a Shirazi prince. In the following centuries, while the island was controlled by the Portuguese, and later by the Arabs and British, a Mwinyi Mkuu continued to be regarded as traditional leader by the people of Zanzibar.

Local legend holds that when Dunga Palace was built, slaves were buried alive in the foundations, while others were killed so that their blood could be mixed with the mortar, to bring strength and good fortune to the house. (There may be some truth in this story as, in the 1920s, a nearby well was found to be half-full of human bones.) Part of the Mwinyi Mkuu's regalia was a set of sacred drums and horns, and these were kept at Dunga during King Mohammed's rule. The drums were carved from mango wood, and inscribed in Arabic. They were said to beat on their own to warn the king of impending trouble. The horns were always kept hidden in a secret place, known only to the Mwinyi Mkuu. When the Mwinyi Mkuu was near death, the hiding place would be revealed to the next in line. Another story holds that when King Mohammed left the palace at Dunga, anyone gathering coconuts or cloves up a tree would have to come down, as nobody was allowed to be higher than him.

Mohammed died in 1865 and was succeeded by his son Ahmed, but he died of smallpox in 1873, leaving no male heir. His two sisters married into prominent families of Arab landowners, but the ruling dynasty came to an end.

Today, only the main walls of the palace at Dunga remain, but it is still an imposing ruin, retaining something of its original grandeur. A few old passages, pillars and staircases can also be seen. The windows are empty and their decorative frames are now in the Peace Memorial Museum.

Places to visit on Zanzibar Island – southern area
Bi Khole Ruins
The Bi Khole Ruins are the remains of a large house dating from the 19th century, situated some 20km to the southeast of Zanzibar Town. Khole was a daughter of Sultan Said (*Bi* is a title meaning 'Lady') who came to Zanzibar in the 1840s, after Said moved his court and capital from Oman. With her sister Salme she helped their brother Barghash escape after his plans to seize the throne from Majid were discovered (see box on the *Escape to Marseilles*, page 154).

Khole had this house built for her to use as a private residence away from the town. Khole is recorded as being a keen hunter and lover of beautiful things. The house had a Persian-style bath-house where she could relax after travelling or hunting, and was surrounded by a garden decorated with flowering trees and fountains. The house was used up to the 1920s, and is now ruined, with only the main walls standing, and overgrown in some places.

The main front door has collapsed, but this is still the way into the ruin, over a pile of rubble. Directly in front of the door is a wide pillar, designed so that any visitor coming to the door would not be able to see into the inner courtyard, in case Khole or other ladies of the court were unveiled. In this room are alcoves and niches with Arabesque arches, although the windows are rectangular.

The Bi Khole Ruins lie a few kilometres to the west of the main road from Zanzibar Town to the southern part of the East Coast, about 6km south of the village of Tunguu. The road passes down a splendid boulevard of gnarled old mango trees, supposed to have been planted for Khole (although they may date from before this period), and the track off to the ruins is about halfway down this.

Unguja Ukuu

This is the site of the oldest settlement known on Zanzibar, dating from the end of the 8th century, and believed to have been founded by early Shirazi immigrants from Persia. Unguja is the local name for Zanzibar Island today, and *Ukuu* means 'great'. It is believed that the settlement may have been quite large, but it was abandoned in the 10th century, possibly because it came under attack. Research at Unguja Ukuu is still taking place and more evidence may yet come to light. The population were probably Muslim. An Arab geographer, writing in the 13th century, recorded that the people of 'Lenguja' had taken refuge from their enemies on the island of Tumbatu, off the northwest shore of Zanzibar Island, where the people were also Muslim.

Today, there is very little remaining that would be of any interest to anyone except the keen archaeologist: just some shallow earth pits and the remains of a few crumbling walls.

To reach this site, you need to pass through the modern village of Unguja Ukuu, reached by turning south off the main road between Zanzibar Town and the southern part of the East Coast, at a junction about halfway between the villages of Tunguu and Pete. South of the village, a small track branches off the dirt road that leads to Uzi Island (reached by a tidal causeway). Follow this to reach the remains of old Unguja Ukuu.

Kizimkazi Mosque

The fishing village of Kizimkazi lies at the southern end of Zanzibar Island. Kizimkazi is actually two villages: Kizimkazi Mkunguni and Kizimkazi Dimbani, both on the coast about 2km apart (3km by road). In Kizimkazi Dimbani there's an ancient Shirazi mosque, dating from the 12th century.

Some of the inscriptions inside this mosque date from AD1107, which makes it the oldest known Islamic building on the East African coast, although the mosque has been rebuilt on several occasions, most recently around 1800. From the outside, it does not appear very old at all, as a corrugated iron roof has been built to protect it.

Archaeological evidence suggests that when the mosque was built Kizimkazi was a large walled town. Tradition holds that it was founded and ruled by a king called Kizi, and that the architect of the mosque itself was called Kazi. Legend has it that when the town was once attacked by invaders, Kizi prayed for divine intervention and the enemies were driven away by a swarm of bees. Later the enemies returned, but this time Kizi evaded them by disappearing into a cave on the shore. The cave entrance closed behind him and the enemies were thwarted once again.

Today, very little of the old town remains, but it is possible to visit the mosque. You can go inside if you find the caretaker (he lives nearby) with the key. Show respect by taking off your shoes and covering bare arms and legs (this part of the island is very traditional so, out of politeness, your

KIZIMKAZI DOLPHINS

Two species of dolphin occur in the area around Kizimkazi. Several pods (groups) of bottlenose dolphin (*Tursiops truncatus*) appear to be resident all year round in the shallow coastal waters. Humpback dolphin (*Sousa chinensis*) seem to have a more sporadic presence. The bottlenose dolphin is more sociable, and more readily observed, whereas the humpback is a shyer creature.

Tourists first started coming to see dolphins at Kizimkazi in the early 1990s. The continued presence of these popular creatures has attracted growing numbers of visitors, so that tourism has become an economic mainstay of the village. Contrary to the practices of other fishing communities in the Indian Ocean, the fishermen of Kizimkazi are very protective of the dolphins and never hunt them. In 1997 men from Kizimkazi helped arrest fishermen from Dar es Salaam who were using dynamite, which poses a deadly threat to dolphins.

For tourists who want to see the dolphins, boat excursions can be arranged with local fishermen through the Kizimkazi Beach Villa guesthouse. Traditional wooden fishing boats are most commonly used, but several fisherman have converted to modern fibreglass boats. Chartering a boat at Kizimkazi costs about $25 for two to three hours – usually enough time to locate the dolphins. You can also book tours in Zanzibar Town which include transport to/from Kizimkazi, or arrange visits from other hotels on the East Coast. Costs vary between $25 and $100 per person, depending on the season, the quality of the trip and the number of passengers.

The most favourable time of year to see the dolphins is between October and February. From June to September, the southerly winds can make the seas rough, while during the rainy season (March to May) conditions in the boat can be unpleasant. However, out at sea you're likely to get wet anyway. You should also protect yourself against the sun.

Dolphin tours are often promoted in a misleading light. Sightings cannot be guaranteed, and swimming with the dolphins is a rare occurrence. It is important arms and legs should be covered anyway – see the *Clothing* section in *Chapter Three*).

The old inscriptions are around the niche at the eastern end of the mosque (facing Mecca). These are Kufic, carved in a decorative style called 'floriate'. Similar inscriptions have been found in old buildings in Persia.

The silver pillars on either side of the niche are decorated with pounded mullet shells from the island of Mafia. The two decorative clocks, which show Swahili time (six hours different from European time), were presented by local dignitaries. The more recent additions of electrical sockets and flex have not been installed with a comparable degree of style or decoration.

Outside the mosque are some old tombs, some decorated with pillars and one covered in a small thatched roof. The pieces of cloth tied to the edge of the tomb are prayer flags. The raised aqueduct which carried water from the well to the basin where hands and feet were washed is no longer used: running water is piped straight into a more recently built ablution area at the back of the mosque.

To reach Kizimkazi Dimbani, turn off the main road between Zanzibar

to remember that the dolphins are wild and their whereabouts cannot be predicted. It is they who choose to interact with people, not the other way around. Generally, however, few people return without seeing any dolphins at all.

Observing dolphins in the wild, as with any other animals, requires time and patience. Shouting and excessive movement will not encourage them to approach your boat. Be satisfied with passive observation – do not force the pilot to chase the dolphins, cross their path, or approach too close, especially when they are resting. If you decide to swim with them, slip quietly into the water and avoid splashing. Never jump in. Rather than swim towards them, attempt to excite their curiosity by diving frequently and swimming below the surface, maintaining your arms alongside your body to imitate their own streamlined shape.

Up to 100 people per day visit Kizimkazi in the high season, all to see the dolphins. The large number, if left unchecked, could have detrimental effects on the animals. The Zanzibar Government's Commission for Natural Resources has recognised this potential threat and invited a study of dolphin related tourism.

The aim of the project is to submit guidelines and recommendations to the authorities in order to sustain a successful development of dolphin tourism in the long term. This is in the common interest of the local tour operators, the visitors and the dolphins. An information centre may be set up in Kizimkazi in response to the many requests received from visitors.

Kizimkazi has the rare privilege of being one of the few places where wild dolphins can be admired in their natural habitat. Please remember that your considerate behaviour whilst watching them will ensure that it remains this way.

Many thanks to the various people involved with the Kizimkazi Dolphin Project and the Foundation Oceana International and to the field staff who willingly gave us their time and information: Francis Plas, George Van Keulen, Jean-Marc Coronet, Angelique Todesco.

Town and Makunduchi at Kufile, and follow this small road to a fork: right goes to Kizimkazi Dimbani and the mosque; left goes to Kizimkazi Mkunguni, which has a small guesthouse (see *Hotels and guesthouses*, page 177, for details).

Zala Park

The Zanzibar Land Animals Park (Zala Park for short) is in the village of Muungoni, just south of Kitogani, where the main road from Zanzibar Town divides into roads to Paje and to Makunduchi. This is a private project run by the tireless and enthusiastic Mohammed Ayoub. Most of the land animals are snakes and reptiles, but there are a few other species on display. There's also a small education centre. Zala Park is only about 3km down the road from Jozani Forest Reserve (see below), and can be combined with a visit there.

Jozani Forest Reserve

Jozani is the largest area of mature indigenous forest remaining on Zanzibar Island, although today it is a tiny remnant of the forest that once covered much of the central part of the island. It stands on the isthmus of low-lying land which links the northern and southern parts of the island, to the south of Chwaka Bay. The water-table is very high and the area is prone to seasonal flooding, giving rise to this unique 'swamp-forest' environment.

Historically, local people have cut trees and harvested other forest products for many centuries, but commercial use started in the 1930s when the forest was bought by an Arab landowner and a sawmill was built here. In the late 1940s the forest came under the control of the colonial government and some replanting took place. Jozani has been protected since 1952 (see the *Vegetation* section in *Chapter Four*) and, as the forest in other parts of the island was cleared, much of the island's wildlife congregated here. The forest was declared a nature reserve in the 1960s, but despite this nominal protection the trees and animals were inadequately protected. Local people cut wood for building and fuel, and some animals were hunted for food or because they may damage crops in nearby fields.

Nevertheless, Jozani Forest retained much of its original natural character, and now forms the core of the Jozani-Chwaka Conservation Area, a partnership between the Zanzibar government's Commission for Natural Resources and the charity CARE Tanzania, with funding by the government of Austria, to protect natural resources and improve conditions for local people and wildlife in the area.

Trees are mainly moisture-loving palms (five species) and figs (two species), plus some introduced species such as Alexandrian laurel and Sydney blue gum. Other trees include red mahogany, which some authorities regard as an introduced exotic, although others point out that this tree is found on other Indian Ocean islands and, like the mangrove, its seeds can float and survive in sea water. With areas of mangrove and saltmarsh, the area contains several diverse habitat types, each with its associated, and equally varied, wildlife.

Jozani Forest's laurel trees were originally imported and planted by the Arab landowner to use for dhow-building timber. More recently, laurels have been planted around the forest to act as a buffer zone. The berries they produce also help to keep the forest's monkey population within the boundaries of the reserve, rather than straying into neighbouring farmland where they damage the crops.

Several rare and endemic species occur in Jozani, making it a major attraction for wildlife fans. Even if you've got only a passing interest, a visit can be fascinating. The main reason most visitors come here to is to see some of the forest's group of red colobus monkey (full name: Kirk's Red Colobus) which are unique to Zanzibar and only found in and around Jozani Forest. Colobus are naturally shy, but the ones in Jozani are increasingly used to human presence and easy to see. You are also likely to see some of the forest's population of blue monkey.

Other residents of Jozani include the Aders' duiker, a species of small antelope found only on Zanzibar and some parts of the Kenyan coast, and the suni, another antelope which is even smaller than the duiker, but both of these are extremely shy and unlikely to be seen. There are even reported to be leopards in Jozani, and elsewhere on the island. Again, they are a local sub-species, smaller than the mainland version, and also very unlikely to be sighted. (For more details on leopards, and the other wildlife in Jozani and Zanzibar, see the *Wildlife* section in *Chapter Four*.)

The entrance to Jozani Forest Reserve is on the main road between Zanzibar Town and the southern part of the East Coast, north of the village of Pete. You can visit at most times of the year, but in the rainy season the water-table rises considerably and the forest paths can be under more than a metre of water. The reserve is clearly signposted, and entrance costs $5,

---

RULES FOR RESPONSIBLE MONKEY WATCHING

Jozani Forest asks all visitors to observe the following rules. They apply to watching primates anywhere in Zanzibar, or elsewhere in Africa:

- You must be accompanied by an official guide.
- Do not approach monkeys closer than three metres, and preferably remain at a distance of five metres. This is for your own safety – the monkeys are wild animals and can bite or pass diseases to you.
- Do not invite any interaction with the monkeys or try to feed them. If they come close, avoid eye contact and move away. Do not make noises to attract their attention.
- You are one of the major threats to the monkeys, as primates are susceptible to human diseases. Do not visit the monkeys if you are suffering from any illness, particularly cold or flu.
- Observe the speed limits if driving through Jozani, and ask your driver to slow down if you're in a minibus. Monkeys are killed by cars every month.

although there are plans to increase this to $10 in spring 1998.

An organised nature trail has been established. It takes about an hour to follow at a leisurely pace, with numbered points of interest which relate to a well-written information sheet which you can buy for a nominal cost at a small reception/information centre. Some other information leaflets and species lists are also available, and there are a few display boards and other exhibits.

The Forest Reserve administrators plan to share revenue from tourism with village communities in the surrounding area. Only if wildlife has a tangible value to local people can its survival be more certain. A large carved wooden chest in the information centre holds the Jozani Community Fund – please donate at least $1.

Many tour companies include Jozani on their East Coast Tours or Island Tours, but you can easily get here by bus, hired bike or car. Alternatively, take a tourist minibus heading for the East Coast, and drop off here. This road is well used by tourist minibuses and other traffic throughout the day, so after your visit to the forest you could flag something down and continue to the coast or return to Zanzibar Town.

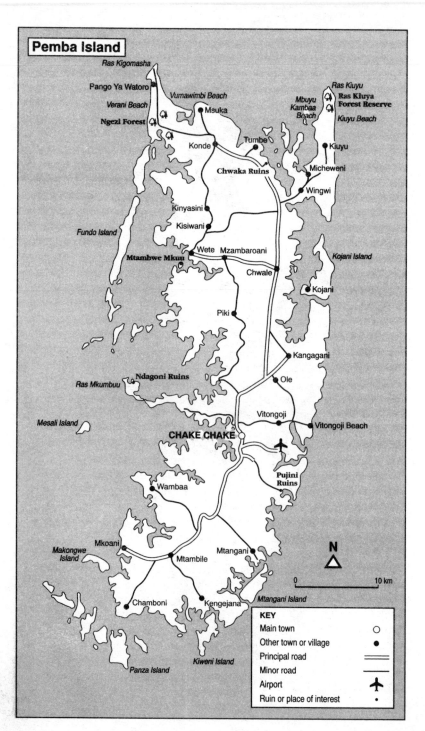

Pemba Island

Ras Kigomasha
Pango Ya Watoro
Vumawimbi Beach
Verani Beach
Msuka
Ngezi Forest
Konde
Tumbe
Ras Kiuyu
Ras Kiuya Forest Reserve
Mbuyu Kambaa Beach
Kiuyu Beach
Kiuyu
Chwaka Ruins
Micheweni
Wingwi
Kinyasini
Kisiwani
Fundo Island
Wete Mzambaroani
Mtambwe Mkuu
Chwale
Kojani Island
Kojani
Piki
Kangagani
Ndagoni Ruins
Ole
Ras Mkumbuu
Vitongoji
Mesali Island
CHAKE CHAKE
Vitongoji Beach
Pujini Ruins
Wambaa
Mkoani
Makongwe Island
Mtambile
Mtangani
Chamboni
Kengejana
Mtangani Island
Kiweni Island
Panza Island

N

0   10 km

KEY
Main town   ○
Other town or village   ●
Principal road   ═══
Minor road   ───
Airport   ✈
Ruin or place of interest   ·

Chapter Seven

Pemba Island

Pemba Island lies about 80km to the northeast of Zanzibar Island (Unguja), and about the same distance from the Tanzanian mainland, directly east of the port of Tanga. Pemba Island is smaller than Zanzibar Island, but it has a more undulating landscape, even though its highest point is only about 95m above sea level. Pemba is also more densely vegetated than Zanzibar (with both natural forest and plantation) and has always been seen as a more fertile place. The early Arab sailors called it *El Huthera*, meaning 'The Green'. Today, more cloves are grown here than on Zanzibar Island.

Pemba is also known as a centre for traditional medicine and witchcraft. The British writer Evelyn Waugh, in his classic travel book *Remote People* (1931), describes Pemba as a centre of 'black art' learning, and goes on to record how '...novices would come from as far as the great lakes [of Central Africa] to graduate there. Even from Haiti, it is said, witch-doctors will come to probe the deepest mysteries of voodoo. Nowadays everything is kept hidden from the Europeans, and even those who have spent most of their lives in the country have only now and then discovered hints of the wide, infinitely ramified cult which still flourishes below the surface.'

As it was in Waugh's time, so it is today. A 1995 travel story in a British newspaper reported that the village of Vitongoji, in the centre of the island, was 'the capital of Pemban sorcery...a place of dark secrets. Some years ago a witch doctor was arrested for eating children in the course of his duties'. This report may have been tongue-in-cheek, but it's an inescapable fact that local people seeking cures for spiritual or physical afflictions still come to the local doctors of Pemba from Zanzibar Island, mainland Tanzania, Kenya, and even as far as Uganda and Zaire. But as a visitor from the West, don't expect to be taken to see any cures or ceremonies; this is strictly for the locals. Even the most innocent of questions about witchcraft will be met with nothing more than embarrassed smiles or polite denials.

The largest town on Pemba is Chake Chake, the island's capital and administrative centre, about halfway down the western side of the island. Other towns are Wete, in the northern part of the island, and Mkoani, in the south – a smaller town, although with a more important port.

Few visitors come to Pemba, so there is little in the way of tourist facilities. Of course, for many people, this is one of the island's main attractions. However, things are changing gradually, and although options are still limited you have more choices now than ever before.

GETTING TO PEMBA
From Zanzibar Island
By air
Air Tanzania (ATC) had suspended flights between Zanzibar Town and Chake Chake in 1997 (although they were still happy to quote us a fare!). There were no immediate plans to recommence services; but as the company is due major restructuring in the next few years, flights may start again in the future.

Your other option is to fly with one of the local air-charter companies based in Zanzibar Town. You can get a group together and charter a whole plane; rates are listed under *Air charter companies* in *Chapter Five* (see page 107) and start at about $400 for a five-seater plane. Alternatively, the charter companies often have spare seats on charter flights to Pemba and sell these to individuals for between $50 and $100. In the high season there are flights most days (or at least every other day) so it's worth contacting the charter companies, or getting a travel agency to do it for you, to see if there's anything going.

By ship
The old government-run Zanzibar Shipping Corporation vessels *Mapinduzi* and *Maendeleo* each go about once a week between Zanzibar Town and Mkoani (at the southern end of Pemba Island). Services are cheap, around $3 payable in TSh, but the timetable is flexible and constantly liable to change. Your other option is the *Lingen,* a cargo ship plying between Dar, Zanzibar and Pemba. There is no timetable but, if you manage to find this boat going your way at the right time, the fare is $6.

More reliable is the passenger ship *Serengeti,* operated by the Azam Marine Co, which runs between Zanzibar Town and Mkoani three times weekly in each direction. The journey takes about six hours and costs $30.

Even better is the new service operated by Mega Speed Liners. Their fast ship *Sepideh* runs between Dar es Salaam and Zanzibar once a day, with a service to Pemba five times weekly in each direction, plus a twice-weekly service to Mombasa and Tanga. There are also plans to extend the service to Lamu. Zanzibar to Pemba costs $30, and the journey takes just under three hours.

For several years reports have circulated that the ships *Flying Horse* and *Sea Express,* which normally run between Zanzibar and Dar es Salaam, are due to extend their services to Pemba some time in the future. If this does ever happen, fares are likely to be around the same as the Dar to Zanzibar trip.

Full details on all these ships are listed under *Shipping companies* in *Chapter Five*, page 108.

By dhow

It is possible to travel by dhow from Zanzibar Town to Pemba. Most dhows go to Mkoani, but a few occasionally go to Chake Chake or Wete. Zanzibar to Mkoani costs about $3 (payable in TSh). There are no set sailing days or times, so you need to make enquiries at the dhow office in the Malindi Sports Club, on Malawi Road in Zanzibar Town. See also page 109.

From the mainland
By air

Unless you charter a plane, there are no flights from mainland Tanzania or Kenya to Pemba, although spare seats on charter flights are sometimes sold to individuals. In Dar or Mombasa, a travel agent will be able to help you – they will probably phone the airport or one of the local charter companies to see if anything is going your way.

By ship

The best (and in 1997, only) way of going by ship from mainland Tanzania or Kenya to Pemba is the service operated by Mega Speed Liners. Their ship *Sepideh* goes from Mombasa and Tanga to Pemba twice a week, then on to Zanzibar and Dar. There are plans to extend the service to/from Lamu. Between Mombasa and Pemba is $45, and the journey takes three hours. Tanga to Pemba is $30 and takes 75 minutes. From Dar to Pemba takes four hours and costs $45.

The ships *Flying Horse* and *Sea Express* (which run between Dar and Zanzibar Town) may start operating between Mombasa, Tanga, Pemba and Zanzibar in the future.

More details on ships from the mainland are also given in *Chapter Three*, page 44.

By dhow

You can reach Pemba by dhow from Tanga (for about $5 to $10, payable in TSh) or from Mombasa in Kenya (for about $10 to $15, payable in Kenya Shillings). Most dhows go to Wete, but a few go to Mkoani. Services are irregular and not idyllic. They may also be illegal for tourists. For more details see page 109.

LEAVING PEMBA
By air

Much of the above information applies here also. If you're in Pemba and want to fly to the mainland, Partnership Travel in Chake Chake will find out if there's anything going on your behalf. Alternatively you can phone the airport control tower (tel: 52238) and enquire yourself. This is a fairly standard procedure – the charter companies often tell the tower if they're looking for passengers to fill spare seats.

By ship

Once again, much of the information in *Getting to Pemba from Zanzibar* and *Getting to Pemba from the mainland* applies here. Partnership Travel in Chake Chake is the agent for the *Sepideh* ship to/from Zanzibar, Dar, Tanga and Mombasa, and can help you out with any other transport enquiries. They also have a small office in Mkoani, and on sailing days run a transfer bus between Chake Chake and Mkoani, leaving Chake Chake about two hours before the boat departs from Mkoani, then returning to Chake Chake after the boat has arrived.

The agent for the *Serengeti* is Hamisa Tourist Agency, an uninspiring shack near the market in Chake Chake.

TRAVEL AROUND PEMBA ISLAND

Options on Pemba are limited compared with Zanzibar Island. However, public transport is sufficient to allow independent travellers to see at least some parts of the island; to get further afield independently you'll have to hire a bike, motorbike, car or boat. It is also possible to arrange a car with driver, or an organised excursion, through a local tour company (see *Travel and tour companies*, page 196).

Car hire

There is no dedicated car hire company on Pemba, but most of the tour companies listed below will rent you a car with driver for about $50 per day, depending on the distance you want to travel, including petrol. If you want to self drive, rates start at $30 per day for a small saloon car, plus petrol.

Alternatively, you can hire a car and driver privately. In Chake Chake, vehicles and drivers wait for business outside the ZTC Hotel. In Mkoani and Wete they can be found near the market. Rates vary according to the vehicle: pick-ups, saloon cars, minibuses, Landrovers and small Suzuki 'jeeps' are often available. Rates are also negotiable and should be discussed fully (and agreed) in advance. As an idea of costs, our trip from Chake Chake to Wete and Ngezi cost us $60 including petrol in a newish pick-up with four-wheel drive. To Mkoani and back in a battered old landrover was $25. Whatever you hire, part payment in advance is usually required, and the first stop is always the petrol station.

When planning your route around Pemba, note that the main road from Chake Chake to Mkoani is tarred but has many potholes. From Chake Chake to Wete, the direct main road (the 'old' road), via Mzambaraoni, is

---

ELECTRICITY ON PEMBA

Remember that power cuts are much more frequent on Pemba than they are on Zanzibar Island, and last much longer. It is not uncommon for the power to be off all night, so when choosing a room remember that having an electric fan is not nearly as important as having some sort of natural breeze.

in fair condition, although it is also possible to take the newer road via Chwale, which rejoins the other road at Mzambaraoni. From Wete northwards, the road direct to Konde (for Ngezi Forest) is in bad condition for cars (although OK on a bike in dry weather). The best route for cars is via Mzambaraoni, Chwale and Tumbe. It seems a long way round, but it's quicker, easier and more comfortable.

Motorbike and bicycle hire

There is no official set-up in Pemba for hiring bikes, although Partnership Travel in Chake Chake plans to offer this service in 1998. Even if they haven't got their fleet established by then, they will be able to set you up with something. The system seems to involve simply finding somebody who is not using their bike and doesn't mind making a few shillings lending it out to tourists. Rates start at about $2 per day for a bike, and $15 for a motorbike.

Alternatively, you can normally arrange to hire a bike or motorbike through your hotel. Tell the reception clerk what you want to do, and they'll inevitably know someone who can help you out.

Bus and dala-dala

Buses are converted trucks with wooden benches and canopies on the back. The main routes are:

Route No 3   Chake Chake to Mkoani
Route No 6   Chake Chake to Wete (on the old road, direct via Mzambaraoni)
Route No 34 Chake Chake to Wete (on the newer road via Chwale, rejoining the old road at Mzambaraoni).
Route No 35 Chake Chake to Konde in the north of the island (on the new road via Chwale and Tumbe

There is usually at least one bus per day in each direction, and the fare on the main routes is about $0.75. Local services include: Route No 10 between Wete and Wingwi, near Micheweni, on the northeastern side of the island; Route No 16 between Chake Chake and Vitongoji, a village about 5km east of Chake Chake; Route No 24 between Wete and Konde.

Dala-dalas (pick-ups) also cover routes No 3, No 6, No 34 and No 35 in between the buses. The fare is the same as the bus, although dala-dalas are quicker and run more frequently with several services each day. The No 34 seems the most frequent service (several times an hour in the mornings) and is also very useful for reaching the Star Inn and Venus Lodge (see page 195).

Most buses tend to run in the mornings, and the dala-dala service thins considerably in the afternoon, but now that Mkoani is linked to Zanzibar Town by a reliable boat service (see details on the *Sepideh* above), it seems that Pemba Island's entire public transport system revolves around the ship's arrival and departure times. On current timetables, the ship arrives in Mkoani from Zanzibar (three times weekly) or Tanga (twice weekly) around 12.30 and leaves at 13.00. Consequently, buses and dala-dalas depart from Wete for Chake Chake from about 06.00. These connect with dala-dalas from

Chake Chake to Mkoani which leave between about 08.00 to 10.00, to reach Mkoani by around noon in time for the boat. Things may be slightly less organised on the days when there's no boat.

Partnership Travel organise a transfer bus between Chake Chake and Mkoani to tie in with *Sepideh* departure and arrival times (details on page 192, *By ship*).

Boat hire

To visit Mesali Island or the ruins at Ras Mkumbuu (see page 202) from Chake Chake, you can hire a boat. Partnership Travel can arrange a small motor boat to Ras Mkumbuu for about $50 (including petrol and captain). To visit Ras Mkumbuu and Mesali, an 'island tour' costs $150 for one person, dropping to $50 per person in groups of four.

CHAKE CHAKE

Chake Chake is the largest town on Pemba, about halfway down the western side of the island. This is the island's capital and administrative centre, and the hub of the bus and dala-dala network. Although Chake Chake has been settled for as long as Zanzibar Town, it never achieved the same degree of importance, and thus has little in the way of an old Stone Town or grand Omani palaces. (Historical remains are pretty much limited to the tower of a Mazrui Omani fort, near the modern hospital.) Nevertheless, it's a pleasant enough town, with a lively market and 'central business district'. The old port, down the hill from the town centre, is worth a stroll around.

Hotels and guesthouses

The Zanzibar Tourist Corporation has three **ZTC hotels** on Pemba, one each in Chake Chake, Wete and Mkoani. These are all exactly the same in style (angular concrete), quality (clean, but slightly dilapidated) and price (singles $20, doubles $35, triples $50, breakfast $2). Some rooms have electric fans. Each hotel has a bar and restaurant, serving meals if ordered in advance. Reservations are not normally necessary but, if you are coming from Zanzibar Island, the ZTC office or any private tour company in Zanzibar Town can make advance bookings for you.

About 4km north of the town centre, on the main road out of Chake Chake towards Wete, are two private guesthouses. Both places can be reached by taking a No 34 dala-dala from the centre. The first one you

---

ACCOMMODATION ON PEMBA

As on Zanzibar Island (Unguja), all accommodation on Pemba must officially be paid for with hard currency: cash US dollars are preferred, and anything else (pounds, francs, marks) may not be accepted. If you have only TSh, these may be accepted at the current rate of exchange. Breakfast is normally included in the room price unless stated otherwise. Other meals are payable in TSh.

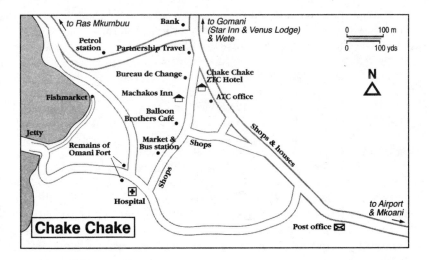

reach, on the right as you go north, is the welcoming **Venus Lodge** (tel: 52294), with pleasant clean double rooms (some en suite) all for $20. Food is also available: chicken and chips is $4.

A few hundred metres further, on the left and directly opposite the huge Gombani Stadium, is the **Star Inn** (PO Box 109, tel: 52190) where rooms range from $10 for a basic single to $30 for an en-suite double. All prices include breakfast, and the restaurant does good-value evening meals from around $3. The staff are friendly and helpful, and speak English. If you're flying into Pemba and contact the hotel in advance, a pick-up from the airport can be arranged. Tours of the island are also available, starting at about $50 per day for the vehicle and up to four people.

Some readers have recommended the **Nassir Guesthouse** (PO Box 385, tel: 52082), about 2km north of Chake Chake centre, in an area called Machomane, near the junction of the road to Vitongoji. Room rates range from $5 to $10 per person, but when we were in Pemba this place was closed (possibly for good, maybe not). We were also told about **Parasini Cottage**, owned by a friendly man called Mr Abdullah, and still under construction in 1997. He informed us that the place is outside town, reached by turning off the Wete road. This place might take a long time to finish, but travellers are still welcome to camp in the garden, or stay in an uncompleted room. The manager at Partnership Travel in Chake Chake will know when this place is properly open and can give you directions (see *Travel and tour companies,* page 196).

Eating and drinking

The **ZTC hotel** in Chake Chake has a dreary restaurant, serving lunches and evening meals for between $6 and $8 (payable in TSh). The food is generally reasonable (especially given that the kitchen staff have to contend with frequent power cuts and cook on charcoal stoves). The ZTC hotels also each have a bar serving beer (usually cold) and spirits.

The other hotels and guesthouses listed above also have restaurants which are open to non-residents, although normally food has to be ordered several hours in advance. Only the **Star Inn** may be able to cut this time to about an hour if you just turn up.

Chake Chake also has the **Machakos Inn**, a small restaurant opposite the ZTC hotel, open lunchtime and evenings, with meals such as chicken or fish with chips or rice for around $4. Local-style meals, such as beans or meat and rice, are also available for around $1. A few hundred metres down the road from here, towards the market, **Balloon Brothers** is the nearest Pemba gets to a pavement café with tables and sun-umbrellas on a small terrace beside the street. They serve drinks and snacks and may start doing meals in the future. There are a few other smaller places around the market and bus station area (the **Bismilahi** seems best), although food (if they have any) is usually only served in the morning and maybe up to lunch time. For the rest of the day your choice is limited to cakes, biscuits and canned drinks.

Travel and tour companies
Partnership Travel (PO Box 192, tel: 52278) is by far the most switched-on agency on Pemba, run by a friendly young man named Tahir, along with several helpful members of staff. The office is on the main street in between the ZTC hotel and the bank. They are the main agency for the Mega Speed Liners ship *Sepideh*, and can also assist with car and boat hire (see *Travel around Pemba Island*, page 192). They offer a range of tours around the island, although there are no fixed itineraries – trips are based on what clients want to do. An all-day trip costs $50 for one person, $30 each for two, $20 each for three and $15 each for four (including lunch). If you don't have lunch, the tour costs $50 for the vehicle, carrying one to four people. Boat trips cost $50 per person in groups of four.

Zanzibar Tourism Corporation, the state travel service, has an office next to the ZTC Hotel. They can arrange tours of the island by car or minibus for around $90 per vehicle, or trips to Ngezi Forest for $65. Boat trips to Mesali cost $90.

The **Star Inn** (see page 195) also runs tours, with prices similar to Partnership's. **Faizin/Inter-Island Investments** (listed under Mkoani) plan to open a Chake Chake office and we were informed by the Zanzibar Tourism Commission that another company called **Pemba Travel & Tours** will open in Chake Chake 'soon'.

MKOANI

Mkoani is the smallest of Pemba's three main towns, but the new boat services linking it to Zanzibar Town, Dar, Tanga and Mombasa make the port the busiest and most important on the island. For most visitors, this is the main gateway to Pemba, and several new guesthouses, restaurants and shops are under construction.

Hotels and guesthouses

Mkoani has a **ZTC Hotel** (exactly the same as the one described on page 194, with the same prices), and the possibility of a small guesthouse due to be opened by Faizin Tours sometime in the future (details available from the Faizin Tours office, listed on page 198). By far the best place to stay is **Jondeni Lodge** (tel: 56042), on a small hill to the north of town, about 15 minutes' walk from the port. This place is a clean white-painted bungalow set in lush gardens, with very friendly staff, singles at $12 and doubles $20. Drinks and meals are available, taken on the shady terrace overlooking the sea.

Eating and drinking

Apart from the hotels which serve food, places to eat include the **Mkoani Restaurant**, on the main street just down from the ZTC Hotel, which serves meals for around $1 or less. Next door, the white nameless building also does meals. Heading out of town, the basic **Nguvu Restaurant** is in the same price-band, and there's another local place opposite the school. Both close at around 16.00. Also worth trying is the **Township Café**, at the top of the steps which lead up from behind the post office.

Down by the port, the **Salsad Café** serves simple local-style meals for around $1 and fruit drinks made with bottled water. Next to Partnership Travel, on the steps which lead up to the main part of town, is another local-style eating house, also with meals around $1. A couple of stalls sell fruit, sweets and biscuits for the passing boat passenger trade.

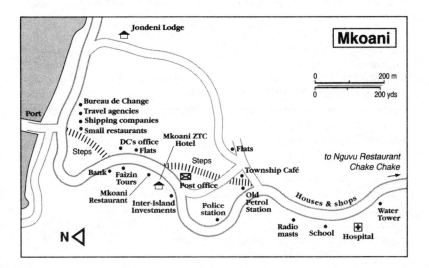

Travel and tour companies

The main operator is **Faizin Tours and Travel Agency,** also trading as **Inter-Islands Investments** (PO Box 70, Mkoani, tel: 56014), with an office on the main street just before it drops down to the port. Faizin/Inter-island was established to encourage small-scale environmentally sensitive tourism on Pemba. They organise tours around the island, to the main towns or smaller fishing villages, and to Ngezi Forest or any other place you want to go. Prices start at $50 per vehicle. They also run boat trips to Makongwe Island, Mesali Island or the beach at Wambaa. Prices start at $60 for the boat. Sea sports, fishing and car hire can also be arranged. Their specialities are bullfighting and devil-dance shows. Traditionally bullfighting takes place on Pemba mostly between August and November after the harvest and before the short rains (for more details see box below) but Faizin/Inter-Islands can arrange a show at any time, with food and transport if required. As the whole package costs $350 this is likely to be of interest only to tour groups. Faizin/Inter-Islands is also the agency for the ships *Canadian Spirit* and *Flying Horse* (details in the *Getting to Pemba* and *Getting to Zanzibar* sections).

At the port are several travel agents, all selling tickets for the *Sepideh, Serengeti* and other boats serving Pemba.

BULLFIGHTING ON PEMBA

During holiday times, mostly between August and November, after the harvest and before the short rains, it is sometimes possible to see traditional bullfighting on Pemba. The origins of this sport are uncertain although it is thought to have been introduced here by the Portuguese during the 16th century. Local 'matadors' put on a brave display in Iberian style, posing in front of the bull, goading it into a charge and then standing aside at the last moment, much to the appreciation of watching villagers. At the end of the fight, the bull is not killed but praised by the fighter, and sometimes decorated with flowers and leaves, then paraded around the village.

This all sounds very grand, but some visitors have reported that in reality some bullfights can be fairly uneventful, and seem to involve a group of local wide-boys annoying an apathetic bull by beating it with sticks while the local girls shriek loudly.

Exactly when a bullfight is about to take place is hard to find out. Ask at your hotel or a reliable tour company for more details.

WETE

Wete is the second largest town on Pemba, at the head of a large inlet on the west coast, in the northern part of the island. There is a large harbour here, used mainly by cargo ships and dhows. Local ferries also sail across the inlet to Mtambwe, from where you can get to the ruins of Mtambwe Mkuu and Fundo Island. For most travellers this town is a good base for exploring northern Pemba; from here Tumbe, Chwaka, Konde and Ngezi Forest can all be reached easily.

Hotels and guesthouses

Wete has a **ZTC Hotel** (exactly the same as the one described in the Chake Chake section above, with the same prices), and two other places to choose from. The **Super Guesthouse** (tel: 54063) is behind the blocks of flats, not far from the ZTC Hotel. It seems to be a converted house, with a few singles at $15 and some doubles at $20. An en-suite double is $25. The **Sharook Guesthouse** (tel: 54386) is in the lower part of town, on a quiet side-street near the market and bus station. It's a small family-run place with single rooms from $8 and doubles for $16 ($20 en suite). Dinner, with local specialities, is $4, but must be ordered well in advance. They have a generator which means constant running water and functioning TV. The friendly staff can arrange bike hire ($5 per day), and also offer a range of tours around the island (see page 200 for more details).

There are plans for a new hotel called the Bomani to open near the Sharook. In turn, the Sharook plans to open Sharook II, a local-style place on the edge of Wete overlooking the sea.

Eating and drinking

All the hotels and guesthouses serve food. Wete also has a choice of local eating houses. Near the ZTC Hotel is the **Four-ways Restaurant**, open evenings only, with local meals around $1 and chicken and chips for $2. Nearby, the **Yarabi Salama Restaurant** is open daytimes only, with local meals like beans and rice for $1. In the same area, on the main street near

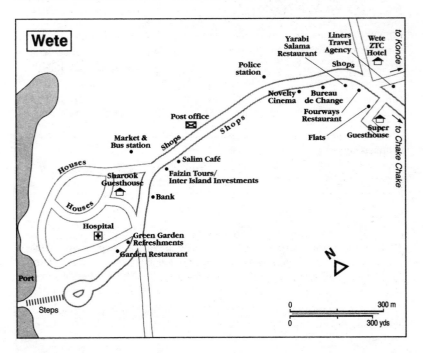

the flats, the **Container Restaurant** (a converted shipping container) is similar.
On the main street, near the market, is **Salim Café**, serving drinks and snacks. The best place we found was the **Garden Restaurant**, a very pleasant open-air café near the end of the main street where it drops down to the port. Omelette and chips or beans and rice are less than $1, and other meals are also available. Next door is **Green Garden Refreshments**, a shop and take-away snack bar, also selling drinks, postcards and stamps.

Travel and tour companies

Faizin Tours/Inter-Islands Investments are based in Mkoani (see that section for details) but have a small office (tel: 54352) on the main street near the market, and can arrange the same kind of services as they can in Mkoani. They may also be able to help with information about dhows to Tanga and Mombasa.

The **Sharook Guesthouse** (tel: 54386) offer a good range of tours: to Mtambwe Mkuu ruins costs $4 per person; a minibus to Ngezi Forest costs $40. Highly recommended all-day trips to Fundo Island cost $35 for the boat (also seating up to 10); or you can go to Mesali Island for $70.

Near the ZTC Hotel, **Liners Travel Agency** (tel: 54139) sells tickets for the *Sepideh* and some other ships. Opposite Green Garden Refreshments, an office sells tickets for the ZSC ships *Mapinduzi* and *Maendeleo* (although these go to/from Mkoani).

PANGO YA WATORO

Pango ya Watoro ('the cave of the fugitives') is a bay on Verani Beach on the west side of the Ngezi Peninsula, north of Wete. A hotel called **Manta Reef Lodge** has been built here by a company which already has three properties in Kenya. It is a dedicated diving place, open August to March (the best time for diving), with most guests coming directly from Kenya, where they also stay as part of a longer tour. There are fifteen double en-

---

NEW HOTELS

When we visited Pemba in 1997 to research this third edition, the Zanzibar Tourism Commission told us of several new hotels planned or under construction on the island. There are two places being developed at Vumawimbe, a beach on the east side of the Ngezi Peninsula, north of Wete and near Pango ya Watoro.

At Wambaa, a beach in the southern part of the island north of Mkoani and opposite Mesali Island, a large up-market dive centre and at least two smaller, locally owned guesthouses (with connections to the Star Inn in Chake Chake and Jondeni Lodge in Mkoani) are planned. At Mtangani Island, off the southeast coast of Pemba, a very smart tented lodge may be built, while at nearby Kiweni Island another up-market place called Kiweni Marine Resort was reportedly almost finished.

More information on all these places will be available from hotels and tour companies in Pemba and Zanzibar Town.

suite cottages, plus a central bar and restaurant overlooking the sea. If you want to dive off Pemba, it might be worth considering this place. Rates are $100 per person full board. Single dives are $32, three dives $66. Partnership Travel in Chake Chake can help with arrangements.

LOCAL SERVICES

Tourist information
The Pemba office of the Zanzibar Tourist Corporation (ZTC), the state travel service, is in Chake Chake (tel: 52121), next to the ZTC hotel. The staff are helpful, and happy to give advice and information about the area, but services they can provide are limited (see *Chake Chake – Travel and tour companies*).

Banks and change bureaux
There is a branch of the People's Bank of Zanzibar in each of the three main towns. They will change money – US dollars are the easiest to deal with – but only the one in Chake Chake will deal happily with travellers cheques. Dollar bills are more useful if you are arriving in Wete or Mkoani.

You are probably better off dealing with a change bureau. The most professional is in Chake Chake, directly opposite the ZTC Hotel. There are also bureaux in Wete (near the ZTC Hotel) and in Mkoani (near the port).

Hospital
The island's main hospital is in Chake Chake. This is a modern place, built with overseas aid. The staff are dedicated, but the hospital suffers from shortages of drugs and other essential supplies.

Post and telephone
Chake Chake, Wete and Mkoani all have post offices, from where telephone calls can be made with the assistance of the operator. Calls to Zanzibar Island or the near mainland cost just over $1 for three minutes. Long distance calls (including to Nairobi) are $2. (If you are phoning anywhere on Pemba, note that all old four-figure numbers are now preceded by 5.)

Food shopping
For lunches or picnics, you can buy fresh fruit at the markets and roadside stalls in Chake Chake, Mkoani or Wete. You can also buy bread. Shops in all three main towns sell a reasonable range of food in tins and packets, imported from the mainland or elsewhere in the Indian Ocean, but in the smaller villages this kind of stuff is difficult to find.

PLACES TO VISIT

Pemba is a place where travel for its own sake, by bus, bike or foot, should be the main reason for visiting. The island's scenery is more varied and some say more interesting than Unguja's. There are, however, a small number of historical sites which add extra interest to a visit here. If you are particularly keen on archaeology, more details on the early history of Pemba are available in the Peace Memorial Museum in Zanzibar Town. Places are described in this section roughly from south to north.

Pujini Ruins

The Pujini Ruins lie about 10km to the southeast of Chake Chake. These are the remains of a fortified town built around the 13th century by Swahili people. Its local name is Mkame Ndume, meaning 'milker of men', derived from the name of a reputedly despotic king who ordered the town walls to be built by local inhabitants who were then forced to carry large stones while shuffling on their buttocks.

Another legend about Pujini tells of a ruler with two wives, who lived in separate parts of the town and never knew each other. A wall was built across the well so that they could not meet if they came to get water at the same time. Little more is known about Pujini (more excavation work is planned); Portuguese records mention the site but describe it as abandoned in the early 16th century.

Today, the remains of the walls and ditches can still be seen, although much of the area is overgrown. It is also possible to see the remains of a walkway that joined the town to the shore, some wide stairways that presumably allowed access to the defensive ramparts, and the site of the town's well.

You can walk from Chake Chake to Pujini and back in a day, but it is easier to travel by hired bike or car. The route goes through farmland and a few small villages and is very pleasant. To get there, leave Chake Chake on the road south, and turn left on to a dirt road just after the tar road turns off to the airport. Follow the dirt road to a fork near a small dispensary, where you go left. At the next junction, go right to reach a flat grassy area which is usually wet. The ruins are amongst the trees and bushes on the far side of the grassy area. (If you get lost, ask for directions to Mkame Ndume.)

Ras Mkumbuu Ruins

Ras Mkumbuu is a headland at the end of a long peninsula about 14km to the west of Chake Chake. The ruins are at the tip of the peninsula and seem also to be called Ndagoni (although Mkumbuu and Ndagoni may have been different places). This is the site of a Swahili settlement, thought to have been one of the largest towns on the coast (and in East Africa) during the 11th century.

Today, the remains of a large mosque can still be seen here, although this is becoming very overgrown, and also several pillar-tombs, graves with a tall 'chimney' at one end, used to mark the burial place of prominent Muslims. Pillar-tombs are found in other parts of East Africa and held to be one of the most distinctive forms of monument built by the Swahili people. The tombs here are in poor condition, although an inscription on one states that they were repaired in 1916.

A road from Chake Chake leads westwards along the peninsula towards Ras Mkumbuu, but it becomes impassable and turns into a footpath for the final 5km which have to be walked. The easiest and most enjoyable way to reach the ruins is by boat (see *Boat hire,* page 194), or on a tour which also visits Mesali Island on the same day. Near the ruins is a small fishing village, and to reach the mosque and tombs you walk through maize fields and a plantation of tall palms with smooth white trunks.

Mesali Island

This small island (also spelt Misali) lies to the west of Chake Chake town, and is surrounded by a coral reef. There is an idyllic beach and it is a good place for a swim, especially if you have a mask and snorkel. The notorious pirate Captain Kidd is reputed to have had a hideout here in the 17th century. In the last few years, the Zanzibar tourism and environment departments have proposed that the island and reef be declared a Marine National Park.

Mesali Island can be reached by boat from Chake Chake or Mkoani (see the *Boat hire* and *Travel and tour companies* sections). Alternatively, some of the dive centres based in the northern part of Zanzibar Island, and the boat-based operators such as Cat-Diving, run trips here. More details are given in *Chapters Five* and *Six*.

Mtambwe Mkuu

This is a small island, joined to the mainland at low tide, directly south of Wete. Silver coins have been found here, one of very few examples of pre-colonial minted silver currency anywhere in East Africa. Despite its rich past, there's now little to see on Mtambwe island, although a trip there from Wete is a very pleasant way to pass the day. From Wete harbour you go by small dhow or canoe to Mtambwe village, then walk south, west and north around a creek and through mangrove swamps to reach the island. Apparently, when the water is high, you can get cut off on the island or be forced to wade through the mangroves, so careful checking of the tides is recommended. Sharook Guesthouse and Faizin Tours in Wete can arrange tours or give you advice.

Tumbe

Tumbe is a large village in the northern part of the island, just off the main tar road about 5km east of Konde. It is the largest fish market on Pemba and people come from all over the island to buy fish here. The mornings are especially busy. Tumbe can be reached by bus or bike from Wete.

Chwaka Ruins

South-east of Tumbe, near the coast, are the ruins of Chwaka, dating from the 16th century and associated with a local king called Harouni, son of Mkama Ndume, builder of Pujini (also now ruined and described above). The most easily recognised buildings are two small mosques, but there are also remains of houses and tombs. Nearby is another group of tombs and an 18th-century fort built by the Mazrui group of Omanis, but very little can be seen, and (to be honest) this site is only likely to excite real history buffs. It can be reached from the main road just north of where it crosses a swampy area on an embankment with metal crash-barriers on either side. The 20-minute walk through the fields and palms is enjoyable, and the view over the bay across to Michiweni is splendid.

Ngezi Forest Reserve

This is a protected area of forest on the Ngezi peninsula in the northwest corner of Pemba Island. Before the introduction of cloves, and the setting up of large plantations on Pemba, much more of the island was covered in natural forest. Although the reserve was established in the 1950s a commercial sawmill extracted timber until the mid 1960s. Through the 1970s and 1980s Ngezi was virtually ignored by the government, and encroachment by local people endangered the forest and its wildlife. In 1995 funds were received from the Forest and Park Service of Finland, to strengthen conservation efforts to the benefit of wildlife and local people, to train forest rangers, and to help develop the forest to attract tourists as a way of raising revenue to ensure future protection.

The reserve covers a relatively small area but contains an interesting range of vegetation, unique in East Africa, with several species more usually found in lowland mountain regions, as well as the palms, figs and other species more often found in coastal areas. The forest is home to several animal species, most notably the endemic Pemba flying fox, actually a large bat. Its name comes from its red fur and dog-like snout and ears. This animal has specialised habitat requirements – dense moist forest, with a ready supply of fruit and tree blossoms – and so only occurs in Ngezi. Even here it is hunted, and is classed as endangered.

Other animals found in Ngezi include vervet monkey, red colobus monkey, hyrax, blue duiker and marsh mongoose, and several bird species. A band of wild European pigs, descended from domestic animals introduced by the Portuguese centuries ago, also live in the forest. As most people on Pemba are Muslims and abstain from pork, these animals are not hunted. (For more details on wildlife, see the *Vegetation* and *Wildlife* sections in *Chapter Four*.)

Ngezi is rarely visited by individual tourists, although you may see groups from the nearby Manta Reef Lodge at Pango ya Watoro. You can hire a car in Wete or Chake Chake to take you right into the forest (and maybe on to one of the nearby beaches), or take public transport as far as Konde and walk the rest of the way. From Konde, follow the tar road (which becomes a dirt road) north and west for a few kilometres, through farmland, until you reach the entrance to the forest, marked by a small barrier and an office.

Entrance to the reserve costs $2. A short nature trail has been established, through sections of moist forest and past several large ponds. You get much more from your visit if you take a forest ranger to act as guide; this costs $10 for groups of up to ten people.

North of the forest, on the east side of the peninsula, is Vumawimbi Beach, which has been recommended. On the west side is Verani Beach. Several new hotels are planned for this area.

At the far northern end of the Ngezi Peninsula, near Ras Kigomasha, is a lighthouse built by the British in the 1800s. Officially, permission is required to visit.

Ras Kiuyu Forest Reserve

Located at the northern tip of the Kiuyu Peninsula (almost an island, joined to the main part of Pemba by a narrow strip of boggy land near the village of Wingwi), this forest is smaller than Ngezi, with a less impressive range of vegetation and wildlife. We heard from two travellers who visited this area, and highly recommended it as a day trip from Wete, as much for the interesting journey through the fields and villages as the forest itself. The nearby beach, on the east side of the forest, was another attraction.

By public transport, catch an early dala-dala from Wete to the village of Wingwi. Some dala-dalas go on to Micheweni, a further 2km. From Wingwi or Micheweni, it's a 5km walk to the village of Kiuyu and another 5km into the forest itself. About 3km beyond Kiuyu village a narrow track branches right (east) to Kiuyu Beach, Nearby, another small track branches left to another small beach on the west side of the peninsula called Mbuyu Kambaa.

Appendix One

Sultans

To help you place the sultans of Oman and Zanzibar in chronological order, the following lists will be helpful. The dates refer to their years as sultan. Note that *bin* means 'son of', and that some sultans were given the name Sultan.

Sultans of Oman and Zanzibar
Ahmed bin Said	1744–1783
Said bin Ahmed	1783–1789
Hamad bin Said	1789–1792
Sultan bin Ahmed	1792–1804
Bedr bin Seif	1804–1806 (regent)
Said bin Sultan	1804–1856

Sultans of Zanzibar
Said bin Sultan	November 20 1804 – October 19 1856
Majid bin Said	October 28 1856 – October 7 1870
Barghash bin Said	October 7 1870 – March 27 1888
Khalifa bin Said	March 29 1888 – 13 February 1890
Ali bin Said	February 13 1890 – March 5 1893
Hamad bin Thuwaini bin Said	March 7 1893 – August 25 1896
Hamoud bin Muhammad bin Said	August 27 1896 – July 18 1902
Ali bin Hamoud	July 19 1902 – December 9 1911
Khalifa bin Harub bin Thuwaini	December 16 1911 – October 17 1960
Abdulla bin Khalifa	October 17 1960 – July 1963
Jamshid bin Abdulla	July 1963 – January 12 1964

Sultans of Oman
Thuwaini bin Said	1856–1866
Salim bin Thuwaini	1866–1868
Azzan bin Qais bin	
Azzan bin Qais bin Ahmed	1868–1871
Turki bin Said	1871–1888
Faisal bin Turki	1888–1913
Taimur bin Faisal	1913–1932
Said bin Taimur	1932–1970
Qaboos bin Said	July 23 1970 – present day

Al Busaidi Family Tree

Ahmed bin Said SOZ 1744-83

Hilal (blind)

Said SOZ 1783-89
— Hamad SOZ 1789-92

Sultan SOZ 1792-1804

Seif

Qais

Said (1791-1856) SOZ 1804-1856 (1)

Salim (1789-1821)
— Hamad
  — Moza (Barghash's first and only wife)

Azze (Said's first wife)

Bedr SOZ 1804-1806 (regent)

Azzan
— Qais
  — Azzan (SO 1868-71)

Ali(5) 1852-91 SZ 1890-93
— Abdid Aziz

Khalifa(4) 1854-90 SZ 1888-90

Saime (1844-1924)
— Rudolph

Khole

Barghash(3) (1837-88) SZ 1870-88
— Khaled

Majid(2) (1834-70) SZ 1856-70
— Farschu

Khaled (1815-54)
— Shembua

Turki SO 1871-88
— Faisal SO 1888-13
  — Taimur SO 1913-32
    — Said SO 1932-70
      — Qaboos SO 1970-

Muhammed
— Hamoud (1847-1902) SZ 1896-02 (7)
  — Ali(8) (1884-1911) SZ 1902-11

Thuwaini SO 1856-66
— Salim SO 1866-68
— Haroub
  — Khalifa (1879-1960) SZ 1911-60 (9)
    — Abdulla(10) SZ 1960-63
    — Jamshid(11) SZ 1963-64

Hamad (1853-96) SZ (6) 1893-96

SOZ Sultan of Oman and Zanzibar
SO   Sultan of Oman
SZ   Sultan of Zanzibar

Only the names of the most prominent family members are given

Appendix Two

Language

USEFUL SWAHILI WORDS AND PHRASES

The language of Zanzibar is Swahili (*Kiswahili* when you're actually speaking the language), although English is spoken in Zanzibar Town and some tourist areas. If you get off the beaten track a few words of Swahili may be useful to help you find your way or even begin a simple conversation.

Pronunciation is generally straightforward: every syllable is sounded and there are no 'silent endings'. In longer words the stress is on the penultimate syllable. Verbs have a 'root' and a prefix which changes according to subject and tense. Nouns and adjectives also have prefixes which denote the singular and plural context. Of course, the best way to learn is to listen to the people around you.

The following basics will help you survive. For more information, use a phrasebook (see *Further Reading*), or visit the Kiswahili Institute (details in *Chapter Five*).

Introductions

Hello (also How are you?)	*Habari* (literally 'what news')
Fine	*Mzuri* or *Nzuri* (the response to *Habari*)
Very fine	*Mzuri sana*
Thank you (vexry much)	*Asante (sana)*
Goodbye	*Kwaheri*

Introductions and salutations are very important in Swahili culture, particularly when speaking to adults (children are not usually greeted by adults outside their family). Even when speaking in English a Swahili acquaintance will ask 'How are you?', 'How are things today?', 'How is your husband/wife/friend?'. You should do the same. Launching straight into any subject without the opening questions is rude. For 'Excuse me' (when attracting somebody's attention) use *Habari*. Traditional Zanzibaris expect women to be less forward than men, although in areas used to tourists this does not apply.

Jambo also means 'hello', but tends to be used only by Zanzibaris talking to tourists.
Hodi means 'Hello, anyone at home, can I come in?' used when knocking on somebody's door. The response is *karibu* meaning 'welcome'.

In Zanzibar, Muslim greetings (in Arabic) are also commonly used:

Aslaamu alekum	Peace be with you
Wa alekum salaam	And peace be with you (the response)

Conversation starters and enders

What is your name?	*Jina lako nani?*
My name is ...	*Jina langu ni ...*
Where are you from?	*Unatoka wapi?*
I am from ...	*Mimi ninatoka ...* (sometimes the *mimi* is dropped)
Where do you live?	*Unakaa wapi?*
I am sorry, I don't understand	*Nisamehe sifahamu*
I don't speak Swahili	*Sijui Kiswahili*
I speak a very little Swahili	*Nazungumza Kiswahili kidogo tu*

Useful words and phrases

yes	*diyo*
no	*hapana*
OK (agreement)	*sawa*
no problem	*hakuna matata*
sorry (condolences)	*pole* (not used for apologies)
where?	*wapi?*
here	*hapa*
there	*hapo*
what (is the) time?	*saa ngapi?*
how much?	*bei gani?*
I want to go to Bububu	*Mimi nataka kwenda Bububu*
Where is the bus for Makunduchi?	*Wapi basi ya Makunduchi?*
I am lost	*Nimepotea*
left	*kwa kushoto*
right	*kwa kulia*
straight on	*moja kwa moja*
near	*karibu*
far	*mbali*
today	*leo*
tomorrow	*kesho*
yesterday	*jana*
where is the ruin?	*wapi gofu?*
shop	*duka*
market	*sokoni*
food	*chakula*
water	*maji*
café, local eating-house	*hoteli ya chakula*

I am ill	*Mimi mgonjwa*
Where is the hospital/doctor?	*Wapi hospitali/daktari?*

The word *soda* means any fizzy drink in a bottle. In the smarter hotels in Zanzibar Town, if you want soda water try asking for a Club Soda.

You may hear the word *mzungu*, particularly by children. This means 'white person', but is not disrespectful.

Numbers

one	*moja*	21	*ishirini na moja*
two	*mbili*	30	*thelathini*
three	*tatu*	40	*arobaini*
four	*nne*	50	*hamsini*
five	*tano*	60	*sitini*
six	*sita*	70	*sabini*
seven	*saba*	80	*themanini*
eight	*nane*	90	*tisini*
nine	*tisa*	100	*mia*
ten	*kumi*	101	*mia na moja*
11	*kumi na moja*	102	*mia na mbili*
12	*kumi na mbili*	200	*mia mbili*
20	*ishirini*	300	*mia tatu*

Time

Swahili time starts at 06.00, the hour of sunrise, and is therefore six hours later than Western time.

What time is it?	*Saa ngapi?*
07.00	*saa moja* (literally one o'clock)
08.00	*saa mbili*
noon	*saa sita*
13.00	*saa saba*

When finding out about bus or boat departures, check if the time you've been told is Swahili time or Western time. This can be complicated further by some buses leaving outlying villages very early in the morning.

Appendix Three

Further Reading

History and background

The following six books are general histories of the region, with sections on Zanzibar. Pakenham's classic history of Africa from the 1870s onwards is particularly compulsive reading:

Coupland, R, *The Exploitation of East Africa 1856-1890: The Slave Trade and the Scramble* (Faber, London, 1939)

Davidson, B, *The Story of Africa* (London, 1984)

Freeman-Grenville, G S P, *The East African Coast: Select Documents* (Oxford University Press, 2nd ed, 1975)

Oliver, R and Mathew, G, *A History of East Africa* (Oxford University Press, London, 1963)

Pakenham, T, *The Scramble for Africa* (Weidenfeld and Nicholson, London, 1991)

Prestage, E, *Portuguese Pioneers* (A & C Black, London, 1933)

The following four books are old guides and histories from the British colonial days:

Gray, J, *History of Zanzibar from the Middle Ages to 1856* (Oxford University Press, London, 1962)

Ingrams, W H, *Zanzibar: Its History and People* (Witherby, London, 1931)

Lyne, R N, *Zanzibar in Contemporary Times* (Darf, London, 1905) Reprinted 1987

Pearce, Mjr F B, *Zanzibar: The Island Metropolis of Eastern Africa* (Fisher Unwin, London, 1920)

The following are modern, post-revolution, textbook-style histories:

Martin, E B, *Zanzibar: Tradition and Revolution* (Hamish Hamilton, London, 1978)

Sheriff, A, *Slaves, Spices and Ivory in Zanzibar* (James Currey, London, 1987)

Sheriff, A and Ferguson, E D, *Zanzibar under Colonial Rule* (James Currey, London, 1991)

The following are modern, very detailed books with specific reference to the Oman-Zanzibar link:

Al-Maamiry, A H, *Oman and East Africa* (Lancers, New Delhi, 1979)

Al-Maamiry, A H, *Omani Sultans in Zanzibar* (Lancers Books, New Delhi, 1988)

Bennett, N R, *A History of the Arab State of Zanzibar* (Methuen, London, 1978)

Bhacker, M R, *Trade and Empire in Muscat and Zanzibar* (Routledge, London, 1992)

Four excellent booklets written and published by Zanzibar historian Kevin Patience. Well researched, they describe in full events which might otherwise be confined to the footnotes of history. The gunship *Pegasus* was sunk during World War I and this book also contains background information on British naval ships in East Africa; while the *Shortest War* describes the 1896 bombardment of the sultan's palace, with several fascinating archive photos:

Patience, K, *Zanzibar and the Bububu Railway* (published by the author, 1995)

Patience, K, *Zanzibar and the loss of HMS Pegasus* (published by the author, 1995)

Patience, K, *Zanzibar and the Shortest War in History* (published by the author, 1994)

Patience, K, *Königsberg – A German East African Raider* (published by the author, 1997). The *Königsberg* was the German gunboat which sunk the British *Pegasus,* fully described in an earlier book by the same author. This painstakingly researched book covers historical events before and after the *Pegasus* incident, including the *Königsberg*'s final sinking by another British ship in the Rufiji Delta, southwest of Zanzibar. The chapter describing the present-day position of the *Königsberg's* relics scattered all over East Africa is particularly interesting.

The next two books are histories of the East African railways, both with good sections on Zanzibar:

Hill, M H, *The Permanent Way* (East African Literature Bureau, Nairobi, 1949)

Miller, C, *The Lunatic Express* (Macmillan, Ballantine Books, Random House Inc, New York, 1971)

The following two books are comprehensive and accessible historical accounts, with an emphasis on readability, sometimes at the expense of accuracy:

Hamilton, G, *In the Wake of de Gama* (London, 1951)

Hamilton, G, *Princes of Zinj* (Hutchinson, London, 1957)

Two books by Emily Reute (borne Salme binte Said Al-Busaidi):

Reute, Emily, *Memoirs of an Arabian Princess from Zanzibar* (Markus Wiener, New York, 1989). Reprint and translation of *Memoiren einer Arabischen Prinzessin*, 1888. A very readable firsthand account by a unique figure in the history of Zanzibar, providing a good overview of the period and several fascinating personal insights. Highly recommended.

Reute, Emily, *An Arabian Princess Between Two Worlds: Memoirs, Letters, Sequels to the Memoirs*, editor E Van Donzel, (E J Brill Publishing, Leiden, Netherlands, 1993). Volume 3 in a series on Arab History and Culture. A very detailed and comprehensive account of Salme's life in Zanzibar, Germany and Syria. Includes a biography of her son Said-Rudolph Reute. Rare.

Travel and exploration

Batchelor, J and J, *In Stanley's Footsteps* (Blandford, London, 1990)

Burton, Richard, *Zanzibar: City, Island and Coast* (London, 1872)

Drysdale, H, *Dancing with the Dead* (Hamish Hamilton, 1991)

Grant, N and Morter, P, *The Great Atlas of Discovery* (Dorling Kindersley, London, 1992)

Moorehead, A, *The White Nile* (Hamish Hamilton, London, 1960)

Mountfield, D, *A History of African Exploration* (Hamlyn, UK, 1976)

Richards, C and Place, J, *East African Explorers* (Oxford University Press, London, 1960)

Royal Geographical Society (Editor John Keay), *History of World Exploration* (Paul Hamlyn, Reed International, London, 1991)

Teal, J, *Livingstone* (Putnam, New York, 1973)

Waugh, E, *Remote People* (Duckworth, 1931), republished 1985 by Penguin Books, UK, as part of their 20th Century Classics series

Large-format photo books

Jafferji, J and Rees Jones, B, *Images of Zanzibar* (HSP Publications, London, 1996)

Sheriff, A, *Zanzibar – Romance of the Ages* (HSP Publications, London, 1996)

Much of East Africa has been covered by publishers of lavishly illustrated 'coffee-table' books, but until recently Zanzibar seems to have escaped their notice. Local photographer Javed Jafferji has made up for this with *Images of Zanzibar* – a portfolio of his finest work showing rich colours and an eye for detail which perfectly captures the spirit of the islands. Jafferji also compiled *Romance of the Ages* – a fascinating collection of archive photos from the late 19th and early 20th centuries – while the text and captions were provided by Abdul Sheriff, Professor of History at the University of Dar es Salaam and Principle Curator of the Zanzibar Museums. Jafferji and Sheriff are working on another book, *Zanzibar Stone Town – an architectural exploration* (The Gallery Publications, Zanzibar) which promises to be as good as the other two.

Fiction

Two historical romantic novels:

Kaye, M M, *Death in Zanzibar* (Penguin, London 1984) (First published as *The House of Shadows*, Longmans 1959)

Kaye, M M, *Trade Wind* (Longmans 1963, Penguin 1982)

Field guides

Kingdon, J: *The Kingdon Field Guide to African Mammals* (Academic Press, USA and UK)

van Perlo, B, *Illustrated Checklist of the Birds of Eastern Africa* (Collins, UK)

Williams, J & Arlott, N: *A Field Guide to the Birds of East Africa* (Collins, UK)

For animals on Zanzibar, a field guide to the more common species of East Africa is of limited use. Kingdon's book is by far the best, as it covers every species in Africa in detail, including those on Zanzibar, with excellent illustrations and background notes.

For birds, the field guide you choose is determined by your level of interest. Of the books listed above, the van Perlo *Illustrated Checklist* is complete, with illustrations of every bird occurring in Africa, including those on Zanzibar, while the classic Williams & Arlott also has fairly good coverage.

Manuals

Hatt, J, *The Tropical Traveller* (Penguin, London 1993)

Shales et al, *The Traveller's Handbook* (Wexas, London 1997)

Tully, C, *The A to Z Guide for Lightweight Travellers* (Writer's Block, Cambridge 1988)

Wilson-Howarth, J, *Healthy Travel: Bugs, Bites & Bowels* (Cadogan, 1995)

Wilson-Howarth, Dr J & Ellis, Dr M, *Your Child's Health Abroad: A Manual for Travelling Parents* (Bradt Publications, UK, 1998)

Phrasebook

Leonard, R, *Swahili Phrasebook* (Lonely Planet, Australia 1990)

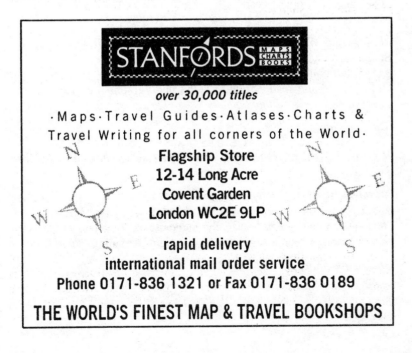

OTHER BRADT GUIDES TO AFRICA AND THE INDIAN OCEAN

Africa by Road   Bob Swain and Paula Snyder
336pp, 8pp colour, 20 maps, £12.95, 1 898323 29 1, 2nd edition

Africa, East and Southern: The Backpackers Manual   Philip Briggs
544pp, 150 maps, £13.95, 1 898323 60 7, 1st edition
Publication spring 1998

Eritrea, Guide to   Edward Paice
192pp, 12pp colour, 16 maps, £10.95, 1 898323 41 0, 2nd edition
'Comprehensive... contains a wealth of practical information and includes
outline maps and a useful basic language section.' *Traveller*

Ethiopia, Guide to   Philip Briggs
368pp, 8pp colour, 59 maps, £11.95, 1 898323 09 7, 1st edition
'A topnotch guide' *The Bookseller*

Ghana, Guide to   Philip Briggs
240pp, 8pp colour, 30 maps, £11.95, 1 898323 69 0, 1st edition
Publication summer 1998

Madagascar, Guide to   Hilary Bradt
368pp, 16pp colour, 43 maps, £12.95, 1 898323 53 4, 5th edition
'The item of choice for any who would embark upon a rugged trip to
Madagascar.' *The Bookwatch*

Madagascar Wildlife: A Visitor's Guide   Hilary Bradt, Derek
Schuurman and Nick Garbutt
144pp, full colour, £14.95, 1 898323 40 2, 1st edition
'Informative and reader-friendly... the photographs are of outstanding
quality.' *African Wildlife*

Malawi, Guide to   Philip Briggs
256pp, 8pp colour, 33 maps, £10.95, 1 898323 35 6, 1st edition
'Excellent... Briggs' information is up to date and reliable.' *Times Literary
Supplement*

Maldives, Guide to   Royston Ellis
272pp, 16pp colour, 8 maps, £11.95, 1 898323 23 2, 1st edition
'Not just another guide book... the authors give their personal accounts
and experiences which makes for more insightful reading.' *Sunday Leader*

Mauritius, Guide to   Royston Ellis
288pp, 8pp colour, 9 maps, £11.95, 1 898323 51 8, 3rd edition
'A splendid treasure house of practical, historical and geographical
information.' *Sun International (Mauritius)*

Mozambique, Guide to   Philip Briggs
240pp, 8pp colour, 39 maps, £11.95, 1 898323 45 3, 1st edition

Namibia, Guide to   Chris McIntyre
400pp, 16pp colour, 30 maps, £12.95, 1 898323 64 X, 1st edition
Publication summer 1998

South Africa, Guide to   Philip Briggs
320pp, 8pp colour, 30 maps, £11.95, 1 898323 52 6, 3rd edition

Tanzania, Guide to   Philip Briggs
320pp, 8pp colour, 34 maps, £11.95, 1 898323 36 4, 2nd edition
'The best for independent travellers' *The Daily Telegraph*

Uganda, Guide to   Philip Briggs
304pp, 8pp colour, 39 maps, £11.95, 1 898323 37 2, 2nd edition

Zambia, Guide to   Chris McIntyre
320pp, 8pp colour, 32 maps, £11.95, 1 898323 50 X, 1st edition

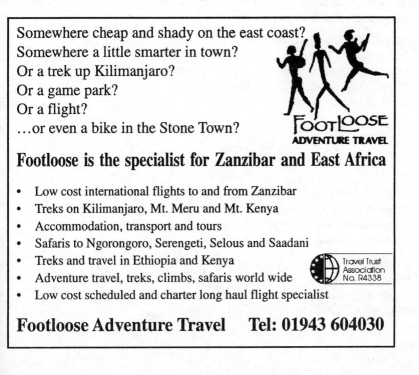

COMPLETE LIST OF BRADT GUIDES

Africa by Road Bob Swain & Paula Snyder

Africa, East and Southern: The Backpackers Manual Philip Briggs (spring 1998)

Albania: An Illustrated Journal Peter Dawson, Andrea Dawson & Linda White

Antarctica: A Guide to the Wildlife Tony Soper & Dafila Scott

Australia and New Zealand by Rail Colin Taylor

Belize, Guide to Alex Bradbury

Brazil: Pantanal, Amazon and Coastal Regions, Guide to Alex Bradbury et al

Burma, Guide to Nicholas Greenwood

Central America, Backpacking in Tim Burford

Central and South America by Road Pam Ascanio

Chile and Argentina, Backpacking in Hilary Bradt et al

Cuba, Guide to Stephen Fallon

Eastern Europe by Rail Rob Dodson

Ecuador, Climbing and Hiking in Rob Rachowiecki, Mark Thurber & Betsy Wagenhauser

Eritrea, Guide to Edward Paice

Estonia, Guide to Ilvi Cannon and William Hough

Ethiopia, Guide to Philip Briggs

Ghana, Guide to Philip Briggs (summer 1998)

Greece by Rail: With Major Ferry Routes Zane Katsikis

India by Rail Royston Ellis

Laos and Cambodia, Guide to John R Jones

Latvia, Guide to Inara Punga & William Hough

Lebanon, Guide to Lynda Keen

Madagascar Wildlife: A Visitor's Guide Hilary Bradt, Derek Schuurman & Nick Garbutt

Madagascar, Guide to Hilary Bradt

Malawi, Guide to Philip Briggs

Maldives, Guide to Royston Ellis

Mauritius, Guide to Royston Ellis

Mexico, Backpacking in Tim Burford

Mozambique, Guide to Philip Briggs

Namibia, Guide to Chris McIntyre (summer 1998)

North Cyprus, Guide to Diana Darke

Peru and Bolivia, Backpacking and Trekking in Hilary Bradt

Philippines, Guide to Stephen Mansfield

Poland and Ukraine, Hiking Guide to Tim Burford

Romania, Hiking Guide to Tim Burford

Russia and Central Asia by Road Hazel Barker

Russia by Rail, with Belarus and Ukraine Athol Yates

South Africa, Guide to Philip Briggs
Spain and Portugal by Rail Norman Renouf
Spitsbergen, Guide to Andreas Umbreit
Sri Lanka by Rail Royston Ellis
Switzerland by Rail Anthony Lambert
Tanzania, Guide to Philip Briggs
Uganda, Guide to Philip Briggs
USA by Rail John Pitt
Venezuela, Guide to Hilary Dunsterville Branch
Vietnam, Guide to John R Jones
Your Child's Health Abroad: A Manual for Travelling Parents Dr Jane
  Wilson-Howarth & Dr Matthew Ellis
Zambia, Guide to Chris McIntyre
Zanzibar, Guide to David Else

Bradt Guides are available from bookshops or by mail order from:
Bradt Publications
41 Nortoft Road, Chalfont St Peter, Bucks SL9 OLA. England.
Tel/fax: 01494 873478   Email: bradtpublications@compuserve.com.
Please include your name, address and daytime telephone number with
your order and enclose a cheque or postal order, or quote your Visa/
Mastercard card number and expiry date.
Postage will be charged as follows: UK: £1 50 for one book; £2.50 for two
or more books; Europe (inc Eire): £2 for one book, £4 for two or more
books (airmail printed paper); rest of world: £4 for one book; £7 for two or
more books (airmail printed paper).

Index

accommodation 57, 88-100, 164-77, 194
agriculture 2
amphibians 71
Anglican Cathedral 147-8
animals *see* wildlife
Arab Fort 56, 136
arrival 39, 49
art galleries 119

banks 120-2
Barghash, Sultan 25-9, 154-5
bars and clubs 105-6
Bawe Island 157
Beit el Ras Palace 151
Bi Khole Ruins 182
bicycle hire 87-8, 162, 193
Big Tree, The 131
birds 71-2
boat hire 194
Britain 14, 15, 18-19, 29-31
Bububu 151-2, 155
bullfighting 201
Burton, Richard 21
business hours 63
Bwejuu 172

cafés *see* restaurants
car hire 88, 161, 192
Chake Chake 194-6
Changuu Island 156-7
Chapwani Island 157
Chuini Palace 151
Chukwani 149
Chumbe Island 67, 157-8
Chwaka 171
Chwaka Ruins 204
climate 1, 39 *see also* weather
clothing 54
cloves 68

clubs *see* bars
coconuts 66
conservation 36, 81-2
coral 75-6, 78, 81-2
currency 4 *see also* exchange rates, money

dala-dalas 86-7, 163-4, 193-4
dance 64-5
Dar es Salaam 44, 191
departure 49-50
Dhow Harbour 130-1
dhows 47, 48-9, 109-10, 190-1
Dimbani 183
diving 40, 114-16
dolphins 182-3
Dunga 21
Dunga Ruins 181

economy 4, 35
electricity 90
embassies 125
entry regulations 50
equipment 54-6
exchange rates 4
explorers 9, 19, 21
Extelcoms Building 129

festivals 63
fishing 40, 77-8, 114-16
food 58-9, 104, 201
forestry 67-8
Forodhani Gardens 137
Fuji Beach 155-6
Fukuchani Ruins 179
Fumba 149
further reading 213-17

geology 65
government 4, 36

Grant, James 21
Grave Island *see* Chapwani Island
guides 87, 112, 114

Hamamni Baths 140
health 51, 60-1, 124, 201
history 2, 5-37
hitchhiking 164
hospitals 124, 201
House of Wonders 135-6, 138

insurance 51-2
Islam 134

Jambiani 174-5
Jamituri Gardens 126
Jozani Forest Reserve 67, 69, 71, 184-6

Kibweni Palace 151
Kidichi Persian Baths 152-3
Kirk, John 25, 148
Kiwengwa 170
Kizimbani Persian Baths 153
Kizimkazi 177, 182-3
Kizimkazi Mosque 183-4

language 3, 127, 209-11
Livingstone 22, 23, 122
Livingstone House 131

Makunduchi 175-7
mammals 69-71
Mangapwani Coral Cavern 153-4
Mangapwani Slave Cave 154-5
maps 125-6
marine life 74-82
market 130
Marseilles Palace 154
Maruhubi Palace 149
Matemwe 168
Mathews, William Lloyd 146
Mbweni 147-9
Mercury, Freddie 132
Mesali Island 203
minibuses 163

missionaries 19
Mkoani 196-8
Mkokotoni 180
Mnemba Island 168
Mombasa 9, 48, 191
money 52 *see also* currency, exchange rates
mosques 134, 183
motorbike hire 88, 162, 193
Mtambwe-Mkuu 203
Mtoni Palace 150
museums 71, 135, 138, 144-6
music 64-5
Mveleni Ruins 180

National Museum *see* House of Wonders
natural history 2, 65-82
newspapers 125
Ngezi Forest Reserve 67, 204-5
Ngoma 65
Nungwi 165-8, 178

Old British Consulate 138
Old Customs House 135
Old Dispensary 131
Oman 11, 17, 21
Orphanage 137

Paje 172
Palace Museum 135, 138
Pango ya Watoro 200
papaasi 87
Peace Memorial Museum 144-6
Pemba Island 1, 188-205
  electricity
  getting there and away 190-2
  local services 200-1
  places to visit 202-5
  tour companies 196
  transport 192-4
people 2
People's Gardens 141-2
People's Palace *see* Palace Museum
pharmacies 141-2

photography 126
police 124-5
population 3
Portugal 9-11
post 123, 201
Prison Island 71 *see also*
  Changuu Island
public holidays 63
Pujini Ruins 202
Pwani Mchangani 169-70

railway 151-2
Ras Kinyu Forest Reserve 205
Ras Mkumbuu Ruins 202-3
religion 3, 134
reptiles 71

safety 61-2, 88
sailing 114-16
Salme, Princess 22, 27, 142-3,
  154
Scramble for Africa 27-9
scuba diving *see* diving
seaweed 80
ship, travel by 44-7, 48, 190, 191,
  192
shipping companies 108-9
Shiraz 7, 8
shopping 62-3, 104, 117-19
slave trade 11-15, 18, 22, 126
Snake Island 157
Speke, John 21
spice trade 66-7
St Joseph's Cathedral 139-40
Stanley, Henry M 23, 29, 121
sultans 207-8

Taarab 64
Tanga 47, 191
taxes, departure 50
taxis 86

teeth 51
telephone 89, 111, 123, 201
Thackeray, Caroline 148, 149
Tippu Tip's House 139
tourist information 120
transport 59-60, 86-8
travel agents 41-3
travel companies 104, 110
Tumbatu Island 180
Tumbe 203
turtles 74-5

UMCA Cathedral *see* Anglican
  Cathedral
Unguja 1, 3, 5, 10 *see also*
  Zanzibar Island
Unguja Ukuu 182-3
Uroa 170-1

vaccinations 51
vegetation 2, 65
visas 50-1

weather 77 *see also* climate
Wete 198-200
wildlife 2, 69-75, 77-81, 185

Zala Park 184
Zanzibar Archives 146
Zanzibar Island 160-86
Zanzibar Milestone 143-4
Zanzibar Town 85-158
  tourist information 120
  accommodation 57-8, 88-100
  bars and clubs 105-6
  guides 112
  places to visit 128-47
  restaurants & cafés 100-4
  shopping 104, 117-19
  transport 86-8